Ple
sho

www.

Renewals
enquiries:

OOOO

Textphone for hearing
or speech impaired

030

ANNAPURNA

14 CLASSIC TREKS INCLUDING
THE ANNAPURNA CIRCUIT

About the Authors

Siân Pritchard-Jones and Bob Gibbons met in 1983, on a trek from Kashmir to Ladakh. By then Bob had already driven an ancient Land Rover from England to Kathmandu (in 1974), and overland trucks across Asia, Africa and South America. He had also lived in Kathmandu for two years, employed as a trekking company manager. Before they met, Siân worked in computer programming and systems analysis, but was drawn back to the Himalayas after her first trek, the Annapurna Circuit, en route from working in New Zealand.

Since they met they have been leading and organising treks in the Alps, Nepal and the Sahara, as well as driving a bus overland to Nepal. Journeys by a less ancient (only 28 year-old) Land Rover from England to South Africa provided the basis for several editions of the Bradt guide *Africa Overland*.

In Kathmandu they have worked occasionally with Himalayan MapHouse and for many winters with Pilgrims Publishing, producing cultural guides – *Kathmandu: Valley of the Green-Eyed Yellow Idol* and *Ladakh: Land of Magical Monasteries* – and a historical look at the Guge Kingdom, *Kailash: Land of the Tantric Mountain*.

In 2007 they wrote the Cicerone guide to Mount Kailash and Western Tibet, as well updating the Grand Canyon guide. During 2011 they revisited Tibet, this time driving the same old Land Rover back from Kathmandu to the UK overland via Lhasa, through China, Kazakhstan, Russia and Western Europe.

It was with great relish that they returned to one of their former trekking haunts in Nepal – the Annapurna region – to prepare this guidebook.

Other Cicerone guides by the authors
The Mount Kailash Trek

ANNAPURNA

14 CLASSIC TREKS INCLUDING THE ANNAPURNA CIRCUIT

by Siân Pritchard-Jones and Bob Gibbons

2 POLICE SQUARE, MILNTHORPE, CUMBRIA LA7 7PY
www.cicerone.co.uk

© Siân Pritchard-Jones and Bob Gibbons
First edition 2013
ISBN: 978 1 85284 699 2
Printed in China on behalf of Latitude Press Ltd

A catalogue record for this book is available from the British Library.
All photographs are by the authors unless otherwise stated.

Dedicated to the preservation of the Spirit of Adventure

The Horizon
All around, the illusory edge of the sky,
Masterpiece of a magical hand,
A faraway line that doesn't exist,
Yet stretches away to the end…

*Translated by Siân and her father John Pritchard-Jones from the traditional Welsh
Englyn poem 'Y Gorwel' by Dewi Emrys (David Emrys James)*

Warning

Mountain walking can be a dangerous activity carrying a risk of personal injury or death. It should be undertaken only by those with a full understanding of the risks and with the training and/or experience to evaluate them. While every care and effort has been taken in the preparation of this guide, the user should be aware that conditions can be highly variable and can change quickly, materially affecting the seriousness of a mountain walk.

Therefore, except for any liability which cannot be excluded by law, neither Cicerone nor the authors accept liability for damage of any nature (including damage to property, personal injury or death) arising directly or indirectly from the information in this book.

Readers are warned that, although there are now local mobile phone networks throughout most of the trekking routes (excluding Nar-Phu), foreign mobile phones may not work. Local lodges will always be able to help and call a helicopter if necessary. In case of emergency self-help may be the only option. Any helicopter rescue would be expensive and payment guarantee required. Be insured. Read, understand and take account of altitude sickness (AMS). See 'Health Matters' in the Introduction.

Front cover: Annapurna III from Braka

CONTENTS

Advice to Readers

While every effort is made by our authors to ensure the accuracy of guidebooks as they go to print, changes can occur during the lifetime of an edition. If we know of any, there will be an Updates tab on this book's page on the Cicerone website (www.cicerone.co.uk), so please check before planning your trip. We also advise that you check information about such things as transport, accommodation and shops locally. Even rights of way can be altered over time. We are always grateful for information about any discrepancies between a guidebook and the facts on the ground, sent by email to info@cicerone.co.uk or by post to Cicerone, 2 Police Square, Milnthorpe LA7 7PY, United Kingdom.

Map Key

~~	ridge
⬭	lake
≈≈	trekking route (various colours)
·····‿·····	alternative route
·‿·‿·‿·	side trip
■	habitation
~∼-∼-	road
~∼-∼-∼	motorable dirt road
ⵣ	camp
⅄	bridge/pass
▲	summit
⬛	gompa
~~	river
🌲🌳	woods
C	cave
-·-·-·-	national boundary
⬭	town/city

7

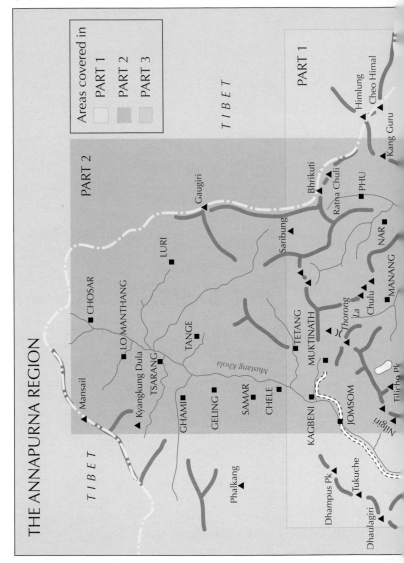

THE ANNAPURNA REGION

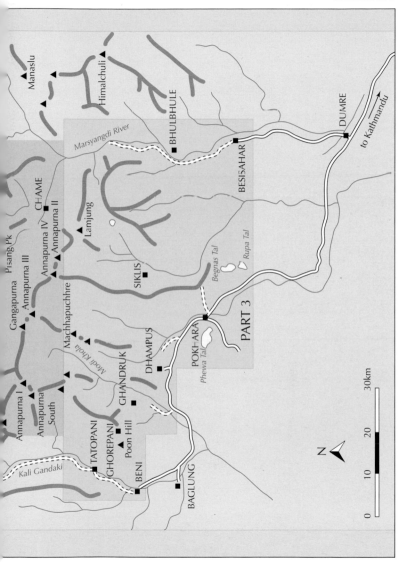

The trail from Tsarang into the Mustang Khola (Trek 5)

ACKNOWLEDGMENTS

We are grateful to Jonathan Williams of Cicerone for allowing us to bring the delights of the Annapurna region to the attention of avid trekkers. Particular thanks must also go to Kev Reynolds, who has inspired us with his books. Thanks also to the team at Cicerone who made it possible.

In Kathmandu we are grateful to Ravi Chandra, Pasang Dawa and Niraj Shrestha; also to Karna, Rajan, Sunil, Sohan, Uttam, Nabin, Kumar and all at the Kathmandu Guest House. Thanks to Pilgrims Book House, where the cultural and historical text was researched, to Mingma Sherpa of The Everest Equipment Shop, to Bhandari's Photo Shop opposite and to KC's restaurant for the superb pumpkin pies. Thanks to Dr Ram Baran Yadav, Dr Kailash Sah and his wife Mina for the medical hints. Also to Christine Miqueu-Baz.

Special thanks to Rajendra Suwal for his contribution about the birds of the Annapurna region. Thanks to Alonzo Lucius Lyons, as well as Bishnu Adhikari and Kate Hargadon at CHOICE Humanitarian for notes on the homestay treks, and to Pawan Shakya at Himalayan MapHouse. In Pokhara, thanks to K B Nembang for his experience-backed knowledge. In Manang, special thanks to Kanchha Ghale, the best pony man in the Annapurnas, and his wonderful pony Kale. In Nar-Phu, thanks to our guide Padam Rai and porter hero Hiro!

Thanks to our parents for putting up with our unusual lifestyle; and many *dhanyabads* to the lodge hosts, trekking staff and porters who struggle daily through such grand scenery, looking only at the trail underfoot.

And finally, thanks for contributing to future printings and editions of this guidebook by sending your suggestions and updates to us through our website www.expeditionworld.com or direct to Cicerone.

Braka and Tilicho Peak (Trek 1)

PREFACE

> It is impossible for any thinking man to look down from a hill on to a crowded plain and not ponder over the relative importance of things.

The Mountain Top, *Frank S Smythe*

Annapurna is the goddess of plenty and abundance, a deity who watches over her devotees benignly, with a smiling face. Rising like a beckoning temptress, the mighty buttresses and ramparts of the Annapurnas touch the heavens and defy description. Only the wildest dreams of nature could have sculpted such grandeur.

The Annapurna giants are sublime in all their moods – whether cast as fiery demons at sunset, shimmering in the starry moonlight, or bathed in the soft light of dawn. They float like benign ghosts above fluffy clouds, are darkened by thunderous storms, or appear reflected as a vision of serenity in the cool blue waters of a lake. Superlatives struggle to do justice to the sensational vistas and contrasting landscapes. It's no wonder that trekkers and mountaineers are drawn, as if hypnotised, to these majestic peaks and their icy bastions.

For centuries Nepal was an isolated and forbidden land. What the early explorers and invited guests found was almost paradise on earth, a lush and plentiful kingdom where the rhythms of life unfolded in daily rituals, strong religious beliefs and a tempo alien to those from more developed societies. People today are drawn to Nepal for many reasons: to seek the solitude of the wild, to scale the Himalayan giants, or look for a spiritual renaissance within its fascinating religious themes. For many the main attraction is the sheer beauty and variety of the landscapes and the mystical Himalayas. Many come for the extreme adventure activities or the elusive wildlife; others are content to delve into its historic byways, discovering the alleys and hidden shrines of the long-fabled Kathmandu Valley.

Today Nepal has become easily accessible and welcomes thousands of travellers each year. Few of them will return to their daily routines unchanged; exploring the country is challenging, both physically and mentally. The sights, sounds and smells of Nepal live on in the memory, and the trails of the Annapurnas are rightly the most popular trekking routes in this very special place.

The simple aim of this guide is to inspire adventure-seeking trekkers to go beyond the familiar, to explore the most mesmerising mountains in the world.

Siân Pritchard-Jones and Bob Gibbons

Porters on the Kimrong hillsides

INTRODUCTION

The power of such a mountain is so great and yet so subtle that, without compulsion, people are drawn to it from near and far, as if by the force of some invisible magnet...

The Way of the White Clouds, *Lama Anagarika Govinda*

We first used this quotation in our Mount Kailash trekking guide, and it is surely no less apt when applied to the Annapurnas. Of all the great Himalayan peaks, the Annapurnas are unique. They are not defined by a single soaring summit but comprise a vast massif, encompassing multiple peaks, spires and impossibly high ridges. The whole range is about 60km in length, with four major peaks and many subsidiary summits. Even the most sedentary soul will wish to get closer, to explore the verdant valleys, discover the mysterious gorges and head for the high passes.

Trekkers come from far and wide to discover Annapurna. Many arrive full of barely controlled anticipation, seeking a new challenge. All will

Misty moods: Dhaulagiri from Kopra (Trek 4)

leave with a renewed inspiration for life – there is something truly uplifting about being among some of nature's most magical arenas. All will lament the poverty of the 'developing' world, but look deeper – do you see many unhappy faces? Nepal's people are her greatest asset: hard-working, brimming with almost child-like humour, boisterous, endearing, versatile and hungry for change, just like most people across our planet.

This comprehensive guide explores the Annapurna massif. Any journey in and around these mountains is a joy, with experiences to treasure for a lifetime. Routes lead around tranquil lakes, through rich farming country, forests of bamboo and rhododendron, cool rainforest, silent alpine glades and rugged, high mountain desert. In the villages, excitable children rush to practise their English. Elsewhere a Hindu god may catch your gaze, or you may hear the chanting of monks in a monastery clinging to a strangely eroded cliff. The Annapurnas may dominate the landscape, but the people and the culture will surprise and delight in equal measure.

One important aspect of this latest Cicerone guide to Annapurna is an update on the impact that the new mountain 'roads' are having on the trails. Initially it might be tempting to write off those areas that have experienced the internal combustion engine for the first time at close quarters. Change is happening in Nepal at a staggering pace, despite its under-developed status. However – and this must be stressed most emphatically – do not believe for one minute that the Annapurnas have lost their shine.

There are many surprising aspects to the Annapurna region, as well as an abundance of exciting trails to discover, in areas new and old. The guide is divided into three parts, covering established routes, restricted area treks and new homestay trekking areas.

Annapurna Circuit

Most of the changes over recent years affect this route, so much of the guide concentrates on this trek, introducing some previously neglected side trips and new alternatives to walking on or close to the new 'roads'. It remains the classic trek and is still a top trekking destination. Roads may change it but will not destroy it (after all, Switzerland has both side by side).

Annapurna Sanctuary

Another classic favourite where little change, other than ever-improving comfort, has occurred. The views from this cloud-bubbling cauldron are still hard to beat.

Ghorepani Circuit

Affectionately known as the Poon Hill Expedition, this has all the ingredients for a short, spell-binding adventure in the foothills. Terraced hillsides, fairy-tale forests and soaring snow-covered spires contrive to make any visit a memorable one.

Mani wall in Mustang

Annapurna–Dhaulagiri

Once a hidden treasure, this route is gradually becoming more popular. Still mainly a camping option, its high isolated ridges will soon see an influx of trekkers, as community homestays open along its lower reaches. The airy belvederes of the Kopra Danda ridge are sensational; even the most experienced trekking hand will be blown away.

Restricted Areas

Many would-be explorers are drawn to the captivating Tibetan culture and the plateau's fantastic scenery. In these remote mountains, specialist trekkers can delve into the natural world, capturing magnificent predators like lammergeyer on camera, tracking the bashful Himalayan bear, sniffing out the elusive snow leopard and even yearning for the yeti.

Mustang

Upper Mustang, with its extraordinary walled city of Lo Manthang, has long been the fabled Shangri-La. Getting there is every bit as fascinating and inspiring. Where in the world can you find such unbelievable variation – the highest peaks of the Himalayas, mysterious canyons, legend-filled settlements, staggering geology and contorted natural landscapes?

Nar-Phu

Perhaps the most astonishing region of all the Annapurnas, Nar-Phu is as barely known as it is inaccessible. Cut off for centuries by the highest passes and the most impenetrable, sheer-sided canyon in Nepal, the medieval villages of Nar and Phu are some of the country's most closely guarded secrets. Trekking here takes one to a new level of adventure and wonder.

Other treks

Long overlooked are two routes below Machhapuchhre: the Mardi Himal Trek and the Machhapuchhre Trek. Both climb above the tree line to the wild, rugged base camps of Mardi Himal.

Lower down the hillsides trekkers can enjoy close contact with local people and their villages; eco-friendly, cultural homestay treks are the new thing. West of Poon Hill on the sunny slopes above the Kali Gandaki River are the Parbat Myagdi treks. Not far from Pokhara is the Siklis Trek; once popular with camping groups, it remains a peaceful and traditional area. The Lamjung foothills – around Chowk Chisopani–Tandrangkot–Puranokot – are the latest area to introduce homestay trekking. A little further north, the Gurung Heritage Trail is sure to be enjoyed by increasing numbers of trekkers in the future.

The joy of discovering these routes must be tempered with some words of warning: no trek to the remote Himalayan region can be underrated in terms of objective danger. Sections of this guide are devoted to the essential advance planning that is required by any potential visitor,

Climbing from Putak with the Thorong La in view (Trek 1)

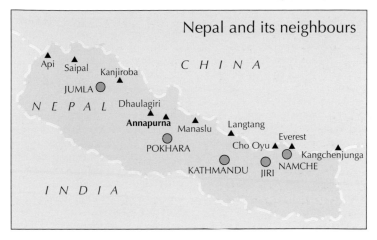

Nepal and its neighbours

especially because of the isolation, difficulty of access, and sheer 'different-ness' of the destination.

Having spent over half our lives trekking in Nepal, we have never tired of the Himalayas. Our youthful romantic notions about these distant, lofty peaks have not dwindled with age – we find ourselves drawn to these mountains, time and time again. It is an addiction that is hard to shed, so beware – you too may find that the 'once-in-a-lifetime' trek becomes habit-forming!

GEOGRAPHY

Stretching over 2500km from the Indian states of Arunachal Pradesh in the east to Pakistan in the west, the Himalayas form an unbroken chain that divides the plains of India from the Tibetan plateau. Nepal is 250km wide on average

and roughly 800km in length. The country's highest peaks, from east to west – Kanchenjunga, Makalu, Everest, Lhotse, Annapurna and Dhaulagiri, all exceeding 8000m in height – are located along its northern borders.

From fossil records in Nepal and Tibet, it is estimated that a sea existed in this area about 100 million years ago. At some time in the following 50 million years India began to 'collide' with Tibet through the process of plate tectonics. Some 40–45 million years ago, the Indian plate continued its northward march, forcing the Tibetan plateau upwards. Around 20 million years ago, the main Himalayan chain was formed by the same process. The Himalayas have continued to rise over the last two million years.

Nepal's border region with India, a narrow, once-malarial jungle strip called the Terai, has been cleared for agriculture and today provides the majority of the population with food. Rising abruptly from the plains of India are the Siwalik Hills: dramatic, steep, yet fragile, being easily denuded by the heavy rains. The steep and forested Mahabharat Hills, rising to over 3000m, mark the southern edge of the middle hills of Nepal, where most of the rural population lives. Most visitors trek through this area – home to the valleys of Kathmandu and Pokhara – marvelling at the impressive farming terraces and rolling hills dotted with quaint houses.

The Himalayan mountains comprise a relatively small zone along the northern border with Tibet/China, but are the visual focus of the whole country. The main Himalayan range is not a watershed; dynamic fast-flowing rivers cut through these mountains, giving access to the inner sanctuaries of the peaks. The main watershed ranges are north of the Nepal Himalayas in Tibet – equally astonishing and alluring mountains – with an altitude range of roughly 3000–8848m (the summit of Everest).

CLIMATE

To see the greatness of a mountain… one must see it at sunrise and sunset, at noon and at midnight, in sun and in rain, in snow and in storm, in summer and in winter and in all the other seasons.

The Way of the White Clouds, *Lama Anagarika Govinda*

The Himalayas are an amazing natural barrier that divides the main weather systems of Asia, affecting the climate in a unique manner. The southern Indian plains experience hot, humid monsoon patterns in the northern hemisphere summer, with cooler, dry, high-pressure-dominated winter periods. In Tibet to the north the climate is harsh, cold and windy. The mountains cause a rain shadow creating a desert-like region, with only the far south of Tibet experiencing any influence of the monsoon. The Annapurna range sits between these two extremes, making a trek in the south very different from one in the north. It is these contrasting climates that make the Annapurna Circuit trek one of such variety. For the specific effects of the climate on trekkers see 'When to go'.

PLANTS, ANIMALS AND BIRDS

Plants

Nepal is a paradise for botanists. With so many climatic zones, it's no surprise to find that there are in excess of 6500 different types of plants, flowers, trees, grasses and growths of all dispositions across the country. Many of the plants favoured by gardeners in the West have their origins in the Himalayas; Joseph Hooker, a noted 19th-century explorer and botanist, discovered many of these as he explored Sikkim.

The lowland jungles and slopes of the Siwalik foothills are home to

Poinsettia

sal trees, simal, sissoo, khair and mahogany. Hugging the Mahabharat ranges and higher you find the ubiquitous pipal and banyan trees, like an inseparable couple shading porter rest-stops (*chautaara*). Chestnut, chilaune and bamboo occur in profusion, and in the cloud forests are a myriad of lichens, ferns, rattens and dripping lianas.

The prolific orchids, magnolia, broadleaf temperate oaks and rhododendron (locally called *laliguras*) colonise the higher hillsides. Higher up are spruce, fir, blue pine, larch, hemlock, cedar and sweet-smelling juniper. Poplar and willow are found along the upper tree line; in the high meadows look out for berberis. Even

Rhododendron

in the highest meadows, hardy flowers and plants, such as colourful gentians, survive.

Animals

With such a wide variety of plantlife and breadth of climatic range Nepal is home to a diverse population of mammals, reptiles and birds. The lowland Terai is home to the spectacular Asian one-horned rhino, elephant, spotted deer and sambar deer, as well as the odd sloth bear, leopard and tiger, which are rarely seen. Gharals, marsh mugger crocodiles, alligators and snakes lurk in the murky waters of the lowland marshes and rivers that drain into the holy Ganges River. These once-thick jungles still host an amazing number of semi-tropical birds, despite clearance for agriculture. The middle hills are extensively cultivated, but still hide a variety of animals. Monkeys and langurs abound in the forests.

At altitude look for marmot, pika (small mouse-like animal, related to the rabbit), weasel, ermine, Himalayan hare, brown bear, wild dog, blue sheep, Tibetan sheep, wolf, thar (species of large deer) and the famed musk deer (a prized trading item in the past). Skittish wild ass, the kyang, are only found in the northern zones of Mustang and Nar-Phu. Wild yaks do still roam in isolated, remote valleys, but most are now domesticated. As well as the infamous butter tea, yak milk is also used by nomads to produce cheese and yoghurt. The dzo – a cross between a yak and a cow – is commonly used as a pack animal. Herders keep sheep and goats, as well as yaks. The snow leopard is rarely encountered and virtually never photographed. Hunting blue sheep in the dawn or twilight hours, they are extremely wary and unlikely to show themselves. Television crews with big budgets have waited many years to get any film of these beautiful creatures. If you see a yeti, do let us know!

Note that trekkers need not worry about encountering dangerous animals in the Annapurnas in general, although domestic guard dogs occasionally show more interest than is desirable.

Birds
contributed by Rajendra Suwal
The incredible diversity of the Annapurnas offers naturalists the perfect environment for discovering a wealth of birdlife. Its unique habitats shelter diverse groups of bird species. Birds move mostly in flocks, hunting insects at different levels in the forest. During quiet times you might spot 5–12 different species, determined by season. There are diurnal, seasonal and altitudinal migrants; birds such as the cuckoo visit during the spring for breeding.

As the first rays of sun hit the **forests**, the insects stir into life and the insectivores, including the colourful long-tailed minivet, and green-backed, black-lored and black-throated tits, begin foraging. Nectarine-, fruit- and berry-eating birds are active early in the day. Trees with berries or flowers are magnets for multiple species, namely whiskered, stripe-throated, rufous-naped and white-browed tits. The forest between Ghorepani and Tadapani is a good place to encounter the great parrotbill, spotted laughing thrush, and the velvet, rufous-bellied and white-tailed nuthatch.

The most rewarding forest habitats are those of Timang, Chame and Pisang, around Ghandruk, Tadapani, Ghorepani, Ghurjung and en route to Annapurna Base Camp. Try to catch a glimpse of the golden-breasted, white-browed and rufous-winged fulvetta. The forest is full of red-tailed, rufous-tailed and blue-winged minla. The tapping of the rufous-bellied, crimson-breasted and pied woodpeckers occasionally interrupts the silence. The forests are alive with the beautiful scarlet, spotted and great rose finch, along with the spot-winged grosbeak. Birdwatchers will be amazed to see tiny warblers, including the chestnut-crowned, Whistler's, black-faced, grey-hooded and ashy-throated warblers. Nepal cutia is found in forests of alder.

Smart sunbirds found in **flowering trees** include the black-throated, green-tailed, fire-tailed and purple sunbird. Fire-breasted flowerpeckers are found near settlements, in the flowering trees and mistletoe. Large-billed crows scavenge on kitchen leftovers or raid village crops. Flocks of red and yellow-billed chough forage **around farms** or high above the passes. The olive-backed pipit, magpie, robin and common tailorbird are found near farms, along with the common stonechat and the grey, collared, white-tailed and pied bushchat.

Streams and riverbanks are teeming with frisky birds. The pristine environment of the Modi Khola is a very rewarding habitat for river birds, including white-capped water redstart and plumbeous redstart; little, spotted, black-backed and slaty-backed forktail; brown dipper, grey wagtail and blue whistling-thrush. Other common birds are the red-vented, black bulbul, great and blue-throated barbet, and also coppersmith barbet in the lower reaches. On some overhanging cliffs below Landruk, Chhomrong and Lamakhet near Siklis are honeycombs made by the world's largest honeybees, where you may spot the oriental honeyguide.

Ravens are acrobatic birds, seen in the **alpine zones**. The blue pine forest is a habitat of the very vocal spotted nutcracker, while orange-bellied leafbirds prefer the upper canopies. More treasures are the tiny Nepal, scaly-breasted and pygmy wren babblers, feeding under the ferns, with their high-pitched territorial calls. With its high-pitched sound, the jewel-like, tiny chestnut-headed tesia is a wonderful bird to see in moist undergrowth

The **mountains** near Lete and Ghasa harbour all the pheasant species found in Nepal, namely the kalij, koklass and cheer pheasant. Shy by nature, one can hear them before dawn. In the rhododendron and oak forest look for ringal, and in cane bamboo watch for satyr tragopan and blood pheasant. The Himalayan munal, the national bird of Nepal, favours the tree line and pastures.

The **Kali Gandaki River Valley** is one of the major 'flyways' of migratory birds, including demoiselle cranes, birds of prey, black storks and many varieties of passerines. Migrating eagles, including the steppe and imperial, as well as small birds of prey, pied and hen harriers and common buzzards also use it. Observing the annual autumn migration of thousands of demoiselle cranes is very rewarding. To gain height and glide over the peaks, they catch the thermals in the windshadow of the mountains. If the weather turns bad, they wait in the buckwheat fields and riverbanks. The golden eagle, the master predator, anticipates their arrival and attacks the cranes in-flight, occasionally separating a young, injured or sick crane from the flock, catching them in the air. This epic migration was broadcast as part of the 'Planet Earth' Mountain Series on the BBC/Discovery Channel.

The **skies of Annapurna** host the vulture and majestic lammergeyers (with 3m wingspans). Himalayan and Eurasian griffons soar, lifting every onlooker's spirit. Some ethnic groups of Mustang practise sky burial and believe the vultures pass the spirits to the heavens. Cliffs are breeding sites for vultures and lammergeyer. All the vulture species of Nepal, including the Egyptian vulture, the endangered white-rumped, the red-headed and the globally endangered slender-billed vulture are found in the foot-hills. Cinereous vultures are seen in winter.

In the **caragana bush habitat** of Muktinath, Jharkot and Jomsom, look for the white-browed tit-bab-bler, white-throated, Guldenstadt's and blue-fronted redstart, brambling and brown rufous-breasted and Altai accentor. Rock bunting and chu-kor partridge inhabit areas between Kagbeni, Muktinath, around Manang and south to Lete, In the air you can observe the speedy insect-hunter white-rumped needletail, Nepal house martin, red-rumped swal-low and Himalayan swiftlet. Finally, near the **Thorong La**, observe the Himalayan snow cock and flocks of snow pigeons foraging near trails, oblivious of passing trekkers.

For more details, contact Rajendra Suwal of Nepal Nature dot com Travels, mail@nepalnaturetravels. com, www.nepalnaturetravels.com.

BRIEF HISTORY

Nepal is one of the most diverse places on earth, its culture and peo-ple as varied as its scenic attractions. With a long history of isolation, the country and its once mystical capital, Kathmandu, has an amazing story to tell. Its history is a complex blend of exotic legend, historical fact and reli-gious influence, suffused with myth.

The original inhabitants of the Kathmandu Valley were the Kiranti people. Around 550BC, in Lumbini in southern Nepal, Prince Siddhartha Gautama was born, later becoming the Buddha, whose philosophy would have such an impact on the country. In the third century BC, Ashoka, one of the first emissaries of Buddhism in India, built the ancient *stupas* (a large Buddhist monument, usually with a square base, a dome and pointed spire) of Patan and the pillar in Lumbini. Around AD300, during the Licchavi Period, the Hindu religion blossomed across the southern and middle hills. Trade routes flourished between Tibet and India, with Kathmandu being the most important trading centre.

When Buddhism declined in India, 'adepts' (masters of Buddhism) crossed the Himalayas to find refuge in Tibet. Tibetan Vajrayana Buddhism later trickled back into Nepal, provid-ing many of the fascinating aspects of the country's religious life. The Buddhist master Padma Sambhava (Guru Rinpoche) travelled around the Himalayas in the eighth century. Few records exist of the period following until the 13th century, when the Malla kings assumed power.

The Malla period marks the golden age of art and architecture in Nepal, with the construction of multi-tiered palaces and pagodas.

Durbar Square, Patan

The people lived in decorated wood and brick houses. Jayasthiti Malla, a Hindu, consolidated power in the Kathmandu Valley and declared himself to be a reincarnate of the god Vishnu, a practice that was considered appropriate for the monarchs of Nepal until 2007. Jyoti Malla and Yaksha Malla enhanced the valley with spectacular structures. Around 1482 the three towns of Kathmandu, Patan and Bhaktapur became independent cities, with each king competing to build the greatest Durbar Square, parts of which still exist today.

From a hilltop fortress above the town of Gorkha (Gurkha) came Prithvi Narayan Shah. His forces swept in from the west, subduing the cities of the Kathmandu Valley and unifying Nepal. Nepalese armies invaded Tibet in 1788, but were later repulsed by Tibet with Chinese intervention. In 1816 the British defeated the Gurkhas and, in the treaty of Segauli, Nepal had to cede Sikkim to India, with the current borders delineated. The British established a resident office, but Nepal effectively became a closed land after 1816.

In 1846 a soldier of the court, Jung Bahadur Kunwar Rana, took power after a bloody massacre in Kot Square in Kathmandu. The queen was sent into exile and the king dethroned. For the next 100 years the Rana family ruled Nepal, calling themselves Maharajas. Family intrigues, murder and deviousness dominated the activities of the autocratic Ranas. The country remained closed to all but a few invited guests, retaining its medieval traditions until 1950.

25

After Indian independence in 1947, a Congress Party was formed in Kathmandu. The powerless king became a symbol for freedom from the Ranas' rule. For those who dared to confront the Ranas, there was a terrible price to pay; many suffered the death penalty. King Tribhuvan finally ousted the Ranas in 1951.

A coalition government was installed, with a fledgling democracy. The country opened to visitors and Mount Everest was climbed in May 1953. King Tribhuvan died in 1955 and his son Mahendra assumed power. In 1960 Mahendra ended the brief experiment with democracy, introducing the party-less *panchayat* system, based on local councils of elders with a tiered system of representatives up to the central parliament. In 1972 King Birendra became the new king, but his coronation did not take place until the spring of 1975, on an auspicious date. In 1980 a referendum was held and the panchayat system was retained. After 1985, rapid expansion brought many changes; the population grew astonishingly, and the traditional rural lifestyle of the valley began to disappear under a wave of construction.

In April 1990 full-scale rioting and demonstrations broke out, forcing the king to allow a form of democracy to be introduced. But political corruption and infighting did little to enhance the democratic ideals, and in the late nineties a grass roots Maoist rebellion developed. Many had genuine sympathy with the need for greater social equality, but violence and demands for a leftist dictatorship met with resistance. In a tragic shooting spree in June 2001 King Birendra and almost his entire family were wiped out by his son, Crown Prince Dipendra. King Birendra's brother Gyanendra became king, but in October 2002 he dissolved parliament and appointed his own government until elections could be held. Meanwhile the Maoist rebellion continued to threaten all parts of the country. Coercion and intimidation were rife in the countryside and no solutions were in sight.

King Gyanendra relinquished power in April 2006 and the Maoist leaders entered mainstream politics after winning a majority of votes in the election. Since then, the government of Nepal has been in freefall, with a political stalemate and paralysis derailing development. Tourism is still one of the main foreign exchange earners, but an increasing number of young Nepalese are seeking work outside the country, particularly in the Arabian Gulf. Despite the political uncertainty, tourists are still made to feel very welcome in the country.

PEOPLE OF NEPAL

At the latest estimate there are around 32 million people living in Nepal. (In 1974 there were a mere eight million.) There are at least 26 major ethnic groups, with the majority of these

Children in Bhaktapur

living in the middle hills. In general, the people in the southern zones are Hindu followers while those from the high Himalayan valleys are Buddhist. However, there is no clear traditional divide in the major valley of Kathmandu, and many thousands of villagers 'escaped' from the effects of the Maoist insurgency to the safety of Kathmandu.

The Newaris – a mix of Hindus and Buddhists – are the traditional inhabitants of the Kathmandu Valley. The Tharu are a major group from the lowland Terai, with their ancestry probably linked to Rajasthan in India. Other people of the Terai, also related to Indian Hindu clans, are collectively known as the Madeshi. The first President of Nepal, Dr Ram Baran Yadav, comes from this ethnic group.

The rural hills of the Annapurna region are home to Magars, Chhetris, Gurungs and Brahmins (technically high caste). Gurung men are particularly noted for their service to the Gurkhas. Thakalis live along the Kali Gandaki. Manangis inhabit the higher reaches of the Marsyangdi.

RELIGION

Holy places never had any beginning. They have been holy from the time they were discovered, strongly alive because of the invisible presences breathing through them.

The Land of Snows, *Giuseppe Tucci*

Religious beliefs and practices are an integral part of life in Nepal. To comprehend the country's culture would be impossible without a

Paintings in Jhong Gompa (Trek 1)

basic understanding of the religious concepts.

Hinduism

Hinduism is the main faith of Nepal; until recently the country was a Hindu kingdom. Evidence of the Hindu faith in the Annapurnas manifests itself mainly through the festivals and celebrations of the people, rather than in an abundance of elaborate temples; it is as much a way of life as a religion. A very definite attitude of fatalism is conveyed to the visitor meandering along the populated trails. The monsoon often brings the destruction of a hillside or village by a giant mudslide, for example; these are seen traditionally not so much as resulting from the uncontrollable actions of nature but

from the vengeance of the gods. Your own bad actions might be the cause of such misfortune.

Many Hindu religious ideals have come from the ancient Indian Sanskrit texts, the four Vedas. In essence, the ideas of Hinduism are based on the notion that everything in the universe is connected through Karma. This means that your deeds in this life will have a bearing on the next.

Despite the apparent plethora of Hindu gods, they are in essence one, worshipped in many different aspects. The trinity of Hindu gods are Brahma, the god of creation; Shiva, the god of destruction; and Vishnu, the god of preservation. They manifest in many forms, both male and female. Brahma is rarely seen – his

THE LEGEND OF GANESH

Ganesh is Shiva and Parvati's son. But why does he have the head of an elephant? Parvati gave birth to Ganesh while Shiva was away on trek. When he returned, he saw the child and assumed that Parvati had been unfaithful. In a furious rage, he chopped off Ganesh's head and threw it away. After Parvati explained, Shiva vowed to give Ganesh the head of the first living being that passed their home – it was an elephant.

work is done. Shiva is the god of destruction but has special powers for regeneration. Shiva can manifest as Mahadev the supreme lord, or as dancing Nataraj, representing the rhythm of the cosmos. As Pashupati he is the Lord of Beasts. Bhairab is Shiva in his most destructive form, black and angry. In his white form he is so terrible that he must be hidden from view, daring only to be seen once a year during the Indra Jatra festival. (He lurks in Kathmandu's Durbar Square behind a gilded wooden screen.)

Parvati is Shiva's wife, with many aspects. As Kali and Durga she is destructive. The festival of Durga takes place during the trekking high season of the autumn, so don't offend her or you may not get your trekking permit on time. Taleju is another image of Parvati.

Other popular gods and goddesses include Lakshmi, the goddess of wealth, and the humorous elephant god Ganesh, worshipped for good luck and happiness.

The third God, Vishnu, is also worshipped in Nepal as Narayan, the preserver of life. Vishnu has 10 other aspects. The eighth avatar, the blue Krishna, plays a flute and chases after the cowgirls. Other notable avatars are Rama, of the Indian epic Ramayana, and the ninth avatar, the Buddha.

Hanuman is the monkey god, sometimes appearing as a rather shapeless stone and often sheltering under an umbrella. Machhendranath is a curious deity, the rain god, hailed as the compassionate one, and has two forms: White (Seto) and Red (Rato).

Buddhism

Buddhists are found in the Kathmandu Valley and in the northern regions of the country. Buddhist monasteries (gompas) and culture are encountered on the Annapurna Circuit beyond Tal, around Muktinath and south along the Kali Gandaki River as far as Ghasa. Mustang and Nar-Phu are also Buddhist.

Buddhism is a philosophy for living, aiming to bring an inner peace of mind and a cessation of worldly suffering to its adherents. Reincarnation

Buddhist gompa in upper Pisang (Trek 1)

is a central theme; the essence of the soul is developed through successive lives until a state of perfect enlightenment is attained. Prince Siddhartha Gautama, the earthly Buddha, was born to riches but his daily life was one of spiritual torment. He left his wife and newborn son to become an ascetic, wandering far and wide, listening to sages, wise men and Brahmin priests. However, he found no solace until he achieved enlightenment through the Middle Path.

Buddhism has two branches: Hinayana and Mahayana. The latter path is followed in Nepal and Tibet, where it has evolved into a more esoteric philosophy called the Vajrayana (Diamond) Path. It blends ancient Tibetan Bon ideas with a phenomenon known as Tantra, meaning 'to open the mind'. Tantra basically asserts that each person is a Buddha and can find enlightenment from within.

The dazzling proliferation of Buddhist artistry and iconography is startling. Even the most sanguine atheist will surely find something uplifting about Nepal's rich and colourful Buddhist heritage.

The following Buddhist sects are found across the Annapurna region:

- **Nyingma-pa** is the oldest Buddhist sect; its adherents are known as the Red Hats. Guru Rinpoche was its founder in the eighth century AD. Today the Nyingma-pa sect is found across the high Himalayas of Nepal, in Tibet, Spiti and Ladakh.

- **Kadam-pa** was developed by Atisha, a Buddhist scholar from northern India, during his studies at Toling Gompa in the Guge region of Western Tibet. He suggested that followers should find enlightenment after careful reflection and study of the texts.
- **Kagyu-pa** is a sect attributed to the Indian mystic translator Marpa (AD1012–97), a disciple of Atisha. Adherents concentrate their meditations on inner mental and spiritual matters, following the wisdom of their teachers. The Kagyu-pa sect split into a number of sub-groups, such as the Drigung-pa, Druk-pa, Taglung-pa and the Karma-pa.
- **Sakya-pa** began in the 11th century under Konchok Gyalpo from the Sakya Gompa in Tibet. Followers study existing Buddhist scriptures and created the two great Tibetan Buddhist bibles, the Tangyur and Kangyur.
- **Gelug-pa** is the Yellow Hat sect of the Dalai Lama. Tsong Khapa, the 14th-century reformer, redefined the ideals of Atisha and reverted to a more purist format, putting more emphasis on morality and discipline.

Bon idol, Kunzang Gyalwa Dupa, Naurikot (Trek 1)

Bonpo

In 1977 the Tibetan government-in-exile recognised and accepted the ancient Bon as a Tibetan sect. The Bon's spiritual head is the Trizin, and its spiritual home is the Triten Norbutse Gompa; anyone interested in Bon should visit the complex near Swayambhunath, such is the rarity of any active Bon culture today. The Bonpo worshipped natural phenomena, like the heavens and mountain spirits, as well as natural powers such as rivers, trees and thunder. The chief icon of the Bon is Tonpa Shenrap Miwoche. The Bon seek the eternal truth and reality of life, as do Buddhists.

See Appendix B for further details. Other religions with a limited following in Nepal are Islam, Christianity, Sikhism and Shamanism.

Festivals

Nepal has an extraordinary number of festivals – any excuse for a good celebration! During the high season for trekkers, the Dasain and Tihar festivals can occasionally disrupt those trying to obtain the necessary trekking documents. During Dasain, the goddesses Kali and Durga are feted and the terrifying white Bhairab is allowed out of his cage in Kathmandu's Durbar Square. (Blood sacrifices are the most noticeable aspect of these celebrations; these are not for the squeamish.) Tihar is a much more light-hearted affair, with crows, dogs, cows and brothers celebrated on different days before a final party night of fairy lights and candles.

During the early spring, trekkers may witness Losar, the Tibetan New Year, celebrated primarily at Boudhanath. Tibetan drama and colourful masked Cham dances can be seen; the Black Hat dance celebrates the victory of Buddhism over Bon. Mi Tsering, the goblin-like clown, mocks the crowd with great mirth.

In spring at Pashupatinath is Shiva Ratri: the night of Shiva. Holi is another festival celebrated across the country. Watch out during this festival, as coloured dyes are thrown at passers-by; tourists and trekkers are fair game! The cavalcade of the white Seto Machhendranath idol also takes place in spring, when a tall wooden chariot housing this rain god is dragged through old Kathmandu, often pulling down power lines and brushing the top storeys of the old brick houses of Asan. A similar festival takes place in May, when the red Rato Machhendranath is hauled around Patan and back out to Bungamati.

CULTURAL CONSIDERATIONS

Despite contact with the outside world since 1950, Nepal remains a conservative country, especially in the remoter hilly districts. Avoid overt expressions of affection and always dress modestly – anywhere in Nepal – to avoid causing offence. Skimpy shorts and tops are fine in St Tropez, but wearing such attire here could cause embarrassment (and invariably some lewd comments from the locals behind your back). In the icy confines of the high mountains, an inappropriate state of partial undress is unlikely to be an issue – unless you have already become an ascetic!

It's a rare thing for a non-believer to be allowed into the inner sanctuaries of Hindu temples anywhere across the country; remember that leather apparel, belts and shoes are not permitted inside. When visiting monasteries, remove trekking hats and boots before entry. Small donations are appreciated in monasteries and photographers should ask before taking pictures inside. On the trail, keep to the left of *mani* walls and *chortens* (religious devotional structures: see Appendix B) and circle them in a clockwise direction. The mantra 'Om Mani Padme Hum' – Hail to the Jewel

Buddhist chortens, Tange, Mustang (Trek 5)

in the Lotus – is inscribed on these walls, on stones and on prayer wheels.

If you are invited into a local house, remember that the cooking area, hearth and fire are treated with reverence. Do not throw litter there. Never sit in such a way as to point the soles of your feet at your hosts, or step over their feet. Avoid touching food, and be careful to eat with your right hand if no utensils are available. Never touch a Nepali on the head.

Begging

Begging is endemic in Nepal, possibly putting a brake on development and local initiative. Seen from the Nepalese point of view, all foreigners are rich, and therefore fair game to be enticed into parting with some of their hard-earned cash. Ordinarily no one will mind this, but in the long term local people need to be helped to help themselves; simply handing out money is not the answer.

Begging is not confined to the poverty-stricken lower classes; even the higher echelons have the same attitude – there will always be some rich overseas government to build a road or desperately needed hydro plant, and so on. Western governments, the UN and large donors continue to ignore the unaccountability of bribery and slush funds, while boasting about how much they give to the poor.

The world still seems to see Nepal as a begging-bowl case. In fact, the wealth of talent in the country is amazing; the 'make something from nothing' and the 'make do and mend' culture shows a level of ingenuity that has almost disappeared in the throwaway societies of the developed world. Given the opportunity, Nepal will flourish and prosper.

Helping the community

The world's big donor organisations and charities hold a soft spot for Nepal. This is in no small part due to its welcoming and charismatic people, many of whom are exceedingly industrious. The effect of these multinational donations is not often felt directly by the majority of the people, so there is plenty of scope for small initiatives to be implemented by visitors who wish to help. Often it is these

projects – improving village water supplies or local electrification, for example – that really make a difference. Check out some of these local projects below.

Kathmandu Environmental Education Project (KEEP) (www. keepnepal.org) was established in 1992 to 'provide education on safe and ecologically sustainable trekking methods to preserve Nepal's fragile eco-systems'. Based down a lane off Tri Devi Marg in Thamel, they give vital information to trekkers, harness tourism for development, run environmental seminars, manage a porters' clothing bank, and help to promote a more professional ethos while improving the skills of tourism professionals. They run volunteer

Local school in the foothills of the Annapurnas

PORTER WELFARE

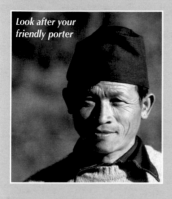

Look after your friendly porter

Every year porters die on the mountain trails of Nepal, and very occasionally some of them are in the employ of foreign trekkers. Fortunately today there is much more awareness about the possible dangers faced by porters, partly because of some high-profile accidents in the past. Exploitation has always been a part of Nepalese society; the caste system, which still pervades the roots of its culture, ensures that each person knows his status. However, visitors need not adopt such attitudes. Following the Maoist insurgency, general wage levels for porters and once badly treated workers throughout society have risen dramatically – perhaps the only benefit of that long reign of violence! Two organisations have made an impact on porter welfare, the International Porter Protection Group (see above) and Tourism Concern (www.tourismconcern.org.uk). Trekking agencies in Nepal are now expected to provide adequate insurance for all their staff.

The following are some outline guidelines for all trekkers.

- Ensure that your porters have adequate clothing and equipment for the level of trek you are undertaking: footwear, hat, gloves, warm clothing and sleeping bags or blankets as necessary.
- Be prepared with extra medicines for your porters, and don't abandon them if they are sick; carry funds for such a situation.
- Group trekkers can make themselves aware of the policy of their chosen agent and keep an eye on the reality on the ground.

Naturally it is hard for trekkers to really know what is going on behind the scenes; the Nepalese are masters at appealing to the sympathetic nature of visitors to the country.

programmes and conduct wilderness first aid training.

Community Action Nepal (www.canepal.org.uk), co-founded by mountaineer Doug Scott, seeks to improve the infrastructure of villages in the middle hills by building schools, health posts and clean water projects, and developing cottage industries.

Choice Humanitarian (www.choicehumanitarian.org) is seeking to end poverty by concentrating on sustainable village development through tourism. The aim is to empower village people, generally with neither funds nor skill, to improve their own prospects.

Mountain People (www.mountain-people.org) 'Helping mountain people to help themselves' is an independent, non-profit, non-political, non-religious and cross-cultural organisation. They help with schools, porter welfare, women's projects and bridge building.

The **International Porter Protection Group** (IPPG) (www.ippg.net) was started in 1997 to raise awareness about the conditions and plight of all-too-frequently exploited porters. Their task is to focus on the provision of clothing, shelter and medical care for often-overlooked working porters in Nepal.

GETTING THERE

Flights to Nepal

The main airlines currently flying to Kathmandu are:

- *Air Arabia* From The Gulf
- *Air India* Via Delhi, Kolkata (Calcutta) and Varanasi
- *ArkeFly* Seasonal charter service from Europe
- *Bangladesh Biman* Via Dhaka; for budget travellers with time to kill
- *Air China* Links Kathmandu with Lhasa, Chengdu and Guangzhou (Canton)

Karjung Kang peak, above the trail towards Damodar Himal (Trek 6)

- *Dragon Air* From Hong Kong
- *Druk Air* From Paro, Bhutan, to Kathmandu and on to Delhi
- *Etihad Airways* Via Abu Dhabi from Europe
- *Gulf Air* Via Bahrain or Abu Dhabi
- *Indigo* Cheap Indian carrier
- *Jet Airways* (India) Good through-service from London to Nepal via Delhi
- *Korean Airlines* From the Far East.
- *Nepal Airlines* From Delhi, Bombay, Dubai and Hong Kong – for those with bags of time
- *Oman Air* Via Muscat
- *Silk Air* From Singapore
- *SpiceJet* Low-cost Indian carrier
- *Thai Airways* Via Bangkok, from Europe and Australia/New Zealand
- *Qatar Airways* Via Doha from Europe
- *Virgin, BA, Turkish Airlines and other major airlines* To Delhi; then one of the Indian carriers to Kathmandu.

This information is, naturally, subject to change. Check the internet or your local travel agent for the latest information.

Overland routes to Nepal

There are several overland routes into Nepal from India and Tibet/China. Land borders with India are at Sonauli/Belahiya near Bhairahawa; Raxaul/Birgunj; Nepalganj; Mahendranagar; and Kakarvitta. The most-used entry point from India is the Sonauli/Belahiya border north of Gorakhpur.

Buses connect Bhairahawa to Kathmandu and Pokhara. The Banbasa/Mahendranagar western border links Nepal to Delhi, but it's a long journey by local transport. Those travelling between Kathmandu and Darjeeling or Sikkim use the eastern border at Kakarvitta.

Kathmandu is linked to Lhasa in Tibet by the Arniko/Friendship Highway through Kodari/Zhangmu. It is a spectacular three-to-four-day journey, climbing over several 5000m passes through Nyalam, Xigatse and Gyangtse to Tibet's once-forbidden capital, Lhasa.

Getting to Dumre and Pokhara

Many trekkers fly to Pokhara – a short flight from Kathmandu. On a clear day, stupendous views of Langtang, Ganesh Himal, Himalchuli, Manaslu and the Annapurnas grace the northern frontier. Airlines serving Pokhara (roughly US$85 single) include Yeti Airlines/Tara Air, Buddha Air, Agni Air and Guna Airlines, departing from the domestic terminal next to the international airport. Planes to Jomsom depart from Pokhara soon after dawn, so an overnight stay in Pokhara is necessary.

Travelling to Pokhara (200km) by bus is quite straightforward these days, since the road has been improved all the way. Normal journey time is six to eight hours, but traffic can get heavy in the afternoon if you are heading back towards Kathmandu. The most luxurious bus is currently the

EARLY EXPLORERS TO ANNAPURNA

Annapurna I sunset from Kalopani (Trek 1)

When Nepal first opened to foreigners in the 1950s a few parties entered through the border south of Pokhara. French alpinists Maurice Herzog, Louis Lachenal, Lionel Terray, Gaston Rebuffat and others were granted access to Nepal in the spring of 1950. Despite having ambitions to summit the higher peak of Dhaulagiri, they settled for Annapurna I. Much of the arduous adventure was spent finding access routes to the mountain and its lower ramparts. Herzog's party succeeded in summiting Annapurna I on 3 June, making it the highest peak over 8000m attained, but the cost of the expedition on his and Lachenal's frostbitten fingers and toes are the abiding memory for readers of his book.

A British-Nepalese Army Expedition succeeded on the North Face of Annapurna I, when Henry Day and Gerry Owens made the top – incredibly it was 20 years later. At the same time an attempt was made on the awe-inspiring buttresses of the South Face, seen from the Annapurna Sanctuary, by Chris Bonington's team. Dougal Haston and Don Whillans tackled this treacherous face on 27 May 1970, just a week after Day and Owens.

Climbers from all over the world have been drawn to the Himalayas of Nepal ever since. The early climbers were backed by vast entourages of porters, cooks and crews to carry their tons of equipment. In the 1960s ex-Gurkha officer Jimmy Roberts decided that the local portering traditions of the country, which allowed goods to 'reach all those parts that were hard to reach', could be adapted for trekking.

Soon all manner of adventurers, hippies and travellers also flocked to the country. You are following in the steps of some illustrious climbers, explorers and yes, ordinary modern-day adventure-seekers like yourself.

Greenline service: US$20 including a great lunch at the Riverside Springs Resort about halfway to Pokhara. Other slightly less comfortable (but generally reliable) tourist buses depart around 7am from Kantipath near Thamel. 'Local' buses, which are even cheaper, leave from the Gongabu bus depot, northwest of the city, but are only recommended for those wishing to rub shoulders (and more) with the locals and their animals all day. The taxi fare to the bus depot is normally more than the bus ticket, so there is little to recommend this option. Local buses often stop in Mugling, an infamous, scruffy village 110km west of Kathmandu – eating lunch here has its risks. In days gone by, dishes of 'hepatitis and rice' were served up.

The road plummets steeply down after leaving the Kathmandu Valley. On a clear day you will see Ganesh Himal, Himalchuli and maybe Annapurna II. The road descends through Naubise then soon follows the Trisuli River, passing through Charaudi, Malekhu and Majhimtar. Buses continue past the Manakamana cable car station for the temple shrine, and on to Mugling. Rafting parties can be observed on the Trisuli. From Mugling the road follows the Marsyangdi River through Ambo Khaireni, the turn-off for Gorkha town. At km135 is Dumre, where Annapurna Circuit trekkers need to wake up and change buses for Besisahar. Otherwise it's on to Pokhara and, with luck, views of Himalchuli,

Lamjung, Annapurna II and IV, along with Machhapuchhre; all are simply dazzling in the afternoon light. From Pokhara at sunset this astonishing panorama is truly heaven-sent – a vision that guests have marvelled at since Annapurna was 'discovered'.

VISAS AND PERMITS

Nepal

All foreign nationals (except Indians) require a visa. Currently visas are available from embassies and overland borders, as well as at Tribhuvan International Airport on arrival in Kathmandu (check that this is still the case before arrival). Entering or exiting the country at the remoter crossing points and from Tibet may be subject to change, with the unpredictable political difficulties in some of these districts.

Applying in your home country is one option, although it will cost more. Be sure to apply well ahead of the time of travel, in case there are any holidays at the embassy related to the festival periods in Nepal. Many people always obtain visas on arrival; at the present time this is the simplest option. The maximum length of stay in Nepal is five months in one calendar year (although the fifth month can sometimes be hard to obtain).

Tourist visas are available for 15, 30 or 90 days, at a fee of US$25, $40 and $100 (payment in cash) respectively. Check the up-to-date

Village house on the trek up to Chowk Chisopani (Trek 12 variant)

fees at www.immi.gov.np. Those staying longer can get an extension in Kathmandu at the Immigration Department at a cost of US$30 (the minimum fee) or pay a daily charge of US$2 per day. All visas are currently multiple-entry, helpful for those heading out to places like Bhutan, Tibet or India and returning to Kathmandu for their flight home.

Note on Indian visas
Although those coming to Nepal from India may hold a multiple-entry 180-day Indian visa, problems have been occurring since the Mumbai bomb attacks in 2008. Visitors entering Nepal from India cannot return to India for two months (difficult if planning to return home via India). It is possible to obtain an Indian visa

before leaving your home country that allows for re-entry, but the visa must state the number of entries. A few people have been able to obtain a re-entry stamp at the Indian Embassy in Kathmandu after a lot of bureaucratic obstacles, but it can take days.

Note on Tibet/China entry
Travel to Tibet from Nepal currently requires special arrangements. **Do not** get a Chinese visa in advance of your visit, as it will simply be cancelled at the Kathmandu embassy. Visas are normally issued on paper only for the duration of the stated itinerary, with extensions not possible. Allow for a few days in Kathmandu and make the application well ahead of your arrival in Nepal. Arranging the visa in Nepal must be through a Nepalese

SOME NEPAL EMBASSIES

UK 12A Kensington Palace Gardens, London W8 4QU; tel: +44 (0207) 229 1594; email: eon@nepembassy.org.uk; www.nepembassy.org.uk

US 2131 Leroy Place, NW, Washington, DC 20008; tel: +1 (202) 667 4550; email: info@nepalembassyusa.org; www.nepalembassyusa.org

India Barakhamba Road, New Delhi 110001, India; tel: +91 (11) 2347 6200; email: connepembdelhi@airtelmail.in; www.nepalembassy.in

China (Consulate) Norbulingka Road 13, Lhasa, Tibet, People's Republic of China; tel: +86 (891) 682 2881; email: rncglx@public.ls.xz.cn

For others, see www.mofa.gov.np.

agent. Independent travellers can still visit Tibet by taking the 'budget tour' on offer through Kathmandu travel agents.

Trekking permits

All trekkers in Nepal are required to obtain permits before setting out on their expeditions. Both the documents below can be procured for a fee by trekking agencies in Kathmandu, or independently at the Bhrikuti Mandap building, south of Ratna Park bus depot, tel: 01 425 6909. The office is open every day except Saturday and public holidays.

Trekkers' Information Management System (TIMS)

There are two types of permits for trekkers: Blue, issued through trekking companies, costing US$10, and Green for individuals, costing US$20 (maybe payable in rupees). TIMS cards can be issued on the spot in 30mins or so. Take a copy of your passport and two photos for the single-use card. Cards are valid for at least one month and longer if requested. See www.timsnepal.com.

Annapurna Conservation Area Project (ACAP)

Visitors to the Annapurna region are also required to pay for entry to the ACAP zone that encompasses nearly all of the trails described in this guide. Currently the fee is Rs2000 per person per single entry.

Note Single entry does mean just that; if you leave one part of the conservation area hoping to re-enter in another (for example, you cannot even get the bus from Beni to Birethanti), you will be refused – this means no rest and recuperation in Pokhara is permitted without payment again in full!

Permits for restricted areas

Prospective trekkers planning a trip to Upper Mustang or Nar-Phu do not require a TIMS card but do need to pay for additional permits and observe

ANNAPURNA CONSERVATION AREA PROJECT

Meeting the locals in the Lamjung foothills

The Annapurna Conservation Area Project was established in 1986. Its aims were to regulate activities within the zone to promote conservation in tandem with community development. The project began work on developing more ecologically sound ways of improving the environment. One major aim was to reduce the destruction of the forests caused by traditional wood-burning cooking; other schemes sought to improve health and hygiene levels, as well as improving basic infrastructure. Bridges, schools, health posts, safe drinking water depots, kerosene dumps and regulation of trekkers have all brought significant benefits to locals and visitors alike. Preservation of the local culture is another key aim, and certainly the monasteries and historic places have seen the results of this sustaining project.

National Trust for Nature Conservation (NTNC)
PO Box 3712, Jawalakhel, Lalitpur, Nepal; tel: 977-1-5526571, 5526573; email: info@ntnc.org.np; www.ntnc.org.np; www.forestrynepal.org.
Trekking Agencies' Association of Nepal (TAAN)
Tel: +977-1-4427473, 4440920, 4440921; email: taan@wlink.com.np; www.taan.org.npSee also www.welcomenepal.com and www.tourism.gov.np.

Lo Manthang harvest (Trek 5)

other conditions for entry to restricted areas. These are normally procured by your trekking agency from the constantly moving immigration office. In addition, both areas require you to take a guide. All places to be visited should be mentioned in your application. Check at www.immi.gov.np/appendix (Appendix 12).

Mustang

Currently a fee of US$500 is levied for the first 10 days, with an additional US$50 per extra day. Trekkers need to be familiar with the rules concerning conservation, ecology and cultural aspects when entering Mustang. Independent trekking in the Mustang region is not yet allowed

Nar-Phu

Your trekking agent will normally obtain your permit, but if you need to go with him to get it be aware of the following anomalies. The permit is issued for one week, but officials will try to insist that it's for seven days and only six nights, which immediately causes problems with the itinerary. The permit should have seven days written on it, but the fixed entry and exit dates might reflect the six nights. (Fortunately the checkpost in Koto is much more in tune with reality and automatically allowed us the correct seven-night period, and they also let one trekker in a day earlier than their permit stated. This means you do not need to be bamboozled into paying

THE EVER-CHANGING REGULATIONS

The trekking regulations have been constantly modified over recent years, so you will need to check the latest changes when planning your trek. Information on the internet is often not up-to-date, so you will need to check in Kathmandu or Pokhara.

Even as this guide was going to press, there was talk of changing the rules to require all independent trekkers to take a guide or porter. Further talks continue on this issue, but as yet no law has been passed. Such schemes (usually instigated by the big trekking outfits) have been imposed in the past, but subsequently abandoned with equal speed. Previous schemes actually harmed many small or fledgling local tourist operatives, porters and guides – particularly all those outside the Kathmandu valley. The reason cited for the latest changes is security – mainly because some individuals who trekked alone and off the main trails sadly came to grief. How these new regulations will affect trekking in Nepal is not clear. Information about the independent TIMs cards is also subject to change.

See also:
- www.immi.gov.np – immigration department for visa and permits
- www.timsnepal.com – information on TIMS cards
- www.taan.org.np – Trekking Agencies' Association of Nepal

for another week, unless you plan some extra days for acclimatisation or additional walks from Phu or Nar; crossing the Kang La will not need an extra week.) It's very unfortunate that extra days cannot be added to this permit, as for Mustang. Theoretically a group must be at least two trekkers, but if you are a lone visitor you can pay double to get the proper papers.

WHEN TO GO

A trek anywhere in the Annapurna range is best undertaken in either autumn or spring. The autumn period, usually the most stable, is the optimum period for trekking in Nepal and will be the busiest time on the trails. Traditionally early October (after the monsoon) heralded the beginning of this season, but in recent years unsettled weather has prevailed. This has given rise to unseasonable rain, heavy cloud and delays for those flying to Jomsom. After mid-October the weather is usually better, with clearer skies and magical views. The harvest is underway, carpeting the hillsides with fabulous colours. November is often the clearest month, with crisp and clear days likely well into December. December is much colder at higher altitude, but trails

Dhaulagiri from a snowy Kopra Danda (Trek 4)

are quieter. The stable conditions expected in autumn can occasionally be disrupted – about once every five years – when a storm blows in from the Bay of Bengal, wreaking havoc with heavy snow in the mountains.

Trekking through the winter is perfectly possible, but heading to high altitude during January and early February might mean encountering more cloud, snow and bitterly cold temperatures; minus 20°C has been recorded in Manang. Trekking into the Annapurna Sanctuary then can bring the risk of avalanche, so check locally with the lodges before proceeding up the Modi Khola. Crossing the Thorong La on the Circuit is also risky – heavy snow makes this dangerous, with a risk of avalanche even before the pass is reached.

The spring trekking season runs from late February to early May. The weather is generally stable, although clouds are likely to cover the mountains more often, and it will be hotter and quite muggy in the lower valleys. Haze is another factor for those who want their mountains crisp and clear for photography. Trekkers interested in flowering plants always favour the spring, when the rhododendrons and magnolia are spectacular. Wind tends to be a factor at this time of year, particularly closer to the Tibetan plateau, north of Manang or Muktinath.

Trekking at the height of summer, July and August, is not recommended

OFFICIAL HOLIDAYS

1 January	New Year
19 February	Democracy Day
14 April	Nepali New Year
23 April	Democracy Day
1 May	Labour Day
28 May	Republic Day

There are also many other religious festive days. For comprehensive listings see www. qppstudio.net and click on *Nepal*.

and is totally frustrating for those hoping to see mountain vistas. Cloud, rain and snow can be expected at any time from mid-June to mid-September. The monsoon also brings landslides, leeches and flooding – so forget it, or keep to the lowest foothills around Pokhara.

STYLE OF TREKKING

The type of trek you are considering will dictate the itinerary. Very little of modern-day Nepal is wilderness. Trekking trails link the villages and are surprisingly busy; local porters, people off to markets, children scurrying about, dogs, monkeys, cows and trekkers all share these routes.

Fully supported group treks

For many this is the preferred option, providing maximum security for visitors. The tour operator removes many of the difficulties and discomforts associated with other ways of organising a trek. Visas and permits can be easily procured, transport does not have to be considered and all day-to-day logistics such as accommodation, food and carriage of baggage will be taken care of. Most trips will be fully inclusive, with few added extras. Clients can relax and admire the scenery around the Annapurnas in as much comfort as possible. Group treks utilise both lodge accommodation and tents; take your pick.

Note that there are some disadvantages to commercial group trekking. Large groups with the support of a Nepali crew have more impact on the local environment. Sometimes clients have to wait at camp for the gear to arrive, although lodges will be well stocked with drinks and refreshments. A major disadvantage is that there is less flexibility on a pre-organised itinerary. You may also be hiking with fellow trekkers who have underestimated the challenges and may not be in the best of spirits. In general, however, most hikers enjoy the conviviality of like-minded fellow walkers.

One other unnecessary danger is the possible effect of 'peer pressure' within the group. At its worst this can overrule common sense, with some members ignoring symptoms of altitude sickness in the unacknowledged race to compete. Do not fall into this lethal trap.

A typical group trekker's day

The day begins at dawn for most trekkers, but fully supported walkers

Pony express: taking the deluxe option from Manang to the Thorong La (Trek 1)

can expect a mug of tea and a bowl of hot water thrust through a tent flap or lodge doorway at around 6am. This is the wake-up call and means 'get up now and pack your bags'. During breakfast, tents will be dismantled and the porter loads organised. Lodge trekkers can luxuriate in a warm dining area. Poor old campers will have to take the weather as it comes. With breakfast over and the loads packed, it's off on the trail.

The morning walks tend to be a little longer to get the best of the morning's clarity. Three to four hours is an average hiking period before lunch, including the odd tea stop along the way. Those on a lodge-based trek will find lunch 'fooding' easily on the main routes. Campers can slouch along until the kitchen boys and the cook come racing by to get ahead of the group to prepare lunch. It might be pancakes, bread or chips, tinned meat, fruit and other tasty goodies – probably a wider selection than available to the lodgers.

Afternoon walks are around three hours, although some days are inevitably longer because of the terrain. Campers should watch the kitchen boys and not get ahead of them. Afternoon tea and biscuits are served for campers (and group) lodgers on arrival at the night's halt. Now is the time to read, rest or explore the locality. Dinner comes piping hot a little after sunset and may be a three-course

47

delight. And that's the day done for campers, bar crawling into that sleeping bag. Lodge guests can utilise the light, enjoying a beer or sampling the often dubiously produced local brews. (Be warned that so doing can adversely affect your health!) Take care with alcohol at altitude. It may be best to avoid it altogether.

Trek crews

Some of the following will also apply to small private groups and to independent trekkers hiring local staff. Normally the trek is lead by a Nepalese guide who speaks good English and has done the trip many times before. Under him will be the most important member of the crew (not counting the cook): the Sirdar. His function (which can also be as leader/guide in a small group) is to organise all the porters, cooks and accompanying sherpas. With as many as 50 staff for a big camping group on a long trek, he certainly is a busy man. The cook naturally is in the spotlight; he will have several kitchen boys with him who will race ahead of the group to prepare lunch, afternoon tea and dinner. They carry all the cooking gear and often sing along the way.

In addition, there will be several sherpas. Some – although not all – may be from the Sherpa ethnic group who live in the Everest region. The term 'sherpa' in this context refers to the job of guiding the group, with one at the front and one bringing up the rear of the party. Big groups often have other sherpas floating between the front and rear guard. They also put

Group trek porters in the rhododendron forest near Siklis (Trek 11)

up the dining tent and tents for the campers. Then there are the porters, as many as 30–40 for a large camping group. In such cases there will also be a Naiki (head porter), who takes some of the responsibilities from the Sirdar, organising and distributing the loads. The Naiki is often seen in the mornings adding items to a lighter load, causing some amusement and embarrassing the culprit who has offloaded a heavy bag on to a colleague in the hope of an easier day.

When booking a trek, be sure to check if all the food and meals are included. In recent years there has been a tendency for some companies to allow members on lodge treks to order and pay for all their own meals. This has happened because of the ever-rising costs in the mountains and because not including food appears to give a competitive edge in terms of the price of the trek. Do check this aspect of the 'fully inclusive' arrangement.

Independently organised trips
For those with more time, or who do not want to be locked into the group ethos, this is a good option, offering a great deal of freedom. Participants will be able to design and follow their own itinerary, according to their preferred length of trip and other special interests.

Organising a trip through an agent in the UK or Nepal for a couple or a small group is not necessarily more expensive than a group departure. Booking directly in Kathmandu is cheaper, but there is an increased risk because you will not be covered by any company liability if things go wrong. Be sure to have adequate insurance cover for helicopter rescue. These days there are a number of excellent local agents in Kathmandu who are very experienced in dealing with trekkers approaching them directly.

Contacting a local operator in Nepal is normally straightforward, although they might be unable to answer immediately at times because of regular, scheduled power cuts (known as load shedding). If you choose to arrange the trip with a Kathmandu agent, you can finalise the trip and pay the operators directly, but remember that if an internal flight is involved – to Jomsom for example – the agent might ask for some advance payment to cover that.

Independent trekking
This style is very popular with those able to carry their own equipment and seeking a closer, more intimate rapport with the local people. It's also a cheaper way to trek in Nepal and ensures that your cash goes straight to the local people. Anyone willing to carry their own gear, with some experience of hill walking, can easily arrange a lodge-based trek on the main routes around the Annapurnas. If you have already been to Nepal or other developing countries you will have the added advantage of knowing roughly what to expect.

Many other trekkers in the Annapurna region hire a local porter/guide through a reputable agency, paying all the living expenses as well as the wage. If you hire a porter, make sure you check and provide all the necessary clothing and equipment for high altitude. In the past porters have died on high passes due to lack of proper equipment. Porters should also be insured – this should already be done if you hire a porter/guide through an agency. Hiring porters off the street and hotel areas is not necessarily a good idea these days, unless it comes through reliable recommendations.

If you decide to head off into the hills alone, be sure to read the sections in this guide on altitude and mountain safety. The points may seem obvious, but every year people are evacuated from or die in these mountains.

An independent trekker's day
Being independent means you could have a long lie-in and make all those group people envious, but more likely you will want to be on the trail as early as possible. In the lodges you may be unlucky and find yourself at a disadvantage to the groups, who will often be served first. After breakfast the day is much the same as for those in groups, except that you can dictate your own pace, itinerary and lunch spots, so there are some positives against the negative of the heavy pack on your shoulders. Living off the lodges generally means a simple diet, but does that really matter? The lodges

Backpacking through Thonje kani (Trek 1)

'FRIED CHAPS'

The Nepalis' use of the English language is a most endearing feature of the country. You'll see this most obviously on signboards advertising the lodges' 'faxsilities', such as inside 'to lets', 'toilet free rooms' and, on enticing tea-house menus, 'fried chaps', 'banana panick' and the like. Watch out for the proudly displayed signs 'Open defecation-free zone'.

can supply all you really need in the way of sustenance. See Appendix E for details of foreign tour operators and local agencies.

ACCOMMODATION ON TREK

Mountains cannot provide bread and warmth, but they can provide secure anchorage for a troubled mind.

The Mountain Top, *Frank S Smythe*

Lodges

The style and condition of accommodation used on trek will depend on the sort of trip chosen. In the past, camping throughout the Annapurnas was the best option, but today lodges are the more popular choice. Lodges en route are relatively basic, but dormitory-style rooms are rapidly being replaced by small but perfectly adequate twin-bedded rooms. Beds tend to be hard, and dividing walls

A trader's house lodge in Tukuche (Trek 1)

allow for a certain amount of communal interaction. Mattresses are getting thicker each year, so carrying a thermarest is not really necessary except on rare occasions (and for some homestays). There are now a few deluxe resort-style lodges in the Ghorepani/Ghandruk area, which are effectively 'normal hotels' with comfortable bedding, carpets and excellent dining areas.

Camping

Camping trekkers can expect a surprising degree of comfort in often with remote regions. Typically, large two-man tents are used and a mess tent is provided. In addition, dining tables, chairs, toilet tents and mattresses come as standard. All food is provided and cooked by the crews.

Homestay

Homestay is a new concept, where trekkers overnight in local people's houses. Normally a room will be set aside for the guests. Most homestays are basic, with outside toilets and primitive washing facilities – much as the first trekkers found. Through local hydroelectric schemes electricity has now found its way to many rural areas, so lack of comfort is not quite on the scale it used to be. Mattresses may be thick or thin! Meals are provided by the household, using wholesome local produce. Don't expect much other than nourishing *dal bhat* (lentils and rice) for dinner, but you could be surprised!

Washing

If there are no proper showers at a lodge you can ask for a bucket of hot water, but you'll have to pay for it. Hot showers in lodges are generally provided by solar systems, but as with many aspects of trekking, utilising scarce resources (wood or kerosene) means conflict with conservation. Camping group trekkers will be given a bowl of hot water at some point during the day, normally mornings, and often now on arrival at camp as well.

Toilets

These will provide endless conversation throughout any trip. Most are outside, often up small, steep steps... be very careful not to drop any valuables down the holes! Increasingly however, loos are becoming quite modern, at least in appearance, with a few lodges offering 'Flash Toilets'. Along the trails, toilet paper should be burnt and waste buried where possible.

FOOD

At one time a liking for dal bhat would have been a great advantage. Today eating on trek has become most civilised, with ample amounts and reasonable choice almost everywhere. Those on fully inclusive group or independently organised treks with full services can expect filling breakfasts, including porridge/cereal, bread/toast with eggs, as well as hot drinks. Lunch is often a substantial affair, with tinned meat, noodles, chips, cooked

The kitchen of a lodge in Phu (Trek 6)

bread and something sweet to round off. At night the lodges are able to provide two- or three-course dinners: soup, noodles/pasta/rice/potatoes as well as a dessert of fruit and so on. Plentiful amounts of hot water/drinks are available on arrival and at all meal times to ensure dehydration is kept at bay, especially at higher altitudes. The further you get from civilisation, the less choice there is, but this far into the trek anything tastes good!

Kathmandu now has a good variety of supermarkets, but don't anticipate many treats elsewhere. Across the city new shopping malls are opening, with familiar food brands and every possible item necessary

IT'S BOILING!

Note that water only boils at 100°C at sea level, and the boiling temperature reduces by approximately 1°C for every 300m, meaning that your tea may not be as tasty nor the instant soups so scrumptious at Phu, 4100m above sea level. Thermometers were used by the early spies in the Himalayas to ascertain the altitude according to the temperature of their tea.

for comfort. Pokhara Lakeside also has a good range of smaller supermarkets now. You might want to take some of your own supplies if venturing into remoter areas. Muesli tastes good even with water; instant soups and tinned fish are a good standby. Everyone should take chocolate, energy bars and snacks to relieve the eventual monotony of lodge food. Make sure as much indestructible rubbish is carried out by you or your crews, or use the places set aside for disposal.

MONEY MATTERS

The currency is the Nepalese Rupee (Rs). Notes come in the following denominations: Rs5, 10, 20, 50, 100, 500 and 1000, and coins: Rs1, 2 and 5.

Approximate exchange rates

£1=Rs125	€1=Rs103
US$1=Rs78	CHF1=Rs85

Banks and ATMs

ATMs are now common in Kathmandu and Pokhara. In Thamel there is one in the Kathmandu Guest House courtyard. Larger sums can be taken from Nabil Bank ATMs. The Himalayan Bank is on Tri Devi Marg.

Moneychangers are very quick to change cash or travellers cheques, and rates are marginally lower than banks. Banks rarely exchange money

these days, and if they do are generally exceedingly slow. Currently there are no banks on the trails, although Jomsom has an ATM that may work, but don't depend on it. Moneychangers there offer poor rates for cash.

Budgeting for the trek

Since all the costs are included in most group treks, there will only be personal expenses such as drinks, souvenirs and tips to be added to the budget, as well as some evening meals in Kathmandu and Pokhara.

Those trekking individually will need to plan for porters (if required), accommodation and food, as well as the above extras. If hiking without a porter or guide, allow at least Rs2000/US$25 per day per person for your own on-trip expenses. Add another US$20–30 per day for a guide, $20–25 for a porter-guide and $15–20 for a porter, and confirm these wages in advance. Get insurance for local staff. Make sure you know if you are expected to cover the guide/porter's sustenance and lodgings. Take more cash than suggested, as there are so few opportunities to change money. Expect prices to rise by up to ten per cent a year in future.

Before planning a fully independent trek, see 'The ever-changing regulations' in Visas and permits (above). Expect to add $10–20 per day if these rules are in force during your trek.

COSTS ON TREK

Chicken curry on the move

Unsurprisingly, the higher you go, the higher the bills for food and accommodation. The authors spent roughly Rs1500 (room with half board for two) in Jagat, while the same in Braka cost Rs2290 and at Phedi Rs2800. On the way down in Tukuche, the equivalent cost Rs1810.

In season (prices in rupees): dorm-bed 100, single room 150, double 250, triple 300, attached (inside loo) 400; dal bhat 300–450, black tea (small pot) 250–400, Coke 100–300, fried egg 90–200, boiled water 80–400, chapatti 100–250, soup 160–350, porridge 150–300, plain rice 180–350, momo (dumpling) 230–450, macaroni 180–450, potatoes 180–450, noodles 180–400, curry 160–450, spring roll 220–450, apple pancake 180–350.

Tipping
Ever since the art of trekking in Nepal was developed in the 1960s, it has been a tradition for group and independent visitors to tip their crews at the end of a trek. It's rare that anyone is dissatisfied with the service they have been offered, so it's no great hardship to budget for this extra. The head cook should get a little more, and the Sirdar and leader/guide more again. Allow around 10–15 per cent

of the wages, or one day's wage per each week on trek. Trekkers may also wish to donate some of their clothing and equipment to the crew.

HEALTH MATTERS

The main problem when discussing health matters in Nepal is the relative remoteness of the trekking regions, and the high altitude. It cannot be emphasised enough that there are virtually no adequate medical facilities en route. The nearest serviceable hospital for the Annapurna region is in Pokhara. Rural clinics are developing, but only the most basic treatments can be expected. There is a Western-manned clinic in Manang that can give limited assistance to those with ailments and those suffering the effects of high altitude. Evacuation is possible from almost all parts of the Annapurnas, but you must have insurance (or pay) before a helicopter will take off.

With relatively fewer bugs surviving at high altitude, the high zones of Nepal are not as unhealthy as some of the more popular lowland destinations, providing you are careful with personal hygiene and what you eat. That said, local levels of hygiene leave a lot to be desired by Western standards.

The following suggestions have been found to reduce health problems significantly:
• Never drink untreated tap water
• Avoid salads

• Peel fruits
• Brush teeth in bottled/cleaned water, or without water
• Wash/clean hands regularly.

Water sterilisation
The biggest problem on trek is the lack of clean running water. Keeping hands clean is paramount in order to avoid the more common ailments. Fortunately lodges on the trails are much more aware of hygiene these days, and those on group treks will be supplied with plentiful boiled water and hot drinks. Others should ensure they obtain the same through their lodge hosts. In the absence of washing facilities antibacterial gel for hands and largish baby wipes for other parts are extremely useful! Bring plastic bags for storing used items and carry out all such rubbish.

Water boils at a lower temperature at high altitude, so some may wish to add sterilising tablets to the water as an added precaution. Iodine or chlorine tablets, or Micropur, can be used. Bottled drinking water can also be bought in Kathmandu, Pokhara and along the trails, although it gets very expensive the higher you go, and there is the added problem of the detrimental effect of discarded plastic on the environment; you will have to crush and carry out the bottles. The preferred option is to drink boiled water where appropriate, or use the safe water stations along the routes. As an extra precaution, you could add sterilising tablets to the 'safe' water!

Vaccinations

Currently no vaccinations are legally required, but always check the situation before travel in case of any recent changes. Consult your GP about which courses you require, and allow plenty of time for the whole series of vaccinations, as they cannot all be given at the same time and some may need to be spread over a number of weeks. It is worthwhile ensuring that all your vaccinations are recorded on a certificate, although this is not a legal requirement.

- **Cholera** Although neither very effective nor required by law, this might be recommended if any recent outbreak has occurred.

- **Typhoid/paratyphoid** Vaccinations are strongly recommended, as these are potential risks.

- **Yellow fever** Vaccination will give cover for 10 years. It is normally only required if coming from an infected area.

- **Tetanus/polio** Recommended.

- **BCG tuberculosis** Vaccination may be recommended by some GPs.

- **Hepatitis** There are various forms of this nasty disease; hepatitis A is the main risk for travellers. New vaccines are continually being developed for all strains of hepatitis.

- **Meningitis/Japanese encephalitis** Sporadic outbreaks occur in rural parts of Nepal, although the risk is minimal. Vaccines

Kang Guru from Phu Gompa (Trek 6)

are available, but are expensive. Clinics in Kathmandu will give vaccinations at short notice for a much lower negotiable fee than payable at home; the CIWEC clinic is the safest option.

- **Rabies** Certainly found in Nepal, but unless you expect to make prolonged or frequent visits, the vaccination is quite an expensive procedure. Seek advice well before (six months at least) the planned trip. Beware of dogs in Nepal – particularly those that guard herding settlements and monasteries – especially in Mustang.

Malaria prophylaxis

Malaria is not found in most of Nepal; it is at present confined to parts of the southern lowlands. However, those spending a night after a trek in Chitwan, for example, or travelling overland to India, will be exposed to malarial risks.

These risks should not be ignored. Using insect repellent at and after dusk, as well as wearing suitable clothing, will give some protection against bites. The three main drugs used in Nepal are Mefloquine (Lariam), Doxycycline and Malarone (Atovaquone/proguanil). Lariam can have very nasty side effects on some people, so it is wise to test it out before travel. In Britain, travellers may be recommended to take Proguanil daily and Chloroquine weekly, if going to a high-risk area. See also www.ciwec-clinic.com and www.masta-travel-health.com.

Other nasty bugs

Giardia is another bug to watch out for, but there is no preventative treatment apart from careful eating and drinking. It is contracted mostly through drinking infected water. It strikes the digestive tracts and lives happily in its host until arrested by a course of Flagyl (Metronidazole), Secnidazole or Tinidazole (Tiniba in Nepal). This unpleasant bug manifests itself in sulphurous foul-smelling gases, cramp and sometimes diarrhoea.

Dengue fever is occasionally reported in Nepal, but the risk is very low in Kathmandu. There is no treatment other than rest and avoidance of mosquitoes.

Common ailments

The most common ailments are colds, blocked sinuses, headaches and stomach disorders. In the event of stomach upsets, the use of Imodium or Lomotil initially is recommended if symptoms are not serious, and also for convenience during long road journeys. The antibiotic drugs Norfloxacin and Ciprofloxacin may be used in more debilitating cases, and are available from pharmacies in Kathmandu. It is necessary to drink more liquids in dry regions. Dioralyte will help rehydration in cases of fluid loss due to stomach upsets.

A good supply of painkillers for headaches should always be carried in Nepal, where the altitude can cause inconvenience. Common remedies (available from the chemist) for blocked noses, sore throats, coughs and sneezes should be easily accessible in any medical kit. The dry air often causes irritations. Stemetil can be used for those prone to travel sickness.

And finally, don't underestimate the power of the sun at high altitude, despite low temperatures; cover up and use sun cream on exposed parts of the body, and wear a suitable hat.

Dental care
Visit your dentist for a check-up before the trip (unless you want to rely on the 'tooth temple god' in Kathmandu for treatment). There are now some very competent dentists in Kathmandu, but you are unlikely to meet one in the Annapurnas. Try Healthy Smiles in Lazimpat if you have a problem in Kathmandu.

FIRST AID KIT

The following list is not exhaustive but an indication of requirements:
Pocket First Aid and Wilderness Medicine Dr Jim Duff and Dr Peter Gormly (Cicerone) – don't leave home without it!

- Antibacterial gel
- Antibiotics (general course)
- Antihistamine cream
- Antiseptic cream
- Aspirin/paracetamol
- Blister prevention
- Dioralyte rehydration sachets
- Dressings
- Eyewash
- Insect repellent
- Knee bandage
- Safety pins
- Scissors
- Sterile gloves
- Stomach upset remedies
- Sun cream
- Tinidazole
- Thermometer
- Water sterilising tablets
- Wet wipes
- Personal medications
- Diamox, coca tablets, ginkgo biloba (for altitude sickness)

Clinics

Check with your GP and with one of the specialist clinics listed below for the latest medical advice for travellers.

- **International Society of Travel Medicine** www.istm.org
- **Hospital for Tropical Diseases Travel Clinic** Mortimer Market, Capper Street, London WC1E 6JB; tel: 020 3456 7890/7891; fax: 020 7388 7645; www.thehtd.org
- **MASTA** (Medical Advisory Service for Travellers Abroad), London School of Hygiene and Tropical Medicine, Keppel Street, London WC1 7HT; tel: 0906 550 1402. MASTA currently have several clinics around the UK; www.masta-travel-health.com
- **NHS Travel website** www.fitfortravel.scot.nhs.uk for advice on immunisations and malaria.
- **CIWEC Clinic** Lainchaur, near the British Embassy in Kathmandu, is an excellent medical centre; www.ciwec-clinic.com

There are always local remedies from self-proclaimed ascetics on the trail, as well as Ayurvedic Indian and Tibetan medical cures, if this lot can't sort you out!

Altitude sickness

Serious altitude problems can occur in the highest mountain regions of northern Nepal. Kathmandu is at 1317m, so no effects of altitude will be felt there, but head straight up to Jomsom and Manang and you will feel lightheaded for a couple of hours. The real risks start at heights above 3400m (11,000ft), especially if you climb quickly. In general, altitude problems in the Annapurna region are confined to the zone above Manang or Kagbeni on the Annapurna Circuit trek, and Machhapuchhre Base Camp in the

Prayer flags at the Thorong La (Trek 1)

Sanctuary. Anyone heading for Mardi Himal along the ridges from Pokhara is probably at the greatest risk of suffering the effects of altitude, due to the rapid ascent. Those conquering Poon Hill will rarely feel any symptoms. Be very careful heading to Nar-Phu; leaving the Nar Valley for Manang presents all the hazards of altitude on the Kang La. And those heading for a trekking peak such as Chulu, Pisang, Tharpu Chuli (Tent Peak), Singu Chuli (Fluted Peak) or the Dhaulagiri Icefall will obviously be well aware of the effects of altitude.

Learn as much as you can about the subject before you go, and check out the medicines on offer to aid acclimatisation (see below). The main symptoms of altitude are headaches, nausea, tiredness, lack of appetite and, later, disorientation. These in themselves are not a reason to stop the trek, but are good indicators of problems that may be overcome by resting when necessary. It is often difficult to sleep. Breathing patterns may be erratic (Cheyne-Stokes breathing) and the heart might thump a bit disconcertingly; however, these are not unusual reactions. It is also a danger to over-exert on arrival at any destination, thinking you have no symptoms; these often only begin to appear after an hour or more.

It is particularly important to walk very slowly, especially when climbing even a small hill. At all times, avoid any hurried walking. Be sure to admit any problems (if only to yourself at first), and don't be pressured by your trekking peers. **Altitude sickness can kill.** If you experience any serious effects before any high pass, consider returning downhill immediately. Carrying on with mild symptoms, perhaps just a slight headache, is acceptable so long as it does not get worse or persist all day and night. The night at Phedi before the Thorong La will determine how well you are acclimatised, although few will sleep well here. Virtually all will feel the effects of altitude above 5000m; some may well feel nauseous and extremely lethargic. This is fairly normal, but symptoms will improve on the descent, so don't worry unduly.

Continuing to ascend with any persistent symptoms can lead to the serious risk of pulmonary or cerebral oedema or even death. There are deaths each year in the Himalayas and Nepal, despite all the warnings. Sometimes complications from altitude sickness can strike very quickly. **Descend immediately, whatever the time of day or night.**

So what else can you do to ward off the effects of altitude? Many trekkers start a course of Diamox (Acetazolamide), a diuretic which thins the blood, makes you urinate more and is generally considered to be of some benefit, although it can have the disturbing side effect of pins and needles in the fingers. Another option is to try coca; not the smoking variety, but a version of the substance used by natives of Peru and Bolivia. Coca is available as homeopathic tablets that some trekkers (including the authors) swear by. It can be difficult to locate these in the UK, but French pharmacies stock them, should you be limbering up in the Alps before your trip. Also recommended by some are ginkgo biloba tablets, which appear to work for reasons not yet defined. It is suggested that these can be taken twice a day for five days before arrival and one tablet a day during the trek, but consult your GP before embarking on a course, as the tablets can affect the blood count and are not suitable for everyone. Finally, avoid alcohol.

Gamow bag and oxygen cylinders

A Gamow bag is a large plastic bag into which a person suffering from serious altitude sickness can be cocooned under higher air pressure to mimic a lower altitude for a limited period. Mountaineers have used oxygen cylinders for years at altitude. These are not generally required on the Annapurna Circuit or lower treks, but in exceptional emergencies may be available at the healthpost in Manang.

MOUNTAIN SAFETY

All mountain walking presents hazards, but with prior awareness and concentration on trek these can be minimised. In Nepal the biggest danger comes from the high altitude, severe cold and bitter winds. Be sure to keep well wrapped up first thing in the morning and make sure you are carrying enough warm clothing for the whole day. Group trekkers will not be carrying all their baggage – just a daysack – and it will not be accessible during the day. In the deep canyons the sun sets very early in the afternoon and temperatures plummet. Take particular care on the rough and rocky trails; bear in mind that the next hospital is hundreds of miles away. Remember that you may not be thinking as clearly as normal at these altitudes; don't take unnecessary chances, such as leaping carelessly across rivers or boulders.

Dehydration is another factor easily overlooked; you may not necessarily feel thirsty in these conditions. Drink frequently, and remember that tea and coffee are both diuretics. Electrolyte powders added to clean water can be of some use. Taking note of the colour of your urine is one good way to keep these problems in check; if it is too yellow, you are not drinking enough. Breathing through a scarf at higher altitudes helps to retain some of the fluid that would otherwise be lost as moisture via the exhaled breath, and also acts as protection against dust and icy winds.

Other less obvious dangers in Nepal are unruly dogs. Normally these dogs are docile and easily controlled by their proud owners, but things may be very different during a night-time visit to the toilet. Better still, don't plan on going out at all at night, but improvise some sort of modern sages who can predict, with surprising accuracy, the patterns to come.

THE SORCERER OF THE CLOUDS

Who is the 'Sorcerer of the Clouds'? How does he weave his magical spell over the mountain ranges of the world?

For a mountaineer there is only one aim, to get to the top, but is their destiny at the mercy of the clouds? Early climbers on Everest in the 1920s argued incessantly about the ethics of using of oxygen on the mountain. Was it sporting, or was it cheating? Today aids come in all forms – better equipment, knowledge and communications technology – but few climbers would openly suggest that any modern device is anything other than an additional source of help in achieving their goal. Debate rages on about the purity and morality of climbing, but is it not safety and humanity that are paramount?

An almost mystical new aid is that of the 'router'. They are dedicated meteorologists, using real time, space age satellite imagery, superb communications and scientific skills to advise climbers about the prevailing weather conditions on any mountain anywhere in the world. They can make incredibly accurate predictions about wind speed and direction, cloud conditions and imminent changes in the weather. The Sorcerer of the Clouds can wave his wand to enhance the safety and the chances of success on any peak, but it is the gods who will cast the final spell.

One such sorcerer has 'climbed' the Himalayas through this technology without setting foot on any slope: Yan Giezendanner has done this from his wheelchair in Chamonix. His extraordinary story is told in the book, *Le Routeur des Cimes*, originally published in French by Editions Guérin, now translated into English as *The Sorcerer of the Clouds*, published by Pilgrims and translated by Siân.

suitable receptacle. Choose a large-necked plastic container, and make sure the lid seal is good!

Don't be put off by all the above advice; just take care and enjoy the trek! Forewarned is forearmed. Trekkers and climbers cannot tame the weather, but there are some

HAZARDS AND SECURITY

At one time it could be said that there was virtually no crime in Nepal, but those days have long gone. However, it is still an amazingly safe country for foreigners to visit. You are very unlikely to encounter any problems in Kathmandu, even well into the night (though night owls might want to avoid grungy dogs in the early hours). Embassies and tourism departments do not recommend trekking completely alone and suggest you register your trip at your embassy or online. Isolated incidents and attacks have occurred in the hills, and theft from tents has increased. Trekkers should not trek alone on the forested trails of the Ghorepani, Tadapani and Ghandruk areas or in any other lonely zones. Individuals are recommended to team up with other trekkers at the lodges when planning to walk through isolated areas. Take sensible precautions, as you should almost anywhere these days.

Other obvious hazards come from ill health, altitude, cold weather and the occasional avalanche or flood; but careless actions like tripping up while walking along trying to take a photo, or looking at a text message, can also lead to trouble. Evacuation by helicopter is not guaranteed: the terrain might be too high, there could be prolonged bad weather or, conceivably, there might be no serviceable helicopter in Kathmandu. Trekkers are still carried out in baskets on porters' backs in an emergency, and might have to endure a few days of this rollercoaster ride. It's best not to fall over!

WHAT TO TAKE

Some of the equipment listed below represents a considerable financial outlay, particularly if it's for a one-off trek. Many of the commercial trekking

Don't become a 'basket' case

Machhapuchhre from the Sanctuary (Trek 2)

companies now provide some necessary basic gear such as sleeping bags, but others do not. These days it's perfectly feasible to turn up in Kathmandu and hire all the equipment for a fraction of the cost. Even buying new gear can cost substantially less than it would at home.

Most will want to bring tried and tested boots, but it is actually possible to purchase boots in the shops of Thamel with confidence and at very low prices (the authors have been buying boots in Kathmandu for a number of years). Boots can cost as little as US$20, although spending a little more is a good idea. Try Mingma at the Everest Equipment shop (near the Kathmandu Guest House) for excellent locally made down jackets and sleeping bags, as well as anything else you might need.

The following list is a guideline only:

- Camera
- Batteries
- Plastic bags
- Toilet rolls
- Torch (flashlight)
- Sunglasses
- Washing kit
- Toothbrush
- Toothpaste
- Sun cream
- Lip cream
- Water bottle
- Ear plugs
- Trousers
- Underwear
- T-shirts
- Blouses
- Cotton skirts
- Socks
- Trainers

Above Bhratang (Trek 1)

- Boots
- Sandals
- Fleece
- Gloves
- Waterproof jacket
- Overtrousers
- Warm sweater
- Scarf
- Sun hat
- Woollen hat
- Sleeping bag
- Sheet liner
- Duvet jacket
- Down trousers
- Penknife
- Tin opener
- Kitbag
- Padlock for lodge rooms

MAPS

An amazingly varied selection of maps is now available. These give a good outline of the routes and features, although they are not always entirely accurate. Place names on maps can also be spelled differently from those seen on lodge signs and so on.

Many maps are produced by Himalayan MapHouse/Nepa Maps (www.himalayan-maphouse.com), who have a bookshop in Freak Street and opposite KC's restaurant in Thamel: the Map Centre. Nepal Map Publisher also has a prolific range of maps. Pilgrims Book House sells a wide selection of maps in its Thamel store, as well as books on all aspects of the Himalayas. Several other book and map shops are located in Thamel.

A selection of titles is listed below.

- Annapurna Base Camp 1:50,000 including Mardi Himal; pocket-size edition 1:65,000
- Annapurna Conservation Area 1:50,000
- Annapurna Region (Milestone Indian series) 1:75,000 with guidebook
- Annapurna, Tilicho and Nar-Phu 1:12,5000 and 1:60,000
- Around Annapurna 1:12,5000 and 1:100,000
- Damodar Kund Annapurna Mustang 1:170,000
- Ghorepani Ghandruk 1:50,000
- Machhapuchhre Mardi Himal Trek 1:50,000
- Mustang 1:100000
- North Annapurna Base Camp (Herzog's route) 1:60,000
- Nar-Phu Area 1:70,000 and 1:60,000
- Pokhara Jomsom Muktinath 1:80,000
- Upper Mustang 1:90000 and pocket 1:60,000

In the UK one of the best places to search for maps of Nepal and the Himalayas is Stanfords in Long Acre, London (www.stanfords.co.uk); see also The Map Shop in Upton upon Severn (www.themapshop.co.uk).

PHOTOGRAPHY

Nepal offers the keen photographer a wealth of interesting subject matter. People, architecture and antiquities, markets and mountains all offer wonderful opportunities. The clarity of light in the mountains is often out of this world.

Keep all photographic equipment in plastic bags, away from heat/cold and dust whenever possible. Bring cleaning equipment. You may need to sleep with your camera/battery to keep it warm and so prevent the batteries' power from draining away when temperatures drop at night. Take particular care on icy mornings; ideally keep the camera tucked up close to your body inside a fleece to warm it up before use.

If you haven't gone digital buy all your film beforehand, as it's virtually unavailable in Nepal now. There are opportunities to recharge batteries on

Don't take photos of people without asking their permission

many trails, but not yet in Nar-Phu. Power supplies can be erratic, so pack extra batteries and memory cards.

Don't take photographs of anything remotely military, such as checkposts, bridges, communication towers, border crossings and so on.

Don't take photographs of people without asking their permission. While some people will enjoy seeing their face on your digital camera screen, others may not be amused. Be careful when taking photographs of yaks – getting up close for the shot might not be a wise move!

COMMUNICATIONS

English is understood to varying extents by all staff involved in tourism. Most people speak Nepalese, and the huge number of ethnic groups each have their own language, including Sherpa, Newari and so on. Everyone understands *'Namaste'* and a smile.

Internet is available in Kathmandu and Pokhara, and in a few places on the main trekking routes, but service is often erratic and uncertain. The international dialling code is +977.

ELECTRIFICATION

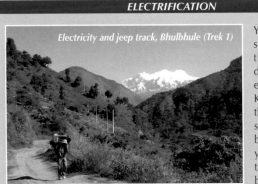

Electricity and jeep track, Bhulbhule (Trek 1)

You might be shocked by the 'load shedding' power cuts experienced in Kathmandu, but in the rural areas the situation is much better. For some years hydroelectric schemes have been installed across much of the Annapurna region. Almost every village on the Circuit, Sanctuary and Ghorepani area has sufficient power for lighting at least. However, you will not find power on the camping trek of Annapurna–Dhaulagiri in the remote northern stages, and a few distant villages do not yet have electricity. The visually and culturally electrifying region of Nar-Phu is also currently completely unelectrified, despite a broken-down hydroelectric scheme in Nar, which will hopefully be repaired and functioning again by the time this book is published.

The **mobile phone** has completely changed the nature of 'getting away from it all' on holiday; Nepal is no exception. Nepal never went through the development of land-based phones across the country, although they did become a novelty for a few years along the trails, with roughly one phone booth every four days' trekking distance. Nowadays it's common to see local people (including monks) all over the country talking and texting on mobile phones. Some may think that this section should be placed under 'Hazards and security', such is the impact mobiles have had! That said, don't expect connection everywhere; mobile network coverage is sporadic.

As for **postal services**, normally the easiest way is to use your hotel or a place like Pilgrims Book House.

Otherwise you will need to trek off into the old city and use the Central Post Office. To send home heavy souvenirs check out the packing agents in Thamel.

KATHMANDU – GATEWAY TO THE HIMALAYAS

Kathmandu (1317m) is the most frequently used gateway to the Annapurna region. The magical city and its welcoming people make it a wonderful home away from home. Numerous excellent hotels and guesthouses cater for all tastes; a myriad of restaurants, cafés and bakeries provide varied and sustaining food. Trekkers should spend a few extra days exploring the city and its environs for, despite some modernisation, the valley holds some enchanting surprises.

Bhaktapur street

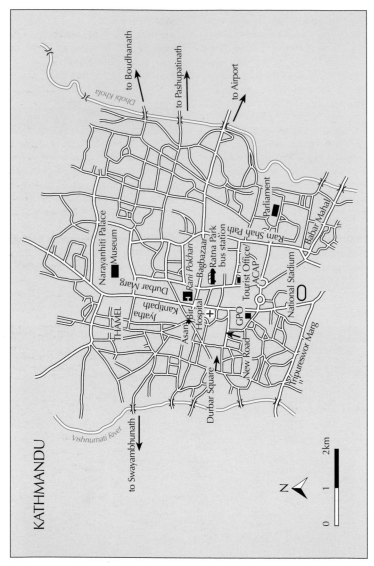

KATHMANDU

to Boudhanath

to Pashupatinath

to Airport

Dhobi Khola

Narayanhiti Palace
Museum

Parliament

Babar Mahal

Ram Shah Path

Durbar Marg

Ratna Park
bus station

Bagbazaar

Rani Pokhari

Bir
Hospital

Tourist Office/
ACAP

Asan

Jyatha

Kantipath

THAMEL

GPO

New Road

National Stadium

Tripuresvor Marg

Durbar Square

Vishnumati River

to Swayambhunath

N

0   1   2km

Kathmandu is still a crossroads of the Himalayas: a trading centre and melting pot of migrating peoples and religious ideas. The cities of Kathmandu, Patan, Bhaktapur and the surrounding valley host perhaps the greatest concentration of temples, shrines and idols anywhere in the world. The religious mingling of Hinduism, Buddhism, Tantra, Vajrayana, Tibetan Buddhism, Bon and Shamanism is a mystery in itself. Legends abound; folktales and myths are the lifeblood of Nepalese festivals and everyday life.

It is still fair to say that idols (but not 'idle' hippies – long may they be remembered as the eccentric pioneers of Nepal's tourist industry) almost outnumber people, and temples outnumber tourists.

What to see

No visit to Nepal would be complete without a thorough exploration of the Durbar (palace) squares of the three great cities, Kathmandu, Patan and Bhaktapur. In **Kathmandu** the central market area of Asan is a kaleidoscope of colour. Close by in Jan Bahal, seek out the glittering courtyard temple of the enigmatic Seto (White) Machhendranath. Buried within the lanes and alleys of the old city are Itum Bahal, a typical Newari courtyard-style housing complex, Sano (Little) Swayambhunath and the temple of Nara Devi.

Patan, across the river, is a city of artisans and quaint, quiet lanes. Deep in the old quarter are the Kwa Bahal (Golden Temple) and the temple of Rato (Red) Machhendranath, as well

A DAY IN KATHMANDU

As a misty dawn breaks over the valley's stupas and temples, the dogs fall asleep. A chaotic cacophony of spluttering sounds erupts; pedestrians compete for space with bicycles, cycle rickshaws, motorbikes, motor rickshaws, taxis and minibuses in the vibrant, colourful streets and alleys. Yet quiet corners, where little has changed for centuries, remain, with a few holy cows lingering beside a grotesque gargoyle or serene idol. Hidden in the intricate maze of narrow alleys, potters spin their wheels by hand and antique Singer sewing machines perform miracles. Buddhists spin their prayer wheels, sending incantations skywards for peace. The rumour mill is in full swing; Bob Dylan and Cat Stevens are always in the café around the corner. People gather in front of a Ganesh idol to offer their devotions for a prosperous day. Trekkers scurry about, getting a T-shirt embroidered with their latest trekking route, or 'Yak Yak Yak'! And the dogs lie dormant, gaining strength for another night of action on the streets...

as many other exquisite temples and shrines.

Bhaktapur, 11km east of Kathmandu, is the least modernised city of the valley. Its Durbar Square is intriguing, but don't miss its other squares: Nyatapola, with a five-tiered temple, and Dattatreya Square, a majestic scene of intricately carved wooden windows and fine brick structures. In the quiet streets of Bhaktapur, time stands still. Its medieval atmosphere is a living relic of a forgotten era.

Not far away are some famous pilgrimage centres. On a hill to the west is the Monkey Temple (Swayambhunath), a picturesque Buddhist stupa surrounded by shrines and temples. At Boudhanath to the east, Tibetans and other Buddhist devotees circle the great stupa, seeking peace. Beside the holy Bagmati River is the Pashupatinath temple complex, where Hindus offer their devotions and where they are cremated before passage into the next life.

South of Patan are Bungamati (Red Machhendranath temple and quaint houses), Kokhana (Shekali Mai temple), Pharping (Buddhist monasteries and Guru Rinpoche cave), Shesh Narayan (a temple devoted to Vishnu) and Dakshinkali (an often-gory temple, where pilgrims offer live sacrifices to the bloodthirsty goddess Kali).

Those with plenty of time can find other enchanting places: Changu Narayan, Kirtipur, Vajra Yogini near Sankhu, the boar-headed Vajra Varahi temple garden of Chapagaon, Bishankhu Narayan and the mountain viewpoints of Nagarkot and Kakani.

Accommodation

Thamel is a backpacker's Mecca, with hundreds of hotels to suit all pockets. Try the famous Kathmandu Guest House, always a lively place. Others are Hotel Courtyard, Garuda, Marsyangdi, Mandap, Manang, Potala Guest House, Utse, Vaisali and the quiet Norbu Lingka. For a taste of Tibet, try the Hotel Tibet in Lazimpat; nearby is the Hotel Ambassador. Those seeking greater luxury can lodge at the Hotel Malla on the edge of Thamel, while further out are the Hotel Vajra, the Hotel Shankar (a former Rana palace) and the palatial Yak and Yeti or Annapurna hotels. Near the airport and Ram Mandir temple is the delightful and atmospheric heritage-style boutique hotel of Dwarika's.

Eating out

Kathmandu (and Pokhara) are a returning trekkers' paradise of overindulgence. A reasonable meal will cost from Rs400 to Rs800 per person for a main dish, pizza, steak, curry and so on.

A word of warning: choose your food especially carefully before your trip to the hills – there is nothing worse than travelling along Nepal's 'roads' suffering from an upset stomach! Even in the better restaurants, avoid salads and unpeeled fruit as a precaution.

Annapurna II and Lamjung from Naudanda

The following are a few of the authors' favourite eating places in Kathmandu (exclusion from this list does not imply any criticism): Pilgrims Feed 'n Read, Rum Doodle, Helena's, KC's, Yin Yang, Third Eye, Dechenling Garden, Kathmandu Guest House, New Orleans, Gaia, Northfield Café, Java Café, La Dolce Vita, Roadhouse Café, Delima Garden, Electric Pagoda, Utse, Le Bistro, Fire and Ice, Kilroy's, Nanglo, Mike's Breakfast and The Factory.

Tourist office/ACAP

This office is located in Bhrikuti Mandap, near Ratna Park bus station; take a taxi! ACAP permits and TIMS are issued here.

POKHARA – GATEWAY TO THE ANNAPURNAS

Once a sleepy village surrounded by rice fields and dense jungle, Pokhara (900m) has boomed over the years into a town of considerable size. The main tourist area is Lakeside, where hotels, restaurants and shops abound. There are a few 'must-dos' in the Pokhara area, such as climbing to the Peace Pagoda, or discovering the lake by boat.

Many visitors head to Sarangkot, a spectacular vantage point, to watch the sunrise or sunset on the Annapurna ranges. Pokhara's number one attraction, the Himalayas, remain untainted, brooding and standing sentinel over the valley.

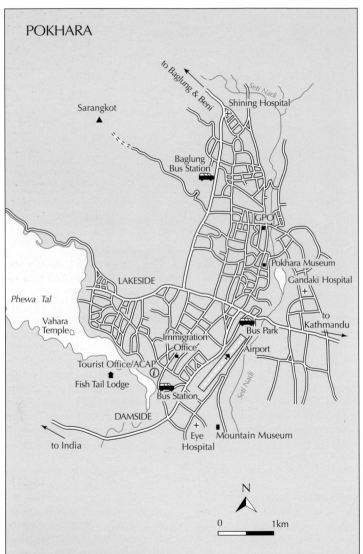

POKHARA

to Baglung & Beni

Seti Nadi

Shining Hospital

Sarangkot

Baglung
Bus Station

GPO

Pokhara Museum

Gandaki Hospital

Phewa Tal

LAKESIDE

to
Kathmandu

Vahara
Temple

Bus Park

Immigration
Office

Airport

Tourist Office/ACAP
(i)

Fish Tail Lodge

Seti Nadi

Bus Station

DAMSIDE

to India

Eye
Hospital

Mountain Museum

N

0   1km

Desert trail to Kagbeni (Trek 1)

Accommodation

All budgets are catered for in Pokhara. The expensive Fishtail Lodge has a great setting. Near the airport is the Himalaya Hotel. In Lakeside is the new Heritage Hotel, along with many old favourites such as Snowlands (originally just a thatched farmhouse veranda), Oju Guest House, Hungry Eye and Trek O' Tel. The Comfort Inn, down a back lane near the Fishtail, has good parking for those driving overland in their own vehicle (still just about possible).

Eating out

Every taste and cuisine is found along Lakeside. The Hungry Eye, Boomerang, Maya and Billy Bunter's are long-time restaurants, but there are also some great new places, too many to name.

Tourist office/ACAP

This office is located in Damside – see the map of Pokhara. ACAP permits and TIMS are issued here.

Pokhara Mountain Museum

The museum opened in February 2004, with sections on geography, ecology and Himalayan culture. There are halls showcasing the Himalayas, International Mountains, Expeditions, a Hall of Fame, exhibitions and features on mountain people. There is also a model of Manaslu and a 21m climbing wall.

HOW TO USE THIS GUIDE

In the following descriptions of trekking routes (and road routes) approximate distances, timings, altitudes and height loss or gain are indicated. Printed maps often give different figures, so a 'guestimate' compromise has been used. Altitude variations within the trekking descriptions attempt to indicate the rough changes along the walking trail. This is a seemingly impossible task, given the lack of accuracy on the maps.

The trekking stages described do not always correlate with day-to-day itineraries. Itineraries reflect the typical and most popular trek route and duration. With time and energy, it's perfectly possible to combine the treks described. Appendix A gives suggestions for trek itineraries based on tradition and personal experience, together with a rough grade of difficulty.

Something of a revelation in the area now is finding some trails marked by painted stripes. Red and white is used for main trails, with blue and white for optional, harder, side treks. In the past locals often used the

Route markers at Kalopani (Trek 1)

odd signposts as firewood. There has been resistance to having signs, as it's thought they reduce the need for local guides. ACAP has been responsible for the new markers, but they are not seen at regular intervals and are at times erratically located. Don't despair if you haven't seen a marker for a while – keep a sharp lookout, as they adorn all sorts of locations. It's a bit like playing 'I spy'!

A source of much debate is the accuracy of daily trekking times for each stage given in guidebooks, and no doubt this edition will be no different. Everyone has their own 'normal' pace, but these vary enormously. The authors have attempted to give an average time for the walk; extra time has been added to cover a few photo stops, pausing to tie up a bootlace, and for those quick visits into the vegetation. In any case, a trek in the Himalayas is supposed to be an enriching experience and a holiday, with time to observe the surroundings. A trek is not, for most hikers, a competition to see who can climb the Thorong La faster than a Sherpa.

Lodges along the trails have deliberately not been named. When it comes to picking where to stay there is very little to choose between them; mostly it comes down to where you happen to be by late afternoon and which place catches your eye. Lodges also have a tendency to change names or be reincarnated with better facilities.

New road near Tal – would you take a bus? (Trek 1)

New 'roads'

It may seem unnecessary to remark on this topic, since a road obviously makes access much easier. However, nothing in Nepal is quite as it seems.

While researching the road access changes for the Cicerone Everest guide in October 2010, the authors were surprised to find that 'new roads' built under the auspices of the UN Food program, ostensibly bringing supplies to rural areas to alleviate food poverty, did not serve the purpose. In that guidebook trekkers are advised to stick to the original trails where possible to avoid the ghastly, bone-wrenching, 'shake-rattle-n-roll' tracks and muddy quagmires – also nominally called the 'new roads.'

The normal effect of a new road in Nepal is to create noise, pollution and inevitably the destruction of the once-pristine environment. Very few of these new roads are sealed, which means rough rides, delays due to avalanches, floods and bridge wash-outs; journey times are never predictable. Bear this in mind when planning your itinerary, particularly on the Annapurna Circuit. Some of those who were lucky to visit Nepal earlier endlessly lament the coming of roads, but from a Nepalese point of view this is progress; no more humping heavy loads along a slippery trail, crossing precarious log bridges or being eaten alive by leeches. According to local people, who are mostly in favour, the Jomsom road has significantly reduced prices of food goods (sugar Rs200/kg down to Rs80). The apple producers are also pleased, because they no longer have to throw away rotting apples; they can be transported quickly to the markets down the valley and in Pokhara.

What gives us, as temporary visitors, the right to bemoan the loss of these trekking routes (except that some 'bypassed' lodge owners also feel the same way)? Why should the

Wide track to Jagat (Trek 1)

local people not have the advantages we all take for granted, such as easy access to medical care and luxury goods such as washing machines? We have to take the treks as we find them now. Nepal is there to change you, and not for you to change it.

Because the definition of a road is so variable in Nepal, the authors have devised the following terms to describe the roads encountered – none of which, as may be expected, gives a smooth, seamless ride. As the locals continue to point out, 'This is Nepal...' – the standard answer for anything not appearing as it might be elsewhere!

- **Sealed road** Speaks for itself, but expect potholes and even broken-up sections.

- **Main road** Applies only to the Beni–Jomsom, Kagbeni 'highway' in all its forms, used by special short wheelbase buses, jeeps and trucks.
- **Jeep track** Any side road used by jeeps and tractors.
- **Wide track/'road'** Trail/track that will become a 'proper road' one day, such as those around Tal.
- **Wide trail** Regular trail, often one that the mule caravans have used for centuries.
- **Trail, paths** As expected, away from the roads.

We apologise in advance if these descriptions are not appropriate during the life of this guide – the situation on the ground is rapidly changing.

PRE-TREK CHECKLIST

- Don't trek alone: hire a guide.
- Don't set off without your ACAP entry permit, TIMS permit or restricted area permit.
- Register your journey with your embassy (if trekking independently).
- Make sure there is adequate insurance for yourself and your staff.
- Carry a photocopy of your passport details page.
- Carry a first aid kit and medications.
- Be forewarned about the dangers of altitude and act accordingly.
- Treat porters properly.
- Register with the checkposts.
- Respect the culture, the environment and local sensibilities.
- Dress appropriately.
- Watch your step!

Mandala in Bungamati Square

THE LAST WORD

It's the beginning that's the worst, then the middle, then the end.
But in the end, it's the end that's the worst.

Samuel Beckett

Annapurna II from the trail to Praken

In the beginning it was a dream, anticipation laced with trepidation – to hike in the Annapurnas – then it became a reality. The smoky, overloaded bus, the impatience getting to grips with the pass, the brutal ascents, the noisy dogs, the knee-breaking steps and then… Back home you soon forget all those hot, sweaty climbs, midnight loo stops and hard beds – the Himalayas can easily become an addiction. Have a safe and happy trek!

1 ANNAPURNA CIRCUIT AND ANNAPURNA SANCTUARY

Green Tarn - Mring Tso

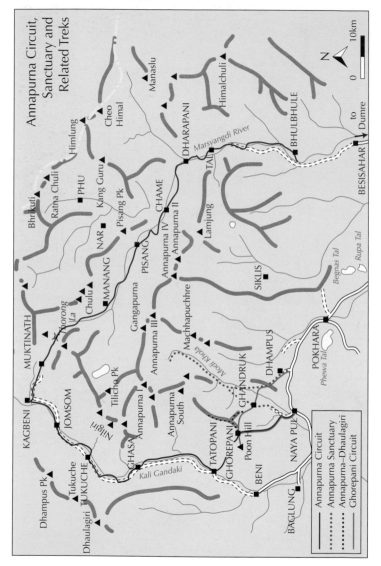

Annapurna Circuit, Sanctuary and Related Treks

Legend:
Annapurna Circuit
Annapurna Sanctuary
Annapurna–Dhaulagiri
Ghorepani Circuit

As well as the two classic Annapurna treks of the Circuit and the Sanctuary, this section also includes the popular Ghorepani Circuit (Poon Hill Expedition) and the Annapurna–Dhaulagiri Trek.

Himalchuli above the Marsyangdi Valley

TREK 1
Annapurna Circuit

Start	Bhulbhule (840m/2756ft)
Finish	Tatopani, Naya Pul or Dhampus Phedi
Distance	190–200km (118–124 miles)
Time	15–23 days
Maximum altitude	Thorong La (5416m/17,770ft)
Transport	Bus, jeep, private car or pony
Trekking style	Lodges or camping

First opened as a complete circular route in 1977, the Annapurna Circuit is one of two classic treks in Nepal (along with the Everest Base Camp Trek). It probably offers the most diverse trekking landscapes of any trek in

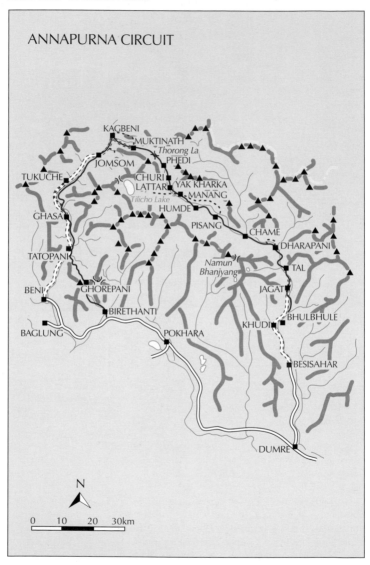

ANNAPURNA CIRCUIT

KAGBENI
MUKTINATH
Thorong La
JOMSOM
PHEDI
CHURI
TUKUCHE
LATTAR
YAK KHARKA
MANANG
Tilicho Lake
HUMDE
GHASA
PISANG
CHAME
DHARAPANI
TATOPANI
Namun Bhanjyang
TAL
BENI
GHOREPANI
JAGAT
BIRETHANTI
BHULBHULE
KHUDI
BAGLUNG
POKHARA
BESISAHAR
DUMRE

N

0   10   20   30km

Nepal, because it passes from the semi-tropical foothills across the main Himalayan range to the rainshadow high plateaux of the north. Hikers experience the lush Hindu lowlands and the dry, arid Buddhist retreats within two or three weeks of walking.

Of course the biggest change to the trek has come with the nominally motorable roads. Various buses link Pokhara with Jomsom and jeeps ferry pilgrims uphill to Muktinath. A rough dirt road to Lo Manthang is virtually finished; it will soon join the existing road from Tibet. In the Marsyangdi Valley, the road, such as it is, is already usable as far as Chame and is expected to go on to Manang. Where trails old and new have been re-routed to enable trekkers to avoid the roads, detailed directions are given in the following route descriptions.

Unless you want to meet every trekker on the route during your trip, it is unwise to do this circuit in the other (clockwise) direction. The lie of the land – especially the steepness and altitude gain on the ascent to the Thorong La from Muktinath – makes that choice unattractive and dangerous.

Kathmandu to Bhulbhule

The highway from Kathmandu to **Dumre** has improved immensely and, once clear of Kathmandu, the 135km journey is generally comfortable. Most buses make it to Dumre in around 5hrs. Unless you are on the direct daily bus to Besisahar, the choice onwards from Dumre is limited to local buses or private transport to get to the furthest roadhead. You can definitely reach Bhulbhule, and getting as far as Chame by jeep is now possible. Beyond this will depend on the latest construction and any avalanche or monsoon damage. The 42km road from Dumre to Besisahar is mainly sealed, but even this (1½hrs+) section is not all smooth going.

The better lodgings in **Besisahar** are at the north end of the long, straggling bazaar. Try the Mount Kailash Hotel. (Recently a chapatti here cost Rs60, a small pot of tea Rs75 and a main course – dal bhat – Rs250.) There is an information office, ACAP entry and TIMS checkpost here.

If you want a jeep, you need to arrange it in Besisahar, because they do not normally pick up trekkers in Bhulbhule. A bombed-out bus runs between Besisahar and Bhulbhule when sufficient customers have waited patiently, costing foreigners around Rs200. The uncomfortable ride on the dirt road takes 1hr, passing through Khudi.

Note that an alternative option can be taken from Khudi to Syange, but that this has not been checked by the authors. From Khudi a little-used trail heads up quite steeply from the village. With views of Himalchuli and Ngadi Chuli, it contours along the west side of the Marsyangdi through the settlements of Dhangai, Ghosing, Sirung, Kalagiring, Sildhunga, Athkhey, Chhapagaon and Mipra before dropping into Syange. Heading off on this path means hiking through settlements that have had little contact with trekkers, so be prepared with some extra food and take a guide. There are only basic teahouse-style lodges in Ghosing and Sirung.

STAGE 1
Bhulbhule to Manang

Start	Bhulbhule (840m/2756ft)
Finish	Manang (3540m/11,611ft)
Distance	70km (43 miles)
Time	5–7 days
Altitude range	840m/2756ft (Bhulbhule) to 3540m/11,611ft (Manang)
Transport	Jeep

Following the drama of the Marsyangdi River as it cuts its way undaunted through the Himalayas, the first few days are exhilarating. Trekkers exchange the humid, lush farming lowlands for the defiant deepness of the gorges that dissect the sheer-walled Himalayan peaks, constantly climbing through the ever-narrowing canyon. The transition to the arid upland of the Tibetan plateau around Manang is astonishing and geologically fascinating. Equally absorbing is the cultural change from Hindu-dominated settlements to the manifestations of the Buddhist peoples.

ANNAPURNA CIRCUIT – Stage 1

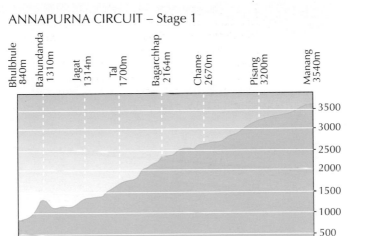

From **Bhulbhule** there are two options. Walk or hitch a lift on one of the jeeps (Rs800 per person or Rs6000–8000 for a whole jeep), along the west bank of the Marsyangdi via Arkhale to Syange, Jagat and Chamje, or follow the old trail through Ngadi to the quaint Brahmin hill village of Bahundanda and on to Ghermuphant. A new dirt track is being 'engineered' from Arkhale to Bahundanda. Heading north on the main route Tal, and eventually Manang, might be the next trailhead.

Bhulbhule to Syange via Bahundanda (6–7hrs)
This option follows the original trail and is on the east side of the valley, completely untroubled by the jeep road. From the bus drop-off area, head down to the right beside a lodge and cross the suspension bridge to the main part of Bhulbhule. There are some good lodges and a check-post. The trail heads relatively benignly up to the village of **Ngadi** (930m). En route up the Marsyangdi are views of Ngadi Chuli (7870m), previously known as Peak 29.

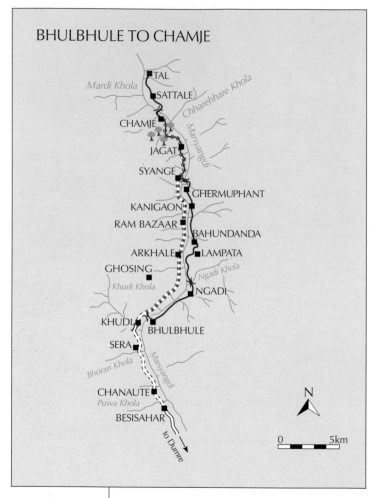

BHULBHULE TO CHAMJE

TAL

SATTALE

CHAMJE

JAGAT

SYANGE

GHERMUPHANT

KANIGAON

RAM BAZAAR

BAHUNDANDA

ARKHALE

LAMPATA

GHOSING

NGADI

KHUDI

BHULBHULE

SERA

CHANAUTE

BESISAHAR

Mardi Khola

Chharehhare Khola

Marsyangdi

Ngadi Khola

Khudi Khola

Bhoran Khola

Marsyangdi

Puwa Khola

to Dumre

N

0   5km

From Ngadi the trail crosses the Ngadi Khola, then climbs rather tiringly up to **Lampata**, through wooded areas and terraces dotted with farmhouses. As work continues on the 'new road' to Bahundanda, there could be some disruption to the trail, so keep an eye out for the right direction wherever the road is intersected. Being the first real big hill, this hike can seem rather long, but **Bahundanda** (1310m) is welcoming. 'Bahun' means Brahmins, who predominate in the village and often paint their houses blue. Brahmins are a priestly caste, but many are also poor. Danda means hill or ridge, thus Bahundanda – hill of Brahmins.

From Bahundanda the path drops on a stepped trail, where care is needed. Continuing more gently, it contours through farms where rice and millet are grown on terraced hillsides.

> **Millet** is a popular crop, providing grain as well as the ingredients of a popular intoxicating drink, *thukpa.*

After **Kanigaon** and **Ghermuphant**, it's not far to the bridge across the Marsyangdi to **Syange** (1100m).

Above the Marsyangdi River near Syange

Bhulbhule to Syange direct (3¼hrs)

The jeep road from Bhulbhule climbs gradually up and then down to **Arkhale**, with spectacular views of Himalchuli ahead. It's a rather hot walk. After Arkhale the 'road' heads up and down past a bridge to the east bank, and up to Ram Bazaar (2¼hrs' walk from Arkhale). There are two lodges in Ram Bazaar and, if you are walking, expect another hour to **Syange**.

Syange to Chamje (3–4hrs)

The cluster of buildings at Jagat has 10 or so good lodges (mattress thickness 10cm, so quite deluxe).

Cut through Syange and then join the jeep road that you have to follow via the settlement of Shree Chour. The 'wide track' to Jagat makes a series of big zigzags up before contouring down to the village of **Jagat** (1314m). ◄

From Jagat, the route heads north on the west side of the Marsyangdi, following the jeep track. Magnificent waterfalls tumble on each side of the ever-narrowing canyon. In less than 30mins there is a red/white marker on the left indicating the 'Old trail to Chamje and Manang'. Following this takes you up beside a pretty waterfall, then right at a junction signed to Manang.

The path climbs on for 15–20mins to an abandoned lodge. At last it becomes flat, leading on to a functioning lodge with a stunning waterfall in view across the valley. This detour on the path takes less than 1hr to **Chamje** (1433m), with the last part gently down. If you are in a hurry, ignore this side trail, as the road is much quicker.

Chamje to Dharapani (5–6hrs)

This stage is characterised by the ever-steeper cliffs that hem in the Marsyangdi River.

> Originally the river was crossed on nerve-tingling **log bridges** that threatened to collapse into the foaming fury at any moment. Those precarious obstacles have now been replaced by new suspension bridges.

En route you will start to see many mule caravans carrying goods.

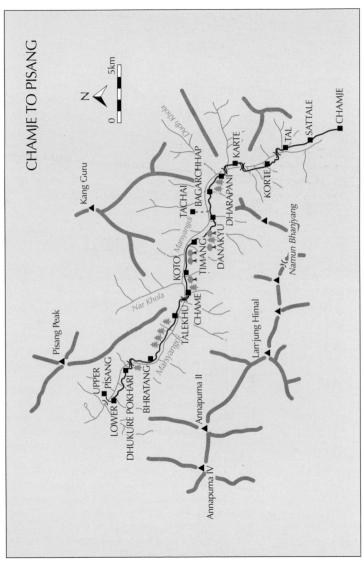

CHAMJE TO PISANG

N
0   5km

The trail climbs towards Tal

At the end of Chamje village, where the new road heads left, watch for a sign 'Way to Tal'. Go down to your right on a very steep path, which is loose underfoot. Cross the Marsyangdi on a suspension bridge then puff your way steeply up steps and a rough trail past primitive teahouses, shady trees and scruffy bamboo groves. The narrow path, sheer canyon walls and the astonishing road construction high above on the opposite bank are enough to keep you enthralled. The gradient of the Marsyangdi River is very steep here, as you embark on the long zigzagging pull up to Tal – this is the very heart of the Himalayan range, dissected by the river over millions of years.

Tal (1700m) is located at the top of this staircase in the Himalayas, a flat area hemmed in by sublimely sheer cliffs. The sky is virtually shut out all day except at lunchtime, when Tal trekkers can bask in the warmth – a little taste of paradise. Tibetans have settled here and run many of the lodges. Tal marks the start of the Buddhist zone, with prayer flags, a mani wall and chortens. It has a small Nyingma-pa monastery, with the iconic triplets – Chenresig, Sakyamuni and Guru Rinpoche – as the main idols. The 'road' on the west bank looks horrendous, with sections blasted from sheer 800m cliffs – anyone fancy a rollercoaster ride?

From Tal, the way soon follows a narrow path below the cliffs; watch out for the mule trains here, and always keep on the safe side (inside). There is a waterfall, junction and sign in about 30mins. For Manang, climb the steep steps over the bluff, then drop under an overhang, keeping on the main trail. The route crosses the Marsyangdi on a suspension bridge then climbs steeply on a sandy, loose trail for 10mins. ▶

Follow the wide track steadily below a waterfall (where a cold shower is free) and continue up to **Korte** with a rustic yet acceptable lodge. The old trail (and possible future trail) is seen across the valley, cutting below more cliffs. Follow the wide track to a suspension

Ignore the old trail on the east side that climbs higher and contours around below cliffs and broken areas – it might be reopened if, or when, the road becomes too busy.

The Marsyangdi gorge en route from Tal to Korte

Anyone wanting to stay at the Dorchester should telephone 97460 14142 for reservations!

bridge and cross to **Karte** with good 'lodgings', including the now famous Dorchester, on the corner by the signposts. ◄

ACAP has marked a **new option** from Karte to the right, via Nache village to Dona (Duna) Lake. It's a five-day, high and wild camping trip to the second-largest lake on the circuit. The lake at 4700m is below Ngadi Chuli, with views of the Thulagi Glacier. On the way, the herder's trail passes through pine forest, where red panda, deer, musk deer and pheasants might be encountered.

Continuing on the trail, it's pleasant but narrow. The 'road' on the west side can now be followed, but since the mules use it, you might find the path much better!

Cross into lower Dharapani then walk for another 10mins up to the checkpost (Tal to Dharapani takes 2–3hrs). The wide track road is complete through **Dharapani** (1960m), with its good selection of lodges, ever eager to encourage you to rest and recuperate. (A small pot of tea costs Rs300 in a Dharapani café.)

Dharapani to Chame (6–7hrs)
Dharapani marks a change in the trekking route direction, towards the west into cooler climes.

This region is **Gyasumdo**, meaning the 'meeting of three highways.' Typically you will see corn, barley, buckwheat and potatoes being cultivated. On the right is the canyon that leads to Bimthang and the high pass of Larkya La bordering Tibet, on the Manaslu Trek.

The walk now climbs steadily. To avoid the wide track from Dharapani, turn right at the sign for Larke in the middle of the village. Cross the suspension bridge and climb up into Thonje village, past a chorten and kani archway to the main junction of Thonje. Bimthang is right and Bagarchhap is left, although it is not marked. Thonje has a small monastery with an impressive central icon, the Sakyamuni Buddha holding his bowl.

From Thonje follow the north bank to a solid bridge (35mins) on a trail that ascends above scruffy bamboo and thinning forest. This high north bank trail passes through isolated villages and, when fully restored, might become a new trail to lower Danakyu, where there is a bridge. Until then you need to cross the Marsyangdi on the high bridge and climb steeply up through pines to rejoin the wide track. It's steadily up all the way to **Bagarchhap** (2164m, 1hr). Bagarchhap was tragically devastated by a mudflow in November 1995. Most of the houses were washed away, killing local people and trekkers; as a consequence it is rather a sombre place, although the monastery above the settlement is worth a few minutes detour.

Soon after Bagarchhap there is a signed junction. Head left for Manang. The climb is steady on a muddy track to some isolated lodges ('even lower' Danakyu) and on to lower Danakyu, with some good lodges (about 2hrs from Dharapani.) The main area of upper **Danakyu** (2300m) is 15mins uphill, with good views east of Manaslu North and the ramparts of Phungi Himal. Danakyu has a 'safe water' station. The cost of nourishment has risen, with dal bhat Rs330. ▶

Tachai village

The best trail heads across the large suspension bridge of 'even lower' Danakyu, 20mins from Bagarchhap. Then, after another bridge, follow the path beside a stream. It zigzags up to a white chorten and climbs steeply on up. The village has been totally unaffected by passing hordes. Houses are traditional stone, mud and wood, people are curious and life continues at a slower pace. Allow 2hrs for this trip.

There is a major change in the route from Danakyu – some maps currently show two routes, the old and the new, as 'roads'. Today the main trail goes to 'upper' Timang, high on a shelf above the river.

Lodge mattress thickness is still 10cm here, so you should sleep well after a solar hot shower.

The trail to Timang

From upper Danakyu, follow the 'road' where it hairpins left. The path up the riverbed is now subject to dangerous landslides. Higher up, if the river is flowing too fast, you'll need to drop to a wooden bridge. A big zigzagging climb commences, with a panoramic view over Danakyu. The route heads up steadily to a small bridge and the pipe of a hydro plant, then climbs through rhododendrons to a woodcutter settlement and steeply up on to the wide track 'road'. Take the trail off to the right, just after the bend, for Timang. **Timang** (2720m) has seven lodges and welcoming sustenance. It's roughly a 300–350m climb from Danakyu to Timang, taking up to 2hrs. The jagged walls of Manaslu and Ngadi Chuli shimmer on the eastern skyline, while to the south is the daunting Namun La.

Continue into mixed forest of pine, fir, oak, maple, walnut and rhododendron on the wide track with glorious unabated views east. The trail is almost level now. The first houses of Thanchok/Lata Marang are reached about 40mins from Timang; there is no road here. The trail then descends to a flat meadow, beside a long mani

Manaslu at sunset, seen from Chame

wall and down a slippery path to a bridge. Inevitably it's steeply up next, on a loose trail around those gnawing rockslides, to a meadow and the main part of Thanchok village. Thanchok is one of the few very traditional old settlements, with 'fooding' and simple lodges as well as more views of Himalchuli, Ngadi Chuli and the Thulagi Glacier above Dona Lake.

The wide track ahead traverses below shady cliffs and forest to Koto (Kuparkodo), taking about 45mins. **Koto** (2600m) has a small monastery and superb views of Annapurna II. At the exit of Koto is a checkpost beside the Nar-Phu trail turn-off. ▸

From Koto the way is delightful en route to Trichyngalta (three lodges). Ahead it's not more than 10–15mins to the kani and prayer wheels of Naya (new) **Chame** (2670m), the regional administrative head-quarters. (Luckily the kani arch is too low for buses.) Sunsets are spectacular here, as Manaslu North (7157m), Manaslu (8160m) and Phungi Himal (6540m) soar sky-wards, glowing a fiery red in the dying twilight.

For more details, see Trek 6 Nar-Phu described in Restricted Area Treks.

Chame has well-stocked shops, a profusion of lodges and a safe water station. Dal bhat costs Rs350 so food prices go up about 10 per cent every 300m (at this rate dal bhat should cost Rs3500 on the Thorong La!) A large pot of lemon and ginger tea in Chame costs Rs1800 in the Shangri La! Inflation – even in paradise.

Chame to Pisang (5–6hrs)
Towering unbelievably far above the whole valley is the slumbering giant of Annapurna II, with its black, rocky ramparts and seas of ice and snow.

After 'passing out' of Chame through the colourful kani/stupa, the route reaches **Talekhu**. Soon the wide track enters the pine forest of the old trail. It's easy to be intoxicated by the sweet scent of pines, the silence disturbed only by the trance-inducing flow of the bubbling turquoise river. The idyllic mood is rudely awakened soon by a couple of disruptive, exposed landslip zones before the breeze into Bhratang (2850m). **Bhratang** (2–2½hrs from Chame) is the only place for a food break before Dhukure Pokhari, a long haul ahead. The settlement used to have extensive cherry blossom orchards, but now it is all-but-abandoned with just one teahouse lodge – the Raju.

Beyond Bhratang the valley narrows, the sheer walls forcing the river to concentrate its flows. The old path was well engineered, etched cunningly into the cliffs. The new road follows this, but trekkers can divert to the west bank. Just beyond Bhratang, go down left, following a sign 'Way to Manang' into the trees. The trail descends and follows the riverbank below. In 10mins you cross the Marsyangdi on a cantilever bridge. Shortly the path climbs and contours before a very steep, slippery but short descent, which needs care. A wooden cantilever bridge is crossed in 5mins back to the east side, before climbing up exceedingly steeply on another very loose path cutting through a soft conglomerate band. Watch out for mule trains here; keep against the rock walls. Shortly rejoin the wide track road (1hr from Bhratang).

The incredible, smooth sweep of the vast rock slab of Paungda Danda appears on the right, gouged out by ice, admirably displaying the forces of nature. The rocky trail climbs to cross a bridge, through more loose bands of rock and then pleasant pine glades interspersed with silver birch. A somewhat relentless but gradual climb follows, which always seems tiring – the first consequences of altitude are kicking in here.

The trail levels off and soon there are some red/white markers where you rejoin the wide track that descends slightly to the much-expanded wayside stop of **Dhukure Pokhari** (3185m, 2–2½hrs from Bhratang). After the tea stop, follow the trail signed to lower Pisang (or take the trail right for upper Pisang). It's a relaxing walk and not far to lower **Pisang** village (3200m), where more comfortable new lodges are being built with unbridled optimism. Clinging to the hillside below Pisang Peak, upper Pisang (3300m) is a stunning, medieval sight, the stuff of dreams. It has a picturesque monastery, a few lodges and lots of

The bridge over the Marsyangdi below Paungda Danda

Upper Pisang: mani wall with prayer wheels

stone houses, with fluttering prayer poles and evocative chortens.

Pisang to Manang

> Known as **Nyesyang**, this region is in the Himalayan rainshadow on the geographic fringes of the Tibetan plateau. A dry desert-like landscape unfolds, with far fewer trees.

There is a choice of trails – the easier low main route via Humde/Hongde, or the more demanding, drama-filled high route via the villages of Ghyaru and Ngawal. If you are feeling the effects of altitude, stay low and enjoy the meadows; otherwise, give the rugged high trail a go. Both routes are very rewarding.

Pisang to Braka via Humde (4–5hrs)

Leaving Pisang through the village, head down across a small cantilever bridge and climb briefly up to an impressive chorten. Following the wide track, it's a long, steady,

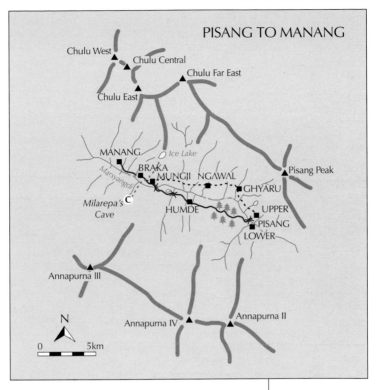

PISANG TO MANANG

▲ Chulu West
▲ Chulu Central
▲ Chulu Far East
▲ Chulu East

MANANG ■ ○ Ice Lake
BRAKA ■
Marsyangdi MUNGJI ■ NGAWAL ■ ▲ Pisang Peak
■ GHYARU
Milarepa's **C**
Cave HUMDE ■ ■ UPPER
■ PISANG
LOWER

▲ Annapurna III

N

0   5km

▲ Annapurna IV   ▲ Annapurna II

seemingly never-ending climb to the Ngoro Danda col (3440m). The view compensates by opening a window on the tranquil Humde Valley framed by the Chulu peaks. From dramatic ochre-coloured cliffs you advance, gently gaining altitude, to **Humde**/Hongde (3400m), an ideal lunch spot (2½–3hrs). ▶

After the checkpost, the route snakes into a zone of strangely contorted turrets and ghostly looking canyon walls, eroded into phantom-like shapes. After crossing the Sabje Khola, you amble though dry meadows. Soaring to the heavens are the sun-bathed, silhouetted outlines of Annapurna II, IV, III and Gangapurna. The

If you're thinking of ducking out of the Thorong La at this stage be prepared to spend US$90, cash only, on a ticket to Pokhara (unreliable flight schedule, not bookable in Manang).

Manang Mountaineering School is on the left, guarded by the snowbound col between Annapurna IV and Annapurna III.

> **Annapurna II** (7039m/26,046ft) was first summited in 1960 by a British-Indian-Nepalese services expedition, led by Jimmy Roberts, putting Chris Bonington, Dick Grant and Sherpa Ang Nyima on the top.

From here, Annapurna III and the northeast flank of Gangapurna utterly dominate the valley. To the northeast are the arid, serrated ridges below the glittering snowy domain of the Chulu peaks. Looking back is the stunning Paungda wall and the petulant Pisang Peak.

> **Pisang Peak** is a popular Trekking Peak, but its upper sanctuary is notorious. In 1994, 10 climbers and a Sherpa were killed on its deceptively benign summit cone.

Across the Marsyangdi is the settlement of **Mungji** (3482m). An ACAP sign suggests the Ice Lake (4600m) to the right takes 3½hrs. The much-promoted Milarepa Cave (4000m) is up to the left and may take 2½hrs. Mungji seems to have more goats than people, as well as a nice stupa and an acceptable lodge. It's a short stroll on to **Braka** (3500m).

Pisang to Braka via Ghyaru and Ngawal (5–7hrs)

This is definitely a tough walk, but for those well acclimatised the panoramic vistas, the culture and the unique villages are the main features of the day. The altitude is showing its teeth in earnest by now, making it hard to predict the walking time. Start early, climb slowly and methodically – there is no gain in rushing on, because the views are sensational all day. This magical, airy balcony of the gods offers fantastic photo opportunities – especially when conditions are crystal clear.

There are two approaches to the main walk:

From lower Pisang From central Pisang, two bridges cross the river, an upper one and the lower bridge accessed from the riverside street. Cross this and head left, looking out for the signpost to Ghyaru and Ngawal. Up past the chortens and across a flat meadow, there is a wide path through sparse trees which climbs to a substantial stone wall and gateway in 20mins. Continue through the gateway and on up. (Ignore a small path on the right to some chortens.) The trail skirts a green tarn on the right and meets the trail from upper Pisang (see below for the onward route).

From upper Pisang It takes around 20mins to climb from the bridges of lower Pisang and another 10mins through the fascinating upper village. Once through the kani, head up, then right and left to a long mani wall with a big prayer wheel chamber. Go right to the Annapurna Hotel and then to the monastery of Urgen Choling; the old gompa dates from 1889. The new monastery is a further 5mins up.

UPPER PISANG GOMPA

This new monastery has been paid for locally, with those unable to afford donations offering to do 54 days' voluntary work. Inside are three magnificent images of the protecting deities – the Ringsum Gonpo Chenresig, Sakyamuni and Guru Rinpoche. On the left are various Buddhas in *mudra*, on the right is another Chenresig, a fearsome Mahakala and a Sakya-pa lama. Learned *arhats* adorn both sides. A dozen monks are currently practising here. Both the monasteries, old and new, belong to the Nyingma-pa sect.

There are three or four lodges here, but they conform to the '4cm-thick mattress' grade only, so if you need more comfort, stay in the lower village.

To take the high route to Ghyaru, go back to the big mani wall down below and turn right (left here if coming up from the lower village). Follow the red/white markers under the exit kani. The path is narrow and bordered on the right by prickly berberis-covered stone walling as far as a chorten. Then it goes down into a ravine and up steeply. Continue across above the meadows, with only the goats

The high route from Pisang to Ghyaru

around to ask the way. It's a peaceful trail through juniper and pine, with a couple more reassuring red/white markers. About 30mins from upper Pisang you see the much-touted brilliant green tarn below, called Mring Tso. The trail descends to join the main trail from lower Pisang.

The long hard slog up to Ghyaru begins after the white chortens. Expect at least 25 zigzags on this ascent. Once the climb (350m) is achieved in about 1½hrs, the path levels as it contours around the barren hillside, peppered with berberis and rough grasses. Goats, sheep, dzopkios and yaks inhabit these high pastures, with the occasional marmot or blue sheep disturbing the grazers. **Ghyaru** (3670m) has typical flat-roofed, stone and wood houses and is one starting point for climbers of Chulu East. From Ghyaru (meaning goat meadows) the path contours around the hillside for roughly 45mins to **Ngawal** (3650m). The inspirational arc of Himalayan giants – Annapurna II, Annapurna III, Gangapurna, Tarke Kang (Glacier Dome) and Tilicho Peak – watches benignly.

Surprisingly for a remote medieval village, some lodges in Ngawal have thick mattresses. The monastery here has the tongue-twisting name of Sanga Dedul Pelgye Ling and is a mere youngster, dating from the 1990s. After Ngawal the path eventually descends to the valley floor of the Marsyangdi. The trail is dusty and care is needed descending to the settlement at **Mungji** to rejoin the main route. From Mungji it takes about 30mins to reach Braka.

Braka (3500m) is located in a semicircular indentation in the cliffs, with a pleasant grassy camping meadow.

BRAKA GOMPA

The Kagyu-pa monastery houses images of most of the sect's major icons: Milarepa, Gampopa, Nilopa, Marpa and Tilopa. When Snellgrove visited in 1956, he noted images of the Buddhas of past, present and future, Dipankar, Sakyamuni and Maitreya. His keen observations also picked out Vajradhara, Prajnaparamita, a red Dakini, Tara and Avalokiteshvara. Mahakala and Palden Lhamo, the ferocious-looking protectors, are in the Gonkhang chamber, but most such chapels are never open to visitors anywhere. The protective deity of Braka is Mentsi, who was revered by the clans of Braka after they fled reprisals from Manang following a suspicious murder. Today three clans remain in Braka, but three clans left for the Narsing Chu Valley to seek refuge. Braka also has a bakery at the Hotel New Yak, with Internet and good food.

Braka (or Braga) was formerly called Drakar. The monastery is astounding, both for its location clinging to the crags among pinnacles and its aesthetic beauty. A visit to the monastery should not be missed, but trekkers will need to be diligent and extremely patient to find the man with the key. The path is on the left side of the meadow, up steep steps.

Ice Lake (5–6hrs)

High above Braka is the Ice Lake (4600m). It makes a good acclimatisation excursion, although it's a tough, dehydrating climb. The route is indicated by blue/white markings.

From the bakery in Braka, head for the white chorten across the soggy meadows and pass the mani wall. Beyond the big tree, cross the small wooden bridge and proceed into the narrow alley. Follow the blue/white markers up and go right up to a sign. This trail can also be accessed from the monastery by contouring east and into the back of the village. At the junction, the Ice Lake path is left and then on up. The path is rather exposed and eroded now as it traverses the hillside, demanding extra care. Only the goats seem to be doing any maintenance on the side trails. Views of the monastery, Braka village, Tilicho and the Grand Barrier are distractingly sensational. The relentless, unforgiving ascent is long – it's not absolutely vital to reach the lakes, as the views are captivating all the way up.

Milarepa's Cave (4–5hrs)

To visit Milarepa's Cave, expect an 800m climb. This cave was a 'penthouse' of the Tibetan hermit poet and magician, Milarepa. According to local folklore, he was deep in meditation when a doe-eyed deer dropped in. A local hunter, Khiya Gonpo Dorje, followed the deer into the cave, to be confronted by Milarepa in soporific meditation. Such was his surprise that he immediately became a disciple there and then. According to one legend, Milarepa lived on stinging nettles that turned his body green.

On the trail to Manang

To get here from Braka, cross the river and head northwest, picking up the trail near some eroded pillars. Apparently the actual cave is located in a gully but the authors have not made this trip.

Braka to Manang (30mins)
From Braka to Manang is a 30min hike, passing chortens to the welcome kani. A steep ascent brings you to the lodge area of the village. **Manang** (3540m), with a permanent population of around 200, is the focal point of the whole region and a village that until recently lived in a time warp. Its ancient stone and wood houses are substantial and a pleasing sight. The lodges are cosy and intimate, but when Herzog's party came here in 1950, they could hardly procure any food at all. Although it's very easy to while away the days in Manang, hopping from

one teahouse to another, it's perhaps not the best use of time. There are many options for the recommended acclimatisation 'day off', which sometimes turn out to be more exhausting than normal days on trek!

Those needing more rupees can normally restock at the Hotel Yeti with Mastercard/Visa in high season. Others with cash can get poor exchange rates from willing locals; a bank may appear one day soon. The Himalayan Rescue Association (HRA) clinic is manned by foreign doctors in season, but by the end of November it could be closed (open 9am–12pm and 1.30–5.00pm). At 3pm daily there is an informative talk about altitude sickness and its dire consequences. A visit to the ACAP tourist centre is worthwhile to see its displays, but it's not always manned.

Anyone contemplating hiring a pony and guide for the Thorong La should check out the options in Manang, where prices can be fixed for the trip in advance. A pony from here to the top of the pass for three days costs Rs9000–10,000 (about US$120). Waiting until you get to Phedi 'bottomside' does not mean you will get a cheaper deal – quite the contrary, if demand is high. Prices are not negotiable higher up, where the pony sharks lurk, awaiting their prey – the flagging trekker. Hiring a pony is a very pleasant and relatively comfortable option, and enables hours of panoramic viewing.

Time in Manang
Even if you spent the previous night(s) in Braka, it's worth spending an extra day around Manang, with so many good options on offer. Enjoy a day trip to Khangsar, hike up a rough track to a wonderful viewpoint, visit the Gangapurna Glacier lake – or even sleep all day. On the northeast side of Manang is the hermit retreat of Praken (Tsamkhang), a half-day monastery excursion.

Three monasteries circuit (3–4hrs)
The suggested itinerary takes in the Bodzo Gompa, the Kama Dorje Gompa and Praken Gompa. From the Manang entry kani cross the riverbed towards the obvious

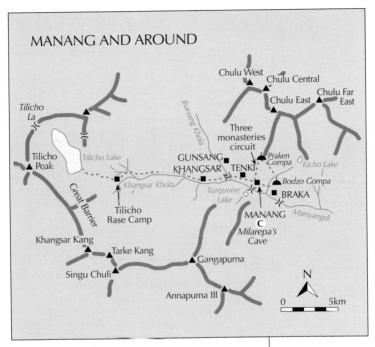

MANANG AND AROUND

Chulu West
Chulu Central
Chulu East
Chulu Far East

Tilicho La

Jharsang Khola

Three monasteries circuit

Tilicho Peak

Tilicho Lake

GUNSANG
KHANGSAR
TENKI
Praken Gompa
Kicho Lake

Khangsar Khola
Bodzo Compa
BRAKA

Turquoise Lake

MANANG
Marsyangdi

Tilicho Base Camp

Milarepa's Cave

Khangsar Kang

Tarke Kang

Gangapurna

Singu Chuli

N

Annapurna III

0   5km

path directly below the orange-painted old fort high above on the crags. The trail zigzags steeply up on a dusty path. The **Bodzo Gompa** (30mins), locally called Vujeck Gompa, was reputedly founded by Guru Rinpoche. The main chamber may be closed, but the courtyard is accessible. The external paintings are exquisite, with a prominent Wheel of Life, the four guarding Lokapalas, the ferocious protectors, Tamdrin and Channa Dorje, and the Harmonious Friends. Take a minute to study the hillside from here towards the white stupa on the ridge to the northwest.

On leaving the gompa go right, descending steeply. It's very loose underfoot, but only 10mins down to the riverbed. Head for the second (of five, left to right) water mill and cross the stream. The Kama Dorje Cholong Karki

Gompa is on the hillside above. There is no obvious path at the moment, so pick the vague trail on the left of the complex around a fence that climbs steeply. Is the monastery ever open? There is no good path from here and the original route, north of the monastery, is very dangerous through strangely eroded outcrops. Head up from the monastery fence; the gleaming white stupa high above is not always visible on this climb. Head towards it as best you can, following poorly defined goat trails.

Beside the white stupa is a signboard for the Kama Dorje Choeko Ling retreat. Two trails lead from here to Praken, seen high above on the sheer cliffs. The two trails meet, then pass walled meadows. Ahead the path goes right towards the five white chortens seen earlier on the skyline.

This track slogs steeply up through an eroded 'organ pipe' area. Continue on, passing the gurgling underground water storage facility. There are absolutely fabulous Himalayan views yet again. Continue up to a sign welcoming you to Praken Gompa; it's still a hard steep slog up to the monastery (3900m). A chorten guards the holy retreat, built into the overhanging cliff. Care is needed on the descent back to the white stupa. From here go down right on a narrow path to a large gnarled tree where two routes drop into Manang; go left for lodges in Manang and right for old Manang. **Praken Gompa** is roughly a 2hr climb directly above Manang.

A high viewpoint

Northeast of the old part of Manang, near a gully and a few chortens, is a roughly defined trail that climbs ever higher. It's pretty steep, but eventually reaches some sharp needle-like outcrops. From this airy vantage point, the panoramic view encapsulates the entire Annapurna barrier, except for the ever-elusive Annapurna I. The descent on loose stones and grit requires care.

Turquoise Lake (30–40mins)

The Turquoise Lake (Gangapurna Lake) below Gangapurna is a popular choice for the day; the creaking, tumbling glacier is tremendous. It takes 30–40mins to reach the lake and, for a different view, head further up to the viewpoint of Papu Chong, high above the lake (at least 3hrs for the round trip).

Khangsar village (4hrs)

Although quite close to Manang, this fabulous village with its ancient houses and traditional culture sees few trekkers. Staying overnight is easy, and standards are rising; and, being on the Tilicho Lake route, it is bound to see an increase in takers.

Initially go through old Manang along the Thorong La route, then turn left at the big chorten, passing the prayer wheels with a sign for Tilicho near the Post Office. The path snakes down from the village and in 10–15mins crosses the new road. Continue to the kani, where you see a sign for Tilicho painted on the rock – go right – this is also the correct path for Khangsar. Ahead is the old trail to Khangsar marked on all the maps, but definitely closed due to landslides.

The Khangsar Valley and the trail to Tilicho Lake

Do not attempt the **old trail**; the authors investigated this, but had to turn back after 3hrs of effort. At the sign for Tilicho, go ahead to the chortens, then down to cross the bridge. The narrow path descends to a meadow before climbing steeply to a plateau area with great views of Pisang Peak – a good enough reason to come this far. Ahead, however, is a dangerous landslide zone that has closed the route from there on.

Trek up steeply from the Tilicho sign and in 10mins you come to a wide track. Contour below **Tenki** village, hiking gently around the hillside bluffs to a suspension bridge. Cross and go steeply up on a narrow path with some overhangs. The Thorong Khola (Jharsang Khola) seems to appear as if by magic from the enclosed canyon. At the top of the rise is a kharka with distant views of Ngadi Chuli and Himalchuli. The trail passes electricity pylons, then drops down to a wide track, then a path around the hillside. It's a steady walk up to a lockable gateway/kani (apparently keeping animals out of crop areas). **Khangsar** (3734m), where little has changed over the centuries, is steeply up and offers a rare view of Kang Guru peak.

Khangsar has four good lodges; a cup of tea costs Rs20 and dal bhat Rs350. Mattress grading is not so sparkling thus far. On the way back to Manang, you can leave the wide track near Tenki and head left instead of down. Be sure to drop three terrace levels as you go and follow the path down a stony streambed before joining the main trail from Gunsang into Manang at the mani wall.

Direct route to Yak Kharka

Note that taking the link trail from Khangsar to Yak Kharka further north on the Annapurna Circuit direct is risky, especially on your own. The route is tough, goes very high and is not marked; the goats have not maintained the trail here. Once across the ridge, the route drops to the Thorong Khola and climbs out to the Khenjang Khola teahouse. It is much safer, easier and quicker to take the main route from Manang via Tenki.

Pisang and Kang Guru peaks from Khangsar

TILICHO LAKE FROM KHANGSAR

This high, lake-filled saddle offers a little-used route to Jomsom that avoids the Thorong La, but the risk of avalanche and frequently bitter weather dampen most notions of taking it for the recreational trekker. Crossing to Jomsom this way is really the domain of well-equipped mountaineers. However, it is not such an ordeal for trekkers to reach the lake from Khangsar. Check that the lodges and trail options en route are open.

During the season, while good weather continues, two lodges are open at Tilicho Base Camp, making an attempt on Tilicho Lake feasible for well-acclimatised trekker. (One very fit trekker did it all in one day from Khangsar, but 'normal' trekkers should plan three, or better four, extra days for a return trip from Manang.) Stay in Khangsar to acclimatise and then head to Tilicho Base Camp, passing Thare Gompa. The high trail to Tilicho can be closed by dangerous landslides. The spectacular lower trail is hard, loose underfoot, unstable and potentially dangerous, especially crossing sands where oddly designed pinnacles stand like sentinels. Allow 6–9hrs for this walk.

From Tilicho Base Camp it's an arduously steep climb, much on loose moraine, to a chorten (5000m) and on to the viewpoint. Tilicho Lake (4920m/16,140ft) is a fabulous spectacle, with its deep blue waters, tumbling glaciers and the great fluted icy wall of the glistening Grand Barrier. Return to Base Camp and the next day head back to Khangsar and/or Manang.

STAGE 2
Manang to Muktinath

Start	Manang (3540m/11,611ft)
Finish	Muktinath (3710m/12,170ft)
Distance	27km (17 miles)
Time	3–4 days
Altitude range	3710m/12,170ft (Muktinath) to 5416m/17,770ft (Thorong La)
Transport	Pony

With the 'lazy' days of Manang behind, attention begins to focus on the crowning pass ahead. This is a high, wild and rugged place, where herders once eked out a meagre living and today's lodge owners do rather better (and some pony men better still!) Unless you have experienced high altitude before, nothing can prepare you for the Thorong La. You'll gasp for breath, wondering why anyone wants to climb a Himalayan mountain – get buffeted by cruel, demonic winds, endure a knee-jerking, endless descent – yet after all that, you'll probably find you can't wait to do it all over again on some other remote pass.

Manang to Yak Kharka/Churi Lattar (4–5½hrs)

At one time Yak Kharka and Churi Lattar (sometimes written Ledar) were isolated stone shelters, almost unnoticed by trekkers heading on to Phedi from Manang. Today, when altitude is treated with much more respect, these settlements have blossomed into lodging spots en route to the foot of the pass.

From Manang the trail begins a dusty 30mins' climb to **Tenki** (Tengi), with its new stupa. As the path continues up, a superb vista opens westwards as the gigantic, fluted wall of Tilicho Peak looms above the Khangsar Valley. New red/white markers guide you around Tenki (3642m), going left around to a tree. From Tenki the trail climbs to Gunsang (2hrs from Manang.) **Gunsang** (3900m) has two good lodges, and staying here to acclimatise on this sunny shelf makes a lot of sense, with great views.

ANNAPURNA CIRCUIT – Stage 2

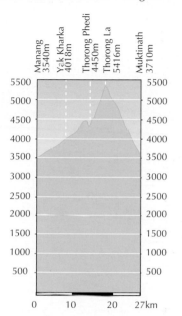

Continue climbing to the Khenjang Khola/Julu East teahouse (30–45mins), distracted by the great amphitheatre of Chulu Central and Chulu West. More red/white markings reassure before crossing a suspension bridge to another teahouse. The gradient is easier now, but tiring due to the altitude. It might take anything from 3½–4hrs to reach Yak Kharka, but do not rush. **Yak Kharka** (4018m), affectionately known as Yak Yak Yak Kharka, has a hydro plant and five or six lodges; unfortunately the sun deserts it rather early in the afternoon, making it a cold place. Some 20mins uphill beyond Yak Kharka is the grand-looking Himalaya Hotel in Upper Yak Yak Yak Kharka!

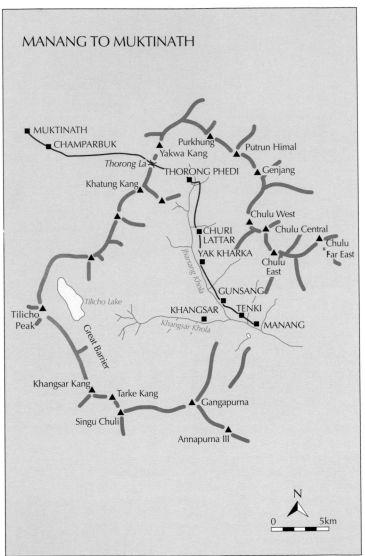

MANANG TO MUKTINATH

MUKTINATH
CHAMPARBUK
Purkhung
Thorong La
Yakwa Kang
THORONG PHEDI
Putrun Himal
Genjang
Khatung Kang
Chulu West
Chulu Central
CHURI
LATTAR
YAK KHARKA
Chulu
Far East
Chulu
East
Jharsang Khola
GUNSANG
Tilicho Peak
Tilicho Lake
KHANGSAR
TENKI
MANANG
Khangsar Khola
Great Barrier
Khangsar Kang
Tarke Kang
Gangapurna
Singu Chuli
Annapurna III

N

0   5km

Chulu West, seen from Churi Lattar

Climb slowly up to the next side valley ravine, noting the stunted juniper as a distraction. It's an energy-sapping amble, but luckily a new suspension bridge over a deep ravine minimises the effort required to reach **Churi Lattar** (4200m). Chulu West is sensational from here at sunset. There is a safe water station, but currently no 'proper' toilets (or electricity – just like Kathmandu!). It's a bit of a shock to have to go to bed so early; make the most of the late afternoon sunshine.

Yak Kharka/Churi Lattar to Thorong Phedi (2–4hrs)

Leisurely it may be today, but the toll of high altitude begins to bite as Thorong Phedi is reached. There's no great panic in the morning to be on the trail – the longer this hike takes, the better will be the chances of adjusting to the increasing altitude. However, during high season, the availability of bed space in Thorong Phedi becomes critical, so don't linger too long or you may end up on the floor overnight.

From Churi Lattar it's relatively gently but slowly up. There is a teashop and the odd red/white marker. Stop and look back, or you might miss yet another spectacular view of Annapurna III and Gangapurna – just another Himalayan sunrise! Continue up to a junction, 1hr or so

117

from Churi Lattar. Go left here and look for the markers down to another junction.

At one time the **'new trail'** was on the east side of the valley and climbed rather tiringly high. Seen to the right, it has luckily fallen into disrepair. The safer way to Phedi has now reverted back to the even older path, which was previously prone to avalanches or landslides and was positively lethal in snowy weather.

Go left at the junction, descending to the new suspension bridge. The other trail before the bridge looks easier, but it is eroded and, out of sight round the bend, has a snappy, steep climb out of the river from the very old lower bridge. The new way is marked and passes the new Buddha Kitchen coffee shop, a great spot for nourishment and contemplation (2hrs). The trail contours and climbs up to where the two paths join near another tea stop – the Deurali Teahouse – another much appreciated rejuvenating tea stop. The way traverses the hillside with some narrow sections, dipping down to a landslide zone with protective stone walls (to duck behind during stonefall). Watch out for Himalayan thar around here, but stop walking before looking up. Ascend briefly up through another landslip area, where it is again narrow; ponies need to be sure-footed here.

After another exposed section, it's on across the final boulder area to **Thorong Phedi** (4450m). This fortress-like enclosure is the old upper Phedi area, not the lower camping area used years ago. There is an efficient hydro plant and, with luck, you will see blue sheep here. The first lodge was opened in 1981 and the current ones are used almost all year round, since the owners stock up in winter for the spring season. ◄

Encircling Thorong Phedi are dark, somewhat forbidding cliffs, crags and ridges. Phedi literally means 'bottom of the pass' in Nepalese; those who rush up too fast may feel it's rock bottom.

The crags above Thorong Phedi invite some trekkers to scramble to a viewpoint, but be aware of the location; think twice about this apparently 'must do' option.

With double-glazing and en suite toilets in one lodge and good food in another, staying at Phedi 'bottomside' can be relatively comfortable if you are well acclimatised. Sometimes the Internet is available; sometimes there is music. With mountain loads of anticipation, relatively crowded lodges and the altitude, it's not going to be the best night's sleep. You are likely to meet trekkers from all over the world, all gathered together in sight of the ungodly pass.

High Camp is roughly 250m further up, about 1hr on a steep and always exhausting zigzagging path. However, do not contemplate heading up there from Yak Kharka or Churi Lattar in one day. This adds greatly to the risk of altitude sickness. Staying at High Camp after a night in Phedi is a good idea for those with time or doubts about their acclimatisation.

Thorong Phedi to Muktinath (6–12hrs)

It's the big day, and the obsessional focus of the last few days. Everyone wants to get on with it, since crossing the pass removes the last major obstacle to making the full circuit. The weather always dominates conversation here: will there be snow, how cold is it, and what time is everyone else departing in the morning?

Waking up – if you've slept at all – is a relief. In the past it was deemed necessary to leave around 3am, but the wisdom now is to avoid the bitter cold of the night and leave just before dawn. Regardless of what was decided the night before, many trekkers do leave early, perhaps because of just wanting to get on the trail. Be sure to cover your nose with a scarf in order to minimise the loss of fluids as you climb, and never ascend at a rate that sets both lungs and heart racing. Those who climb slowly and methodically often get to the pass more quickly. There is an altitude gain of almost 1000m to be conquered, taking 3–6hrs. If snow is encountered higher up, the trek is more exhausting and potentially dangerous. ▶

Remember that altitude can kill. Do not trek alone over the pass. Don't attempt to cross the pass in any

You must always know the limits of the possible. Not so that you can stop yourself, but so that you can attempt the impossible under the most favourable conditions.
Romain Gary

If you are on horseback put on extra socks to keep your immobile feet warm and avoid frostbite.

Porters approaching Phedi

storms, especially if there is snow. Getting stuck here is lethal, with arctic winds and poor visibility. Take adequate warm clothing, emergency snacks and plenty of water. Bad weather is the usual reason for tragedy. Turn back if you get a very severe thumping headache and start to become disorientated.

By torchlight – or in the first flush of dawn – most will be climbing relentlessly on this first section. The path zigzags up and up. After a while a rhythm sets in and, with each step, the realisation of the achievements ahead brings inspiration. Initially the route is right of the boulder scree and below the cliff on the right. The first hour is a seriously tiring climb to a narrow gully, where you might hear the snowcocks awaking. Once the sun comes up, the fantastic panoramas are your wake-up call as Annapurna III and Gangapurna welcome the first rays. Their icy ramparts rise like the great godly sentinels that Nepalese folklore has attributed to them. It's easy to appreciate the beliefs of the local people about these peaks as homes of their feared and benign gods.

High Camp lodge (4800m) with 110 beds is a sort of deluxe mirage, but it's good to top up on much-needed fluids here. ▶

From this cosy spot there is a narrow path to a somewhat exposed viewpoint – it passes the time if you overnight here.

Soon after dragging yourself away there is a short, exposed section with drops on the right; take great care, especially in snow. The peak of Yakwa Kang appears in view; the way is up, steeper and around a bend. A large sand conglomerate ridge is seen ahead and the trail climbs to a bridge. Be careful traversing the loose sandy ridge upwards. Soon go around the bend again.

The amphitheatre of peaks show off their finest – the captivating cirque of Purkung (6126m), Putrun Himal (6500m) and Genjiang (6111m) to the north and northeast, with tumbling glaciers in abundance. The great mass of the whole Chulu range appears to ever-greater fanfare on the eastern horizon. The path climbs to another warming teahouse about 1hr up from the last stop. It is highly recommended to drink more tea here. Porter services are on offer. The next section is a bit of a killer, so pony men hover around like vultures from here to the pass. Don't be surprised to be quoted US$300 (to be paid in five rupee notes of course!) for a 30-minute gallop to the top. (Just think how much would you ask for, if you had to hang around up here to make a living?) The path climbs steeply now, through rough ground up and up towards the sky.

Climbing to the teahouse on the Thorong La trail

The final approach to the pass can be rather frustrating, as a number of false summits are encountered. Be sure not to speed up in anticipation of bagging the summit cairn, as these false demons are guaranteed to extract the last vestiges of energy. Continue to plod on, however slow the pace seems; keep a good rhythm and try to breathe with a diligence that constrains an over-extended heart – the pass is at hand and all the effort will soon be rewarded. There is a great mound of a stones and a briefly joyful respite – downhill for a minute or two. With immense relief it is followed by the final pull to the prayer-flag-draped **Thorong La** (5416m). Don't sit on the pass 'topside' too long, because the effects of altitude can creep up quickly, either here, or as you begin the long and tiring descent – the bitter, icy wind is ferocious and never abates.

It's not a bad idea to take an expensive brew in the tiny teahouse at the pass – it's a very long way down to the next at Champarbuk or Charbarbu (4300m). At Rs60 per cup, it's a bargain. Two trails head down from the summit of the pass but soon meet. Then it is necessary to swing down towards the left side of the wide valley. Be sure to stop for a rest out of the wind and admire the wondrous panorama on display – the amazing changes in the landscapes across the Kali Gandaki Valley of Eastern Dolpo and Upper Mustang. The mood lightens as dramatically as the view offers its drama. Slightly to the northwest you can see four snowy peaks in a roughly symmetrical line, although they are not shown on any current Nepalese map. Roughly translated, they are named Rum, Dum, Tara and Rara. The distant peak behind them is rarely visible, save on the most sparklingly clear days – and, according to trekking folklore, has been climbed just once.

The descent to Muktinath (3–5hrs) begins in earnest immediately, as the trail snakes down moraines and ridges. The mountains in view are Dhampus Peak and Tukuche Peak, but before long Dhaulagiri will reveal itself in majestic glory. Be careful to watch your footing and stop occasionally to admire the views. Dropping

Siân descending from the Thorong La

constantly, the trail can be rough and loose in places, with some pole markers.

At a junction the route heads left on the wider trail steeply down to a meadow viewpoint just over 1hr from the pass. It is very steep down to a ruin and a cairn with panoramic views over Muktinath. Continue the relentless descent. Look for red/white markers to avoid the long loops of the disused and disconnected new road before reaching **Champarbuk** (at least 3½hrs down). A tea stop is obligatory here; your knees may be trembling. Continue down through the cafés to a new suspension bridge high over the ravine. The temple area of **Muktinath** (3710m) is a welcome sight, then it's down to the kani gate of Ranipauwa. Note the path for Jhong here on the right, marked by the familiar red/white marks. If you spy the quirky Hotel Bob Marley with the Rasta-rock café you might think you are still suffering from the altitude, but it's real enough. Enjoy the spicy enchiladas!

Muktinath/Ranipauwa

The old street of Ranipauwa is rapidly changing, but it is jeep-free and there are still some old traditional structures such as the police checkpost building. The jeep depot is 5mins west of the main street. Jeeps to Jomsom for foreign tourists cost Rs660 per person and currently depart at approximately 9am and 4pm; it's possible to hire a complete vehicle (or as 'complete' a vehicle as can be found in Nepal!). Muktinath now has a dozen decent lodgings and more can be expected with the influx of Indian tourists via the new road from Jomsom. Internet costs Rs10 per min. Four Tibetan monasteries are to be found in the vicinity, and there is a multi-activity trail-biking possibility down from Muktinath along the jeep tracks.

The pilgrimage centre of Muktinath has **shrines** sacred to both Hindus and Buddhists. Many Hindu pilgrims come from India; some walk all the way. The Hindu temple is devoted to Vishnu, flanked by Lakshmi and Saraswati. Around the main shrine are 108 cow-headed waterspouts, the focus of the

Hindu pilgrimage shrine at Muktinath

pilgrims. Scantily dressed holy men – *sadhus* – often congregate here. Buddhists are attracted to the sacred flame, hidden in the corner of the Dhola Mebar Gompa (also referred to by its Hindu name, Jwala Mai). It is a temple of fire – a natural gas jet and a spring that traditionally represent earth, fire and water, which is why this place is seen as a holy spot. The monastery of Sarwa (Marme Lhakhang) contains images of Avalokiteshvara, Sakyamuni and Guru Rinpoche, whose footprints are said in legends to be imprinted on a stone outside. There is also a Bon deity on site called Sengye Droma (lion), which is generally likened to the Hindu avatar of Vishnu, Narsingha. See www.muktinath.org for more background information.

STAGE 3
Muktinath to Tatopani

Start	Muktinath (3710m/12,170ft)
Finish	Tatopani (1190m/3904ft)
Distance	60km (37 miles)
Time	4–6 days
Altitude range	1190m/3904ft (Tatopani) to 3710m/12,170ft (Muktinath)
Transport	Avoid it all!

Crossing to the west side of the Thorong La brings a spectacular change in landscape, as the upland pastures of Manang give way to desert. Looking north towards Upper Mustang are barren vistas, snow-touched peaks, multi-coloured cliffs, strangely eroded crags and outcrops – an exotic, remote and once-forbidden destination. The trek down the Kali Gandaki canyon will blow your mind as much as the wind will bowl you over. There is history and culture aplenty, thankfully unaffected by that much-talked-about modern intrusion – the road.

ANNAPURNA CIRCUIT – Stage 3

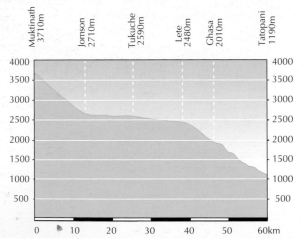

THE ROAD

It's a huge shame that the arrival of the road from Pokhara to Jomsom has been viewed so negatively by many trekkers. It is relatively easy to avoid and most visitors wouldn't classify it as a road anyway. Only around 5 to 10 vehicles per day ply the routes, and the buses are some of the worst in the country, with very poor maintenance. It's far better to trek out if you have the time, enjoying the exceptional scenery instead of suffering a bumpy and dangerous ride on the highway to hell. The only other alternative is to take a flight out of Jomsom to Pokhara, but these can be unreliable because of bad weather. Winter fog closes the airport in Pokhara in the early mornings, and by 10–11am the howling winds in the Kali Gandaki prevent any form of flight except for the Himalayan Griffon and other dramatic birds of prey.

Muktinath to Kagbeni (and on to Jomsom)

It's invariably a very relaxing walk down through the arid countryside from the holy shrines of Muktinath to the dry, stony, windswept Kali Gandaki Valley, once a major trading route. There are two main routes between Muktinath

Putak village with the Thorong La beyond

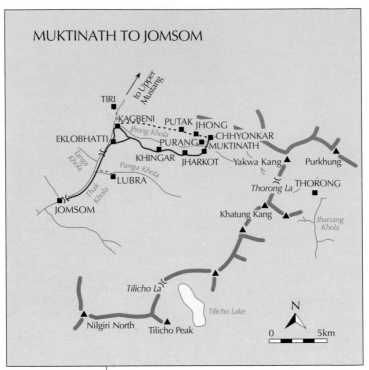

MUKTINATH TO JOMSOM

TIRI

KAGBENI — PUTAK — JHONG
Jhong Khola
EKLOBHATTI — PURANG — CHHYONKAR
KHINGAR — JHARKOT — MUKTINATH
Thanga Khola — *Panga Khola*
LUBRA
Thak Khola
JOMSOM

to Upper Mustang

Yakwa Kang — Purkhung

Thorong La — THORONG

Khatung Kang

Jharsang Khola

Tilicho La

Tilicho Lake

N

Nilgiri North — Tilicho Peak

0 — 5km

and Kagbeni. The traditional trail descends via Jharkot
as the new jeep road keeps its distance. More exciting
is the newly permitted trail that heads through monastic
villages like Jhong, reminiscent of Upper Mustang, and
on across arid desert landscapes to Kagbeni. The whole
area is dotted with caves once used by hermits, sadhus
and sages seeking contemplative meditation and austere
conditions to find enlightenment.

To Kagbeni via Jharkot (3–3½hrs)

Just past the jeep depot on the right is the walking trail
to Jharkot. The road goes slightly up to the left and loops
away from the old route. It is about 25mins down to

Jharkot (3550m), a medieval mud-walled village with a Sakya-pa monastery and a Tibetan medical centre. The village has retained its traditional ambience. **Khingar** (3200m) is the next settlement, with a few lodges. Further down the trail divides; the right-hand trail goes to Kagbeni, a traditional fortified village that should not be missed. ▶

The trail down is as wide as a jeep track (it might even be a jeep track by now) to **Kagbeni** (2800m), characterised by mud houses and tunnels, dry fields and small orchards.

The left-hand trail heads over the dry plateau and down to Eklobhatti.

To Kagbeni via Jhong (about 6hrs)

The following notes are more detailed, since you may not meet any other trekkers on this route. Plan on a long day: give yourself time to absorb the spectacular sights (and sites) on offer.

Head back to the entry kani of Muktinath and go down to the left at the signpost. The path crosses a stream

Jhong village with Dhaulagiri in the distance

and passes the hydro station. Go left and down at the junction, by the sign for Chhyonkar/Jhong. There is a great mountain view and a monastery below. Head up briefly and join a wide track; cross the river on the wide track and look out for the red/white marks. Continue around and left at the next junction. The trail goes up into the village of **Chhyonkar** under trees. The Tantric monastery is at least 200 years old, but expect it to be closed (the key was probably lost years ago). The village houses are brightly painted. Follow the markers; go left at the monastery by the chortens and then down (1hr from Muktinath).

Continue down; the route is blocked ahead beside a mani wall, so go sharply right into a narrow alley and then into a low tunnel. Out of the village, pass the chortens, with a tremendous canyon below on the left. Descend to the long suspension bridge and follow the wide track/road, contouring around the hillside to the superbly located village of **Jhong** (3600m, 2hrs). Continue through the village, passing a café on the left, and go down to the open area with the monastery complex and fort left up past a basic lodge (the trail to Putak is to the right here).

> The **fort at Jhong** dates from the 14th century and is called Rabgyel Tse Fort, meaning 'Peak of Supreme Victory'. Jhong (or more correctly Dzong) used to be the capital of the whole valley. Pondrung Throgyal, the son of Amapal, who ruled Upper Mustang, founded the small fiefdom of Dzong.

The Jhong Gompa has a great view of the Thorong La and the intriguing-looking Purang – the village in the middle of the valley that is missed on this route. ◄

The trail from Jhong to Purang is unmarked and hard to find, so ask directions if you want to visit the villages on a day trip from Muktinath.

From Jhong follow the wide track for 20mins to **Putak** village. Look for the red/white markers on the roadside and take the path down left. In the village is a prayer wheel mani wall. The route out is ahead through a narrow alley then down left to a prayer wheel. Go right

JHONG GOMPA

The Wheel of Life

The monastery, called Dzong Chode Shedrup Chopephel Ling, belongs to the Sakya-pa school; the main idol is a red-hatted Sakya-pa lama. Lo Kenchen Sonam Lhundrup, a disciple of the noted master, Ngorchen Kunga Sangpo, established the gompa in the 15th century. Until the 18th century the monastery housed monks from all over the region, including Upper Mustang. Today the monastery acts much like a school, as a retreat for preserving ancient learning and promoting Buddhist traditions. Inside the main chamber note the Black Buddha and his three consorts or disciples. Other clear images include Chenresig and a Medicine Buddha. Outside note the typical four guarding Lokapalas and a Wheel of Life.

and leave the village under the three-chorten kani. Now you need to keep left, down the rough, rocky trail into the glade, with a reassuring sign. In 10mins go right at more red/white marks and contour around the hillside to a suspension bridge over a deep, dark mysterious ravine, once home to troglodytes. The route climbs for 15mins to a small col and another amazing view of the Thorong La between its two sentinel peaks. The jagged spires and ridges of the Muktinath Himal are well displayed to the southeast.

The route follows a wider track down and skirts an area of saline ponds, where white salt crystals form weird patterns around the edges. Hiking on through arid country, the trail sweeps across open and lonely desert, with some long bends that ease the descent. Continue gently down on the wide double track to a junction. This is a wild and desolate zone; the views to the north of the Mustang Thak Khola Valley are tantalising. Go left, down through a sort of spaghetti junction of trails, with all heading roughly down. Losing more height, the trail comes to a viewpoint of the Kali Gandaki River far below; behind is the last view of the Thorong La.

The new trail to the Kali Gandaki viewpoint

The trail loops, with prayer flags on the left above a massive drop – Kagbeni is seen below. Look for a solitary pole with markers and follow the path near it. A dirt road circles away and below – take it if you don't like exposure, although it will be a long loop around to Kagbeni. Looking north, you can see into Upper Mustang as far as the red Chele cliffs. The route drops down into a small chasm with a cave on the left. Be extra careful on the loose stones underfoot. Further down it is virtually necessary to sit down and drop on to the dirt road. Follow it left and down into **Kagbeni**, stepping back into medieval times as you pass under the kani entrance arch.

Kagbeni

Kagbeni (2800m) is a classic Mustang-style village with mysterious alleys and tunnels leading to prehistoric courtyards. It is the gateway for the Upper Mustang Trek (see Trek 5). Founded by Tenpe Gyaltsen in 1429, the large monastery with a new residential building is known as Tubten Samphel Ling. Imagery includes Sakyamuni Buddha, Chenresig, a white Tara, the Four Harmonious Friends, some wise arhats and an image of the main deity, the red-hatted, Sakya-pa lama Tupten Samphel Ling (entry Rs100). The village has camping spots and fine lodges with great character, like the Nilgiri View Hotel, built in typical Thakali style (normally doubles for Rs500, with 'toilet-free' rooms cheaper at Rs200). Check out the YakDonalds café.

Tiri village

West of Kagbeni is a trail to the restricted region of Eastern Dolpo, leading westwards to distant Do Tarap. The village of Tiri is north of Kagbeni on the opposite side of the Thak Khola and can supposedly be visited as a day trip (1hr each way). Its main attraction is the Sumdu Choide Gompa (Snellgrove called this Tingri Gompa).

The historic heart of old Kagbeni

Kagbeni to Jomsom (3hrs)

From Kagbeni the trail goes along the stony bed of the wide valley. By mid-morning, the wind is beginning to whip up the dust and by early afternoon it can be quite unpleasant battling along the riverbed.

The old path from Kagbeni to Jomsom used to cross the river on the suspension bridge, but the trail has suffered severe erosion and it is now a bridge to nowhere. However, it is still possible to walk mostly on east side trails, since the road is invariably high above the valley. Jeeps to Jomsom costs Rs300 (+Rs30 for bags; for Muktinath expect to pay Rs550). It's only a short hike to Jomsom, so there is time to take a side trip to Lubra (Lupra) if you're feeling fit. Those with keen eyes might find ammonites and shaligram fossils in the riverbed; about 100 million years old, these objects are revered by Hindus.

Leave Kagbeni passing the big chorten on the south side near the Nilgiri View Hotel on to a wide track just above the fields. It's a quiet walk once the jeeps have gone (around 9am). Just 15mins along a wide trail, begin a short climb. Take the path on the right and note the red/white markers as you continue down along the riverbank, still well away from the jeep road high above. Soon you reach **Eklobhatti** (*ek* meaning one and *bhatti* meaning shelter), which now has about five (rather than one) lodges.

Beyond Eklobhatti is a long suspension bridge across the Kali Gandaki to Pakling/Phalyak, set on a sunny shelf on the west side.

> The **route across the bridge** is marked in blue/white and heads high under the forbidding, twisted strata of the cliffs above the villages, but in reality it goes nowhere, as the path down into Jomsom over the high col (marked by a mobile phone mast) is very badly eroded and appears unsafe. Don't expect to be able to follow this alternative anytime soon.

Follow the red/white marks for Jomsom, with the Nilgiri peaks ahead. Soon you come to a wide river valley on the left; this is the entrance for the mysterious Lubra (Lupra/Lubrakpa) Bon Gompa side trip.

Lubra (Lupra) Bon gompa (3hrs)

The sign on the south side of the Lubra side valley indicates the path to be south of the river, but it soon goes nowhere below cliffs. So you have to head up-valley *before* the river – however, you will need to cross it at some point. Cross the stony valley floor, keeping to the dry, cracked mud areas that are easier to walk on. Do not climb out of the riverbed on to the left (north) bank, where an old, disused trail runs beneath the pylons. The river eventually meanders across to the north side of the stony valley and it's here you'll find a couple of crossing points (varying with the seasons). Log bridges are used at times of higher water, but nothing is certain.

It is about 20mins to the base of the hillside on the south side, where the trail can be seen leading up to Lubra. The climb is steep and there is a junction in a few minutes. Do not stray too far to the left towards the unstable cliffs, but try to keep right. Once past a double pylon, the trail keeps near, but mostly above, the power lines, climbing steeply to a tree and fence. Go around the fence and the walls above to see two buildings. Climb up towards the flags to find the Bon monastery, some chortens and scripts on rocks (about 1hr from the main trail.) The Gonpak Gompa is guarded by a big dog – beware.

Lubra

Lubra has been a Bon settlement since the 12th century, when it was established by Trashi Gyaltsen. He was the son of Sherap Gyaltsen, a disciple of the Bon 'Master' Lo Rongom Kokme Zhikpo. Karu Drupwang Tendzin Richen from Western Tibet founded the Puntsokling here. It apparently houses nine notable clay images, including four prominent ones: Tonpa Shenrap (the Buddha figure of the Bon), Nampar Gyelwa, Drupa Namkha and the Lubrakpa icon (Trashi Gyaltsen, to whom the Gonpak Gompa is dedicated). The Danish Embassy in Kathmandu funded the Puntsokling restoration. The Gonpak Gompa

The spectacularly located Bon village of Lubra

has many wall paintings that show the life of the Bon. The main icons here are the Red Apse, Dungmar, Shangshung Meri and Sipai Gyalmo. The multi-armed and multi-headed deity is Kunzang Gyalwa Dupa.

Chiara Bellini has documented the monastery and her findings are published by the Radhika Sabavala Marg Foundation in Mumbai as *Wonders of Lo, The Artistic Heritage of Mustang*.

The suspension bridge over the main Lubra Valley seems to be surrounded by collapsing cliffs, but a fragile trail heading north to Kagbeni or Muktinath is discernible. If contemplating this be aware that it will be difficult, and preferably only try it with a guide. When returning to the main trail for Jomsom seek out the safest crossing point of the river again. Allow 3hrs or more to discover all the sights of Lubra.

The trail to Jomsom hugs the eastern side of the valley, or cuts directly across the stony valley floor in the dry season. Continue around the hillside, passing a new small, isolated monastery. It's quite a tiring 1hr walk into Jomsom (Dzong Tsom, meaning 'fortress of Tsom').

Jomsom
Always a bustling trading centre, **Jomsom** (2710m), with its STOL airfield linking it to Pokhara, now has the added facility of a bus depot, for better or worse. The jeep depot is on the north side near a new monastery. Follow the paved street and cross to the right at the wooden bridge. Bus tickets for Ghasa (Rs790), and maybe beyond to Tatopani and Pokhara, can be purchased here. The contraptions depart on a whim at around 9am or 4pm and possibly at noon in season. It's claimed to be a 3hr ride to Ghasa. Buses are rumoured to depart for Beni at 7am and 8am if there is enough demand (which means probably not at all, since on the authors' last visit the bus syndicates were making everyone change vehicles in Ghasa).

The main trekkers' lodges are a few minutes left from the bridge along the nicely paved main street. Jomsom has a Machhapuchhre Bank ATM, and moneychangers opposite will change cash at lower rates. Internet is available here, and the museum by the checkpost is well worth a look.

Jomsom to Thini and Dumba (4–5hrs)
Take this route as a half-day trip from Jomsom just to Thini, Dumba Lake and Ngatsapterenga Gompa, or use it to continue south avoiding the road (see alternative option below).

Pass the Jomsom airstrip and at a big rock go left around the airfield to see the sign for Thini and Dumba Lake. Cross the river on the long suspension bridge and go right. Thini is signposted up and Dumba Lake is ahead, right. Going to Thini it's a devilishly steep climb through a weird sandstone band. Above this zone there are a number of tracks to Thini around the meadows – it's best just to head towards the village following the wider routes. ▶

The main trail from Jomsom to Thini is near the main central wooden bridge where you first arrived in the town.

THINI GOMPA

The Buddhist icons feature the Sakyamuni Buddha, Guru Rinpoche, Chumpi, Chenresig, Channa Dorje, Tsepame, Dorje Tsangpo, a fearsome three-faced Heruka, Avalokiteshvara, a Green Tara and a yabyum image of Kundo Tsangpo. However, the two strangest idols are the Bon deities that predate the rest. The dark blue idol is Welse Ngampa 'fierce, piercing deity', representing power and ferocity. Note his nine heads of white, red and blue. His middle heads are the tiger, lion and leopard, and his top heads the dragon, garuda and makara (aquatic monster). His 18 arms help to destroy demons. He makes an amazingly evocative sight embracing his dark green consort – the lady of boundless space. Welse Ngampa sometimes stands on five animals: lion, elephant, horse, dragon and garuda. The other idol is the white image of Kunzang Gyalwa Dupa. In his right hands he holds a royal banner, a swastika and a wheel. In his left hands are the bow, arrow and noose. His two hooked arms join to hold the sun and the moon. The gompa also is said to house a shawl of Guru Rinpoche. There were 13 monks in residence when the authors visited.

Once on Thini 'high street', follow red/white markers to find the monastery above an open area. Tilicho Lake is also signposted here. **Thini** (2820m) has a lodge and school. Thini Gompa is amazing, being once a Bon place of worship and now a Nyingma-pa Buddhist sanctuary.

The path to Dumba is straight on below the monastery from the open area, indicated with the usual red/white markers. At a junction go down right, around by a water channel then steeply down on a wide track. The route crosses the Thini Khola to climb up around the bluff, marked with a sign for Dumba. Go through Samle and climb. Dhaulagiri looks supreme from the ridge above, beside a fence. The lake is ahead, a brilliant green-turquoise expanse (about 2hrs to this point).

From Dumba Lake (2830m) you can head back to Jomsom; otherwise continue around the lake and climb to the next ridge and a kani. The 17th-century Nyingma-pa Ngatsapterenga Gompa is about 15mins along the ridge from the kani, close to various stupas and

Dumba Lake

chortens. The name means 'five treasures' – actually clay statues carried here from Samye in Tibet. There is said to be a foot imprint of Guru Rinpoche here. Go left from the kani, down to **Dumba** village (2900m). A wide track goes down from the village and back around the cliffs to Jomsom, with a crossing point over the Kali Gandaki to lower Syang.

The Jomsom–Tatopani route

Some intriguing sites and places are found along the Kali Gandaki Valley. It is easy to walk – although rarely necessary – on the main road after 9am, as there is virtually no traffic. You are also unlikely to encounter many trekkers on the Kali Gandaki trail because of the misconception that the new road has ruined the trek. This is patently not the case, with fascinating villages like Marpha, Tukuche and Larjung en route. Between Jomsom and Tatopani the road can be avoided almost all the way, but to find lodging and some more interesting sights you might need to follow it for just a couple of hours.

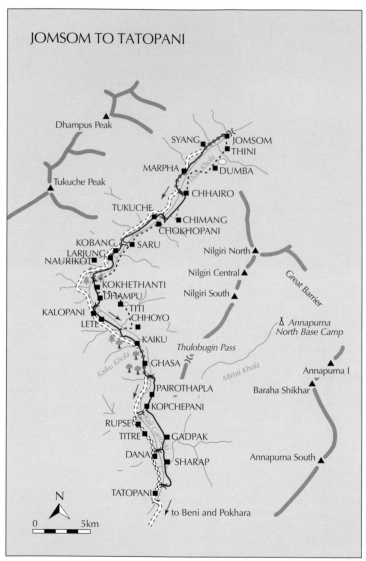

JOMSOM TO TATOPANI

Dhampus Peak

SYANG
JOMSOM
THINI

MARPHA
DUMBA

Thaia Khola

CHHAIRO

Tukuche Peak

TUKUCHE

CHIMANG
CHOKHOPANI

KOBANG
SARU
LARJUNG
NAURIKOT

Nilgiri North

Nilgiri Central

KOKHETHANTI
DHAMPU

Nilgiri South

KALOPANI
TITI
CHHOYO

Annapurna
North Base Camp

LETE

KAIKU
Thulobugin Pass

Kaiku Khola

GHASA
Miristi Khola

Great Barrier

Annapurna I

PAIROTHAPLA
Baraha Shikhar

KOPCHEPANI

RUPSE
TITRE
GADPAK

DANA
SHARAP
Annapurna South

TATOPANI

N

0   5km

to Beni and Pokhara

Jomsom to Marpha (1–1½hrs)

It's possible to avoid the road most of the way from Jomsom to Marpha. Look out for Himalayan pheasants in the undisturbed forest sections.

About 10mins along the road out of Jomsom, head down to the left. After a small wooden bridge, keep on the east side of lower **Syang** village (wall on your right and Kali Gandaki on the left).

> In October a butter festival is held in the Nyingma-pa Iashi Lha Kang Gompa in **Syang**. Syang also has a Nyingma-pa nunnery – the Dhi Che Ling.

You should pass through a wood yard. Soon go right on a path towards a house and then rejoin the main road near a water stand. Follow the road for 10mins and then take the old route, left on the lower wide track that soon begins a gradual ascent to Marpha.

Jomsom to Marpha via Dumba and high route (5–6hrs)

Only diehard trekkers and guidebook writers are likely to be seen on the high trail from Dumba to Marpha. Fully laden backpackers should note the dangers of the exposed, high path to Marpha. (If done as a side trip from Jomsom, allow 6–7½hrs.)

From Jomsom, it is probably best to head to Dumba village directly (avoiding the steep climb to Thini); see description above. From Dumba, continue to Marpha by crossing the wide, stony riverbed below the village. Head for the obvious trail seen on the far bank hillside (about 150m downstream from an isolated tin roof complex). Climb up the hillside trail, passing a couple of markers, then zigzag left and then right. Now the path is almost level. Ignore a trail up to the left and watch for red/white markers. Around the corner the way follows an airy belvedere with a great view over the river and Marpha, far, far below. However, great care is needed now, as it gets narrow and very exposed in places. Watch out for gusts of wind, especially if you have a wide backpack. The path climbs over a bluff, then down, with more exposure and scary drop-offs. Some sections are very loose underfoot. **Don't come this way if you suffer the slightest vertigo.** Eventually the trail cuts down around the cliffs to some fields. There is, however, no crossing point here unless you can tiptoe across a water pipe. You need to head south for 20–25mins to a good bridge in Chhairo village.

A lodge is under construction in **Chhairo** village, where Tibetan refugees have lived for many years. Go right at the small village monastery and then through trees beside the river to find the suspension bridge. **Marpha** (2670m) lies over the bridge back up the valley, with a choice of comfortable lodges. Daytrippers can return from Marpha to Jomsom, taking 1–1½hrs more.

Marpha

The incredibly clean streets of picturesque Marpha

Marpha is an amazing traditional Thakali village, with quaint houses, paved streets and a large, imposing Potala-like monastery called Samtenling. The Nyingma-pa

complex has a fine dancing Mahakala with skulls as well as the 1000-armed Avalokiteshvara; hundreds of books sit in the atrium. Above the monastery is the Guru Pandita Anand meditation centre. Internet is available in Marpha. It is also famed for its plentiful orchards, which provide the ingredients for the apple brandy sold locally and across Nepal.

Marpha to Tukuche via Chhairo and Chimang (5–6hrs)

With the motorable road hugging the west side of the Kali Gandaki, south of Marpha it is better to follow the trails on the east bank to Tukuche. This route also suffers much less from the winds than the road. Don't expect to see many red/white markers regularly on the east side route after Chhairo.

Head to the Marpha bypass road, passing the jeep/bus ticket office. Continue along the main road and, if you need sustenance, stop at Rita Lodge before leaving the main road. Continue downhill, cross the suspension bridge on the left and walk for 10mins through trees and beside the river to the centre of **Chhairo** on the east side of the Kali Gandaki. Follow the red/white marks, including one on a pole, from the village centre, south from the small monastery into the forest and then around to the right to another larger monastery being restored by the Heritage & Environment Conservation Foundation.

CHHAIRO GOMPA

This Nyingma-pa monastery, originally called Tsherok, is 400 years old and was founded by Nawang Tiling, a Tibetan monk. It is now under the guardianship of the Thakali family of Subba Bhatarchan. So far the restoration has taken eight years, with the project highly rated by the National Geographic World Volunteer Tourism programme. The gompa has superb imagery, including Chenresig, Sakyamuni and Guru Rinpoche, with the donor, the golden figure, in front. There are many terracotta idols and some tablets. The other chamber has a large, imposing Guru Rinpoche with frescoes of arhats. A festival takes place annually in December to placate the powerful local ▶

deity Gyalwa Puja. Dhekepchey, a masked dance festival where astrological predictions are made, is also celebrated here.

For the extraordinary story of Karl Hendrick (1911–2007), who became known as Anagarika (homeless one) Sugata (walking happily), and his association with Chhairo, see www.dunya.be/sugata.html. See also www.resto rationworksinternational.org if you are interested in volunteering here.

From the monastery, head south over a stream to the mani walls, then walk between the meadow walls to the settlement of Lucky. This village has a large chorten, where the route goes left for Tukuche. Once on the wide track, look for the sign to 'Chimang' on the right and continue to another junction. Go left, then almost immediately another junction is reached – left for Chimang and right for Chokhopani. (Going to Chimang is recommended if you have time –this trail climbs steadily through meadows up to the village at the top.) Going right (Chokhopani), the forest trail drops around beside the Kali Gandaki. It's a great walk and in about 10mins you pass through a settlement reminiscent of the 'old Nepal' below towering crags of crumbling conglomerates, etched into turrets by wind and water. The path circles around to a big side canyon that drains the Nilgiris. You come to a sign, right to Chokhopani, with Chimang now marked ahead up the valley.

The village of Chimang appears perched precariously high on the cliffs above. This is a second chance to visit this incredible place, and a diversion is called for here.

Chimang (about 1hr)

Follow the wide track uphill (15–20mins) to a path on the left. ◄

The path zigzags up beside a tumbling waterfall in spectacular fashion. At a junction go left (the right links to the jeep track). In about 10mins you come to a traditional wooden ladder. Scramble up this and come on to the top of the meadows (view north here towards Chhairo and Marpha). Go right to a watermill and two more ladders.

The wide track also continues up to Chimang; it's a little-used jeep road, used mainly for the apple harvest.

The small Thakali village of Chimang

Use these to enter the village near a chorten and mani wall. **Chimang** (2750m) is a typical, small Thakali village, a 'mini Marpha', with narrow paved streets, beautifully clean stone houses and brown wooden doorways.

At the top of the village is a new school and signs indicating a path down to the right, along the wide track to Chokhopani/Tukuche. Return this way or take the zig-zag path back down. At the bottom a different way along the valley floor allows you to rejoin the main Tukuche trail that you abandoned at the river crossing sign. Cross the wide track and take the small path down to a log bridge, continuing down valley.

Rejoin the direct trail from Chhairo. Go left and follow the wider track below the Nilgiris ('blue mountains'). After isolated buildings there is a sign to Chokhopani (see alternative trail below). Going right to the bridge for **Tukuche** is a more interesting choice. Once on the main road, it's just 30mins to the first part of Tukuche village. In 10mins go left at the signs for 'old Tukuche/Way to Kalopani' (about 3hrs' walk from Chhairo).

Tukuche

Don't miss Tukuche (2590m). It was originally called Dhu Tshe, meaning fertile plain. Famed for its former prominence in the salt and wool trade with Tibet, it boasts four monasteries and many exquisite houses. Tukuche Guesthouse is a typical Thakali merchant's trading house, with ground-level storage for goods and stables. The upper floors are the living areas and under-table coal buckets provide warmth and comfort in the superb restaurant. A museum housed in the old distillery, down by the riverbank, celebrates the time that the Japanese monk Ekai Kawaguchi spent here in 1899. There are also great apple pies at Sunil's. Tukuche's Nyingma-pa Qupar Gompa is 400 years old. Entry is from the east side upstairs; donations are gratefully accepted. The main idol is the ancient classic, 1000-armed Chenresig with 11 heads. There are side trips from Tukuche to the vantage points of Yak Kharka, Buddha Lake and Shyokong Lake; guides are needed.

Typical Thakali whitewashed houses with wooden windows in Tukuche

Tukuche to Kokhethanti

Always a classic in the past, this stage shows off Kobang, Larjung and Naurikot, as well as the magnificent grandeur of Dhaulagiri. Larjung is a base for tackling the Dhaulagiri Icefall. The route used to cross the wide expanse of the Kali Gandaki, making it a long, arduous and stony section, especially if the wind was strong. You might want to stick to the main trail/road through Larjung; the new alternative trail offers solitude but is less interesting and little used.

Main trail route (2½–3½hrs)

Leave Tukuche at the far west end and turn right into the riverbed; cross an old bridge near the road bridge. This route keeps below the main road and takes short-cuts along the stony riverbed of the valley. Head roughly towards a lone house to join the road where the river-bank permits. Follow the main road that goes around the cliffs. After 1hr or so you come to the 'conurbation' of Kanti/Kobang and Larjung. A long new footbridge to Saru is under construction across the wide expanse of the Kali Gandaki here. **Kobang** (2560m) centre is a further 10mins. The Makila Khang Gompa is worth a look – it's on the left past a watermill near the riverbank. The main idol is Guru Rinpoche. Note the fading old painting outside of a chain and a tiger – the vehicle of Guru Rinpoche.

Continuing from Kobang, go left at the sign for Larjung/Beni across the suspension bridge to find the main street of **Larjung** and a junction. (Naurikot is signed to the right.) Going left brings you to the main lodges of Larjung (1–1½hrs from Tukuche.)

Larjung to Naurikot (2hrs)

From the signpost in Larjung (see above) go up left and around a house, then right to cross the main road. Take the steps opposite here past chortens and head up. Look for a big rock with writing on and scramble up right. This path continues up to two Nepali pagoda-style temples. Cross the wide track and go up steep steps, passing a

Naurikot village

small gompa on the right. There are more steps up into forest, zigzagging for a while. At the top is a new lodge on the left, a chorten and the Thakali-style village sitting on this sunny shelf.

The Bon monastery is on the left after the kani tunnel. It's simple inside, but the site is said to be more than 1000 years old. Of the three images, Kunzang Gyalwa Dupa is on the left, Welse Ngampa is central, with Namse on the right. The Guru Sangbo cave linked to Guru Rinpoche is beyond the village. On the return route you can divert directly through Larjung to the lodge area by way of the narrow street off the main road.

Leaving Larjung, go west across the mudflats briefly to rejoin the road. The road undulates around the hillside to a wide valley with a stony riverbed. The road loops a long way to a bridge and around the west side of the valley, so it's quicker to cross the riverbed area on log bridges. ◄ Be careful on these; some are narrow, others could roll.

After the monsoon the river may be uncrossable, in which case you will have to follow the road.

Once back up on the road, walk around the spurs to the main trekkers' suspension bridge over the Kali Gandaki – it squeezes through a narrow gorge here

(1½–2hrs from Larjung). There is a sign on the other side indicating Sirkung to the left, but you should now go right for Kokhethanti. It's another 10mins to **Kokhethanti** (2560m), where there are a couple of lodges.

Tukuche to Kokhethanti (about 3hrs)
For the trail on the southeast bank of the Kali Gandaki, ask locals in Tukuche where to cross, as the log bridges move with the seasons. The route offers a full-on view of Dhaulagiri. You may need to retrace your steps northeast from Tukuche for 30mins to the bridge for Chokhopani (see above). In general, the way crosses alluvial fans and goes through forest relatively low down by the river. After a short climb around bluffs, the route drops to an isolated house and on to the village of **Saru**. Another alluvial fan is crossed here, and to Sirkung the way is mostly just above or along the riverbed. The authors have not walked this section, which joins the main trail by the Kali Gandaki suspension bridge well before Kokhethanti. As yet there are no facilities on this trail, so be prepared with water and snacks. (The new footbridge from Saru may be open if you want to recross to the west bank.)

Kokhethanti to Kalopani (1hr)
From Kokhethanti continue to **Dhampu** on a good stone trail that has been used for decades. It's best to keep above the river here on this pleasant contouring route, although during winter when water levels are low the route dips into the riverbed, saving a few minutes. Ahead is the crossing point of the Kali Gandaki, with a choice of two suspension bridges. (There is a trail from these bridges up through the forest to Titi Lake, but it's a lonely prospect and best done with a guide.) Shortly after rejoining the road, you see a sign on a big rock; turn left for Ghasa or go straight ahead to Kalopani/Lete.

Kokhethanti to Kalopani via Titi Lake (3–4hrs)
If you are considering a variant to the main route via (or side trip to) Titi Lake, be aware that, according to locals, you need a good 3hrs to climb up and then down to

Kalopani/Lete. This makes it best tackled earlier in the day, particularly as the afternoon weather is often cloudy or windy. You might need to stop in Kokhethanti overnight. Views of Dhaulagiri in the mornings are reputedly ravishing. Lodges are being built along the route. Shortly after Kokhethanti you will see the trail, actually a jeep track to **Titi** village and nearby lake. It's about 45mins up to the village; ACAP has marked it in the usual red/white dashes. Konjo is a traditional village up here; it's necessary to detour to find Taglung Gompa. The descent heads to **Chhoyo** through forest close to power lines. It's a short walk from Chhoyo to the main trail at Kalopani across the Kali Gandaki.

Kalopani (2530m) is the only place on the whole Annapurna Circuit from where the elusive Annapurna I peak is visible; it's mind-blowing at sunset. Little of the old village remains, but with good lodges, Kalopani makes a nice stopover (although it is noticeable that some mattresses are thinner on this side of the Thorong La). Some lodges close for winter around mid-December. ◄

Note that some maps are wrong here, as the main road is always on the west side of the Kali Gandaki river.

Kalopani to Tatopani (9–11hrs)

Following the road is much quicker and the volume of traffic is still light, but taking the alternative marked trail is not to be missed. Currently there are no good facilities along the trail, except basic lodgings in Pairothapla and Kopchepani, so be aware of your timings and don't get caught out in the bush.

Return to the big rock (see above) and take the new alternative Ghasa trail, now on the right. (There is also a shortcut to this new trail from the central part of Kalopani, on the east side, which joins the trail near a clearing with a single building nearby.) The way is serenely peaceful in the forest of blue pines with early morning birdsong – it's an entrancing walk, but watch your footing! The trail drops into fields and comes to a junction (30mins). Dhaulagiri, with its spectacular icefall, and Tukuche Peak are stunning from here. Head on and look for a boulder painted with signs – Ghasa is ahead and Lete is right (the Titi Lake trail described above joins here from the left).

Keeping warm and fed in Kalopani

Continuing, the trail comes to a farmhouse and junction. Turn right into the forest, ignoring a vague path to the left. Watch for monkeys along here. The village of Chhoyo is visible across the main river. Soon you rejoin the main road (1hr).

> Chhoyo is also close to the starting point for the trail to **Annapurna North Base Camp**, a route that is currently wild and dangerous. The route crosses the Thulobugin Pass (4310m) to a base camp at 4200m. ACAP hopes to upgrade the 'upside' of this trail eventually.

Having followed the road, now south of Lete, for less than 10mins, look for a trail steeply off down to the left – oddly, it's not marked by ACAP. There is a suspension bridge and an abandoned lodge below here. The road does a long loop northwards towards Dhaulagiri – a last look – but you should carefully drop to the sad, empty lodge and bridge. This was a popular stop in the old days. Cross the suspension bridge and climb steeply back up to the road. About 2hrs from Kalopani you reach the teahouse of Ghumaone, where a red/white marked trail heads sharply up and around a landslide, but it seems a waste of effort for the time being and is a very short but hard way to avoid the quiet road. Across the valley a vast avalanche zone provides visual geological evidence of the continual degradation of the mountains. **Kaiku** (2085m) is the first part of Ghasa, but follow the road down to the path left into the main part of Ghasa, with good lodges (2½–3hrs from Kalopani).

Ghasa (2010m) is the last of the Thakali villages, with some picturesque houses and a small monastery of the Nyingma-pa sect. The checkpost men will be waiting to pounce here. This section of the trek is now in the deepest part of the Kali Gandaki gorge and towering cliffs dominate the landscape. The rugged and spectacular

East bank trail along the Kali Gandaki near Kopchepani

Thulobugin Ridge and the route to Annapurna I Base Camp are thousands of metres above.

Join the main road near the empty bus depot and continue to the lower area of Ghasa, with more lodges. The road here is above to the west, while the old trail turns off to the left at the end of lower Ghasa. You could follow this path briefly, but it's easier just to continue on the road for a few minutes by going right. Come to a sign soon, indicating Tatopani to the left across the suspension bridge – a trail you should take to avoid the road. It is marked in red/white here – this is the old trail with very basic facilities, and the next crossing point is not until near Kopchepani, leading to Rupse Chhara on the road.

Having crossed the Kali Gandaki, the path is narrow and heads into trees with dry scrub and spindly bamboo. It undulates to an isolated house, then climbs up around the hillside for a while. You get a great view of the road below, with mules making fast headway. Eventually the trail descends to **Pairothapla** (1890m), 1hr from Ghasa, with one basic lodge. Go up through the village and then lose height once more in the scrubby forest. Climb around a small landslide before making a steep descent on loose surfaces down to the sunny fields of **Kopchepani** (1620m) (1½hrs from Ghasa). At a marked junction, turning right leads below the eroded cliffs to the bridge at Rupse Chhara – an escape route to the main road.

Going left means another steep climb, but there is a great view of the dramatic Rupse waterfall across the valley. A sign indicates the next adventure: 'To Tatopani' and 'Way to Gadpak' (Gadpark). Climb uphill; at the top is an old settlement. A small shed-like shrine indicates the presence of traditional animistic beliefs here, with Shaman-style, morbid-looking fetishes outside. Ahead is a view to Dana, as well as another glimpse of the Rupse waterfall. Continue down quite steeply, with care needed over the landslip section, to the riverbank and into the traditional settlement of **Gadpak** (sometimes spelled Gadpar). Continue below a substantial bouldery,

Gadpak village

rock-walled zone to the suspension bridge leading to Dana (1400m) and the main road (allow 3–4hrs for the walk from Ghasa).

Dana

The trail to Tatopani is to the left here, but it could take another 3hrs this way, with no facilities en route. If it's getting late, save it for another day, since Dana is a worthwhile short detour. The main part of **Dana** is right, off the road, up into a quaint old street decked out with flowers, lined by beautiful old merchants' houses and a few reasonable lodges. The other area of Dana is across another suspension bridge 10mins further on. You could then rejoin the main road and follow it much more quickly to Tatopani. However, you'd be missing out on the section that takes in the famous Miristi (Mristi) Khola and the gateway for mountaineers to Annapurna I – following in the tracks of Maurice Herzog.

From Dana, cross back over the Kali Gandaki and go right, not up the forbiddingly steep steps, but along the riverbank on a muddy section. There is a junction soon where you need to go right, then shortly go left uphill following the red/white markers. In 15mins scramble over a wall and pass a football 'pitch'. Another wall stile is negotiated, then it's a great walk along the river in rainforest, serenaded by the ever-harmonic cicadas. The traffic noise – if there is any – is drowned out by the sound of the Kali Gandaki plunging headlong towards the heaving, holy city of Varanasi.

There are frequent markers now as you climb up steps, but wake up for the exposed narrow bit above the river. Sharap is the next settlement and, just beyond the quiet village, you pass the Tatopani mini-hydro plant. Cross a small concrete bridge and at the junction go right. There is a suspension bridge over the Kali Gandaki here; however, continue straight on and climb around the cliffs, with a short exposed area. Down and then left, go uphill at the next junction to a farmhouse (1½hrs). Yet again you climb steeply, now with some stone steps and more farms. Finally you descend and suddenly there is a view up the mysterious gorge of the Miristi Khola: rugged, densely forested, incredibly sheer-sided and extremely hard to navigate. There is a hint of the Baraha Shikha peak (Fang) in the sky above but, as ever, Annapurna I is hiding her face.

Cross the Miristi Khola; the bridge was donated by the Agricultural Association of the British Gurkhas in 2002. Next the sign points right to Tatopani. Pass a school with an unusual, sad-looking temple above it. Follow the level path at a small intersection and then the wide track around to a massive rock and, finally, some markers. After a farm you reach a long suspension bridge and cross to the main road. The view of Nilgiri South is superb from this bridge, with poinsettias gracing the foreground. Tatopani is only 10mins along the road; go right for the main street and left for the bus stop.

Tatopani

Tatopani (1190m) has some pleasant lodges with gardens, and finally a bank, the Nilgiri Vikas. It is famed for its hot springs, which have long been a magnet for

High above the Tatopani road

sore feet and aching bones. You might be running out of steam in Tatopani, that is, until you see the bus to Beni, making the 1600m climb to Ghorepani a more attractive proposition. Another small bus area is south of the main bridge beyond Tatopani, if no transport is found in the village. Buses leave when overfull and rarely pick up people en route, so it's take the bus from here, or walk. Stage 4 describes the trekking route from Tatopani to Naya Pul, but the Circuit can be cut short if you wish by following the road from Tatopani to Beni on foot or by bus (see below).

Leaving the trail: Tatopani to Pokhara via Beni

The new motor road enables those short of time to make a dramatic and at times unnerving exit down the Kali Gandaki to Beni, a large, rapidly expanding trading town. An equally hairy road takes you on to Pokhara. You can walk to Beni in 6–7hrs and it's not that unpleasant following the empty road. Note that you will be deemed to have left the ACAP area after Tatopani on this road and will not be allowed back in – at Birethanti or elsewhere – even on the same day.

About 45mins from Tatopani there is a great view north of Fang and ahead is a spectacular narrow defile, where the Kali Gandaki is almost choked off. It can be muddy, so be careful, and in less than 2hrs you reach a bridge over the river. Tiplyang (1040m) offers some refreshment and basic lodging. The following forested section is pleasant through to Naya Baishari, where some real tea is on offer at the blue-painted café. Unfortunately after this it starts to seem a long slog, hauling past the Beg Khola Valley and forever on to Galeshwar. ▶

Use the suspension bridge in Galeshwar to avoid a long road detour. The Hotel Riverside looks passable for lunch and there are plenty of bananas around. The Mahakala Shiva temple is not normally accessible to foreigners. It's a dusty road to Beni (830m), 45mins further. The bus and taxi stand is at the entry to town. Hotels here include the Yeti and Deep Shikha, but none are overly enticing. The Beni–Pokhara road is still not sealed as far as the Baglung turn-off, a rough 40mins' drive. The surface is then fine to Kushma, even if the driving standards are not (taxi Rs2500–4000 to Pokhara). With some exposed corners, a good road (unfortunately perhaps, as the drivers speed up) continues to Pokhara.

Just before Galeshwar is the bridge that leads to the start/end point of the homestay Parbat Myagdi Circular (see Trek 10).

STAGE 4
Tatopani to Naya Pul via Ghorepani

Start	Tatopani (1190m/3904ft)
Finish	Naya Pul (1070m/3510ft)
Distance	28km (17 miles) to Naya Pul
Time	2–4 days
Altitude range	1070m/3510ft (Naya Pul) to 2850m/9348ft (Ghorepani)
Transport	Bus or taxi to Pokhara

To follow the traditional Annapurna Circuit trail, get ready for a big slog. Say no more! When we first trekked the Annapurna Circuit before roads were invented, the trekking route continued from Birethanti through Chandrakot, Lumle and Naudanda to Sarangkot above Pokhara. According to some, Sarangkot had the finest view of the entire circuit – what a lot of wasted effort, then!

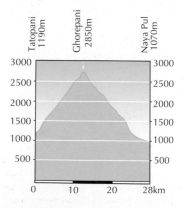

ANNAPURNA CIRCUIT –
Stage 4

Tatopani to Ghorepani (6–8hrs)

It's one very long day to Ghorepani, so many overnight in Chitre en route. There is now a jeep/tractor track snaking its way as far as Sikha (and further up soon enough). The trail heads up in the cool morning shadows into countryside dotted with fields and quaint, picturesque farmhouses. Energetic kids scurrying about and the daily life along the trail are a constant distraction. Forests give some shade higher up, and the views of Dhaulagiri are sensational. Ghorepani means 'horse water', harking back to the days when long mule trains dallied here on the long march from Pokhara to Tibet. Two homestay

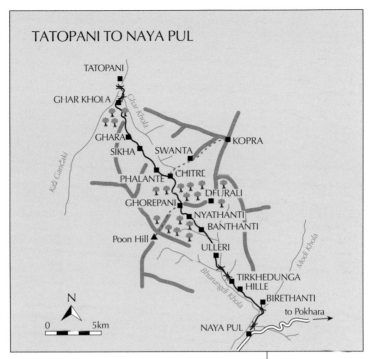

TATOPANI TO NAYA PUL

treks (Parbat Myagdi: Treks 9 and 10) can be accessed from Stage 4.

From **Tatopani** there are two options: follow the road to a suspension bridge on the left across the Kali Gandaki (you can go this way, although it's not signposted). Cross here to the small settlement and a junction. ▸

Go right to cross another smaller bridge and head up to Sundar's restaurant in Gharkholagaon village.

Alternatively, continue along the main road. Crossing the Kali Gandaki on the road bridge further down the valley takes you to an interesting Hanuman temple devoted to the monkey god, who stands on watch. Shortly after the temple, turn sharp left at a sign for Ghorepani (which also leads to Sundar's restaurant).

Going left at this junction is an obscure trail that leads eventually thousands of feet up to the Kopra Danda Ridge (see the Khayer Barah route under Trek 4).

159

From Sundar's, follow the jeep track quite steeply up. Ignore a small path to the left, and around the bend zig-zag up again to a scruffy sign painted on the rock, 'Way to Ghare and Ghorepani'. Follow the steep and dusty (sometimes muddy) track and look for shortcut paths. One goes up steeply on the left. Watch for the new bright red spot markers that indicate the way (if they haven't been washed off by the monsoon rains!).

At a tree, follow the jeep track briefly then head off to the right on a stone path with more red spots – the old trail. The jeep track is crossed again beside a house, then it's the trail for a while, steeply up, passing a porters' resting place (chautaara). Continue to another old porters' rest spot below the two signature trees of the typical chautaara – the Banyan and Pipal. It's quite a steep pull uphill on steps and soon it's even steeper, around the right side of a huge new landslide area. Follow red spots up to the jeep track and the teahouse of Durbin Danda (1550m). The jeep track descends a little to a sign for Ghorepani, left on a grassy trail. This heads into the village of **Ghara** (1700m) and avoids the jeep track. The

Farmhouse on the trail to Ghara

trail climbs on through sections of meadows and patches of forest up to the large village of Sikha (Shikha). ▶

By mid-morning the village of **Sikha** (1940m), with its excellent lodges, makes an inviting refreshment stop before the long slog continues ever-upwards. Fortunately, the at-times gruelling climb is broken by views of Dhaulagiri. Soon after **Phalante** (2300m) is **Chitre** (2390m). Between these two villages is the new homestay trail of the Parbat Myagdi Link trek, heading southwest. This trek (see Trek 9) can be integrated into the Annapurna Circuit as a variant, ending in Beni, starting from Chitre or Poon Hill.

From Chitre the path enters the somewhat degraded rhododendron forest on the final push for the top. **Ghorepani** (2850m) has a number of good lodges and 'foodings'; unfortunately, it can get very chilly here in the afternoons when clouds hug the ridge tops. An early night is advisable, with the pre-dawn objective of sunrise on Poon Hill.

The jeep road circles off away to the west, but expect sections of it to reappear in the future, even up as far as Chitre.

KOPRA DANDA

From Chitre it is possible to head northeast on to the Kopra Danda (ridge), since a couple of new homestay lodges have opened. This 3–5 day diversion takes you to the panoramic viewpoint of the Kopra Danda – much higher than Poon Hill, with correspondingly more impressive views. The trail heads through the settlement of Swanta (Someta) before making a very steep assault on Kopra Danda. Kopra has a new community homestay, providing those with bags of time the opportunity to witness the very special sunrise here (without the obligatory early morning hike up that Poon Hill demands). Spending two nights in Kopra (3800m) will allow you to trek up the dramatic ridge crest towards Annapurna South and Khairetal Lake (see Trek 4 Annapurna–Dhaulagiri).

Poon Hill (2hrs round trip)
The daily ritual of witnessing sunrise on the Annapurnas from Poon Hill (3193m/10,473ft) should not be missed. Trekkers have been embarking on this climb for years, with total justification – it still ranks as one of the most

accessible sunrise points in the Himalayas. The panorama stretches from the tangled knots of Churen Himal in the west, through Dhaulagiri, the Kali Gandaki gorge, the Nilgiris, Fang and Annapurna South. The path is well used and obvious, but bring a torch for the pre-dawn light.

Ghorepani to Naya Pul (7–9hrs)

Sticking to the classic Annapurna Circuit, the day offers a return to warmer climes as the trail drops another 1600m to Birethanti – the roadhead near Naya Pul. Leaving **Ghorepani**, the trail descends into rhododendron and magnolia forest, a gentle warm-up in the cool of the morning. Snaking down and around, the path emerges from the misty, atmospheric forest through Nyathanti to reach the small settlement of **Banthanti** (2300m). From here Machhapuchhre shines out, its twin-peak 'fishtail' exhibited to maximum effect. The trail contours around the hillside then descends, providing endless vistas of terraced hillsides. The largish Magar village of **Ulleri** is a good place to take lunch or break the long descent into the Bhurungdi Khola. Almost all the way down to Tirkhedunga is a well-engineered path of around 3000 steps (known as a Gurung staircase). Take your time, or your knees will revolt long before the bottomside. **Tirkhedunga** (1540m) is well used to the needs of trekkers, so enjoy the warm evening while you reflect on the last stage of the trek.

It's little more than a couple of hours via **Hille** (1475m) and Sudame to the trailhead at Naya Pul (1070m) beyond Birethanti, and a bus or taxi to Pokhara. After Hille expect to find a jeep track being carved out en route near Sudame. **Birethanti** has two new lodges and a road bridge for transport to Syauli and beyond Kimche up to Ghandruk. ACAP has a checkpost before **Naya Pul**. From here cross the stream on the rustic bridge and, once in the bazaar area after the Muktinath Bikras bank, look for a tiny path on the left going steeply up between walls. The road is up here after you've passed through all the rubbish! A taxi to Pokhara from Naya Pul typically costs around Rs1500 and takes 1½hrs; there are also plenty of cheap buses.

ALTERNATIVE STAGE 4
Tatopani to Dhampus Phedi via Ghorepani and Ghandruk

Start	Tatopani (1190m/3904ft)
Finish	Dhampus Phedi (1130m/3706ft)
Distance	38km (23 miles)
Time	5–6 days
Altitude range	1130m/3706ft (Dhampus Phedi) to 2990m/9810ft (Deurali)
Transport	Bus, jeep or taxi to Pokhara

If you want to join Trek 2, Annapurna Sanctuary, take this trail as far as either Tadapani or Ghandruk; trails from both these villages head to Chhomrong.

Follow Stage 4 as far as Ghorepani (6–8hrs).

Ghorepani to Ghandruk (6–7½hrs)
Take the trail east from **Ghorepani**; it keeps close to the ridge-top meadows for the initial 1½–2hrs. The path eventually drops into little-disturbed forest; in spring this section is ablaze with flowering rhododendrons – a botanist's paradise. In winter the next section steeply down beside a waterfall can get icy, especially after snowfall, so be very careful. The waterfall is often frozen by late December. Continue down to another **Banthanti** (2520m),

ANNAPURNA CIRCUIT –
Alternative Stage 4

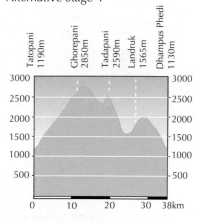

163

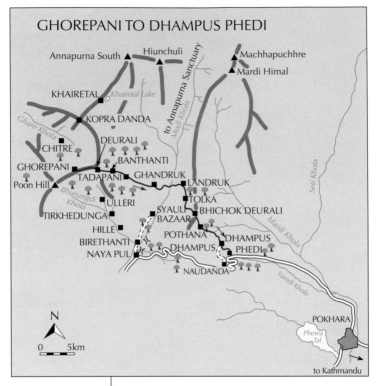

GHOREPANI TO DHAMPUS PHEDI

Annapurna South ▲ Hiunchuli ▲ ▲ Machhapuchhre

▲ Mardi Himal

KHAIRETAL ■ ○ *Khairetal Lake*

to Annapurna Sanctuary

Modi Khola

KOPRA DANDA ■

Ghare Khola

DEURALI ■

CHITRE ■

BANTHANTI

GHOREPANI ■ TADAPANI ■ GHANDRUK ■ LANDRUK ■

Poon Hill ▲ *Bhurungdi Khola*

TOLKA ■

ULLERI ■ SYAULI BAZAAR ■ BHICHOK DEURALI ■

TIRKHEDUNGA ■ *Mardi Khola*

HILLE ■ POTHANA ■ DHAMPUS PHEDI ■

BIRETHANTI ■ DHAMPUS ■

NAYA PUL ■ NAUDANDA ■

Seti Khola

Yamdi Khola

POKHARA

Phewa Tal

to Kathmandu

N

0   5km

built below a massive cliff (2½hrs). Take a break here; the trail then drops through forest high above the Bhurungdi Valley.

After crossing a small bridge, the path climbs steeply up though dense, dripping woods to **Tadapani** (2590m, about 4hrs). Surrounded by dense forest, often damp and cold in the afternoon, Tadapani is basically a trekkers' settlement with lodges. There are three trails from here. One heads north for the Kopra Ridge (see Trek 4 Annapurna–Dhaulagiri); another goes to Chhomrong via the Kimrong Khola and on to the Sanctuary (see Trek 2, Alternative Stage 4 Chhomrong to Naya Pul via Ghorepani, in

Annapurna South from Tadapani

reverse). The other trail is the one most commonly used, to Ghandruk, described below.

Dropping from Tadapani, the route continues through dank, dense forest. Most of this stage is spent in dripping rain-cloud woodland, characterised by ancient moss-covered trees, hanging vines and Langur monkeys. Be careful in the damp sections – the path is often slippery, muddy and covered by tree roots. A few small clearings with isolated teahouses provide trekkers with respite en route. Eventually the trail emerges into terraced hillsides for the last stage down to **Ghandruk** (1940m). The well-used eroded path gets muddy after rain. Ghandruk is one of the larger Gurung settlements, with a traditional old section of slate-roofed houses and neat pathways. A new 'trekkers' section has grown now, with modern structures. Here you find two Gurung Traditional Museums and the ACAP area office, which has a regular video show about conservation and ecological matters.

Ghandruk to Dhampus Phedi via Landruk (7½–9hrs)

There is still a very long descent and ascent to negotiate en route to Landruk. The trail snakes down steeply for much of the way, mostly on steps and terraces. The valley of the Modi Khola is always hot and humid. Cross the suspension bridge and start the long climb up the other side of the valley.

As you begin the climb watch out for **beehives** clinging to the underside of overhanging cliffs. These hives are famed both for their quality honey and for the 'honey hunters' who gather the spoils, hanging from precarious ropes as they smoke out the bees. It's a dying art and a rare sight these days.

The trail climbs through mixed forest and up through terraces to **Landruk**/Landrung (1565m) – another Gurung-dominated village. The soul-stirring sunset views are of Annapurna South and Hiunchuli.

The last stage is no slouch – crossing the Bhichok Deurali Ridge opens up distant panoramas towards Pokhara, but it is Machhapuchhre that utterly captivates the eyes, overwhelming every other vista with its dynamic grandeur. From Landruk the trail contours around the steep hillside to **Tolka** (1700m). Around the next bluff, it's a steep climb on an energy-sapping path through humid forest to **Deurali** (2100m). Here trekkers gather to celebrate the last climb of the trek with a drink, while porters rest their heavy loads, catch their breath and light their cigarettes.

Years ago long lines of porters rested here (and on similar hilltops) smoking their **bedis** – rolled tobacco leaves typically found all over India and Nepal that always needed a whole box of matches to keep them alight. Deurali, meaning top-of-the-pass, is also a local brand of cigarette.

The route passes the souvenir sellers of **Pothana** and continues down through trees to **Dhampus** (1650m) and **Phedi** (1130m). The Annapurna range is seen from Dhampus in all its glory at dawn and dusk.

Leaving the trail:
Dhampus Phedi to Pokhara
The final run from Dhampus Phedi into Pokhara is by jeep or bus along the road, through Hyangja, past the Tibetan refugee camp. These places once hummed to the tune of trekking boots squelching along through the rice fields under a hot, wearying sun – but no more.

And so from the hills we return refreshed in body, in mind and in spirit, to grapple anew with life's problems.
The Mountain Top,
Frank S Smythe

Annapurna South from Landruk

TREK 2

Annapurna Sanctuary

Start	Dhampus Phedi (1130m/3706ft)
Finish	Naya Pul (1070m/3510ft)
Distance	80km (50 miles)
Time	10–12 days
Maximum altitude	Annapurna Base Camp (4130m/13,550ft)
Transport	Bus, jeep or private car from Pokhara
Trekking style	Lodges or camping

Machhapuchhre from Pokhara

Still one of the most popular hikes across the region, the Annapurna Sanctuary Trek has changed little over the decades. Once the sole domain of sheep and goat herders, the barren meadows of the lower Sanctuary were 'discovered' by the outside world in the mid-fifties. Since then, climbers, adventurers, trekkers, lodge owners and porters have carved a trail through the once-formidable bamboo forests and thickets to open up the

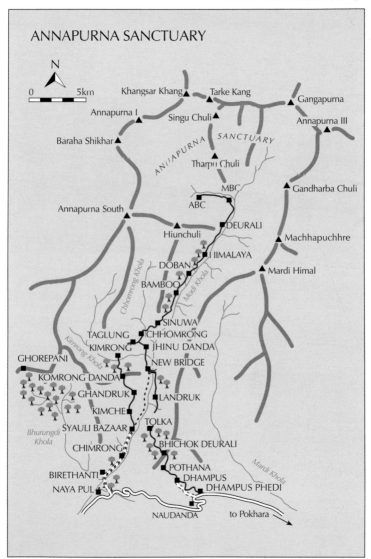

ANNAPURNA SANCTUARY

N

0   5km

Khangsar Khang ▲   Tarke Kang ▲   ▲ Gangapurna

Annapurna I ▲   Singu Chuli ▲   ▲ Annapurna III

Baraha Shikhar ▲   *ANNAPURNA*   *SANCTUARY*

                         Tharpu Chuli ▲

                                              MBC ■   ▲ Gandharba Chuli

Annapurna South ▲   ABC ■

                                    ■ DEURALI   ▲ Machhapuchhre
         Hiunchuli ▲

                              ■ HIMALAYA

                     DOBAN ■   ▲ Mardi Himal

                  BAMBOO ■

                                   Modi Khola
         Chhomrong Khola

                              SINUWA ■

           TAGLUNG ■ ■ CHHOMRONG
           KIMRONG ■   JHINU DANDA ■

GHOREPANI ■   NEW BRIDGE ■

   Kimrong Khola

■ KOMRONG DANDA

     ■ GHANDRUK   ■ LANDRUK

       ■ KIMCHE

Bhurungdi SYAULI BAZAAR ■   TOLKA ■
Khola
     CHIMRONG ■   ■ BHICHOK DEURALI

BIRETHANTI ■   ■ POTHANA   *Mardi Khola*
NAYA PUL ■   DHAMPUS ■
                              DHAMPUS PHEDI ■

                     NAUDANDA   to Pokhara →

Typical terraced hillsides

great amphitheatre of the Sanctuary for recreational use. Being accessible from Pokhara in less than a two-week time frame makes it a perfect destination for those with limited vacations. It can be done in as little as eight or nine days and certainly in just under two weeks, including the Ghorepani add-on routes. Lodges and camping areas are frequent, making this destination ideal for all styles of trekking.

STAGE 1
Dhampus Phedi to Chhomrong

Start	Dhampus Phedi (1130m/3706ft)
Finish	Chhomrong (2170m/7117ft)
Distance	18km (11½ miles)
Time	2–3 days
Altitude range	1130m/3706ft (Phedi) to 2170m/7117ft (Chhomrong)
Transport	Bus, jeep or taxi from Pokhara

Although a jeep track has now been constructed up to the Dhampus Ridge, it does not take much longer to walk up on the old trail. From Pokhara take a bus, jeep or taxi to Phedi (or Dhampus). The hike up can be rather sweaty through the forest of sal trees with sections of stone steps. Brahmins, Chhetris and Gurungs inhabit the area.

Dhampus Phedi to Landruk
(6½–7½hrs)

ANNAPURNA SANCTUARY –
Stage 1

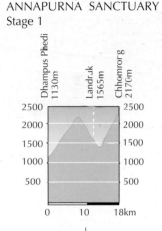

To Dhampus (1650m) takes no more than 2hrs from Phedi. 'Australian Camp' is the rather odd name of another starting point used by groups located north of the road, close to the villages of Khare and Lumle. From **Dhampus** (1650m) the route climbs the ridge, passing farmhouse and meadows up to **Pothana** (1890m). The trail from 'Australian Camp' joins around here. Pothana has lodges, but it is much more memorable for its astute sellers and souvenir hawkers. When you've pulled yourself away, continue the steady climb to Bhichok **Deurali** (2100m), marked by a few rustic shelters and a forest canopy that threatens to obscure the view of Annapurna South.

The path for Landruk descends through rhododendron forest, often colonised by inquisitive monkeys screeching overhead, to the area of Bheri Kharka/Bhichok. After rainstorms at the beginning of October, this section of trail seems to be inhabited by every blood-sucking leech that ever lived in Nepal – so watch out during those unavoidable loo stops! Contouring around the hillside, the trail goes through cultivated fields to **Tolka** (1700m), high above the Modi Khola. To the south there are distant views of the whole valley as it cuts through the middle hills. The path drops a little as it circles around to the Gurung village of

The Modi Khola Valley view near Ghandruk

Landruk (1565m). At sunset you are likely to get a superb view of Annapurna South and Hiunchuli.

Landruk to Chhomrong (5–6hrs)

At one time it was necessary to head to Chhomrong via Ghandruk, but the opening of the new bridge in the 1980s made that energy-sapping descent and ascent a thing of the past. The route follows the Modi Khola and, after the bridge, climbs relentlessly to a small pass before reaching Chhomrong.

Leaving Landruk in a northerly direction, cross a bridge and pass the hydro pipe, following the well-defined trail that descends gently down the hillsides. ◄

The trail to the left in Landruk goes down to the Modi Khola and up to Ghandruk.

As the path approaches the river, fields give way to cool, leafy woodlands; the raging torrents of the river break the silence. Once across the 'new' bridge over the Modi Khola to the settlement of **New Bridge** (1340m), the trail begins to climb around to the Kimrong Khola before the hard part begins up to **Jhinu Danda** (1780m). If you take a side trail from here you can visit the hot springs; alternatively make it a short day by overnighting here; otherwise there's a climb of over 400m to **Taglung** village.

With the one of the toughest stages over, it's a pleasant respite ambling on to **Chhomrong** (2170m). The trail drops into this prosperous farming and lodge community. Many of the newer lodges have spread up the hillside before the old village. Chhomrong is the last permanently inhabited village on the route to the Sanctuary.

THE GURKHAS

The term 'Gurkha' applies not to any ethnic group of Nepal, but to the tradition of soldiering. The town of Gorkha in central Nepal was the birthplace of Prithvi Narayan Shah, the unifier of modern Nepal, and his armies were known as the Gurkha army. Today the role of the Gurkhas in the British (and Indian) Armies is well known. There is one recruiting base for prospective soldiers near Pokhara, and another near Dharan in the eastern hilly tracts. Chhomrong is home to many ex-Gurkha soldiers (like the famous 'Captain', the jolly Captain's Lodge owner), who retired here and set up the first well-appointed lodges in the 1970s.

ALTERNATIVE STAGE 1
Naya Pul to Chhomrong

Start	Naya Pul (1070m/3510ft) or Syauli Bazaar (1170m/3840ft)
Finish	Chhomrong (2170m/7117ft)
Distance	16km (10 miles) or less if jeep taken
Time	8–9hrs or less
Altitude range	1070m/3510ft (Naya Pul) to 2170m/7117ft (Chhomrong)
Transport	Jeep from Birethanti

It's also possible to get to Chhomrong from Naya Pul by taking a jeep to Syauli Bazaar. The valley is heavily cultivated and dotted with typical farms and small settlements.

A new trail now skirts below the Ghandruk bluff along the Modi Khola directly from Syauli Bazaar (1170m) to

ANNAPURNA SANCTUARY –
Alternative Stage 1

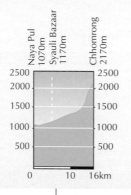

New Bridge, a better option for the inbound trek to Chhomrong (16km, 10 miles). Depending on your luck with transport, Birethanti to Chhomrong via New Bridge can be done in one long day, but it's better to take two days and stay at **Jhinu Danda** for a hot bath.

In Syauli you'll need to ask the way, particularly with the new jeep track making for even more confusion. Allow 2–3hrs to reach New Bridge along the riverbank and watch out for the beehives of the famous honey hunters. Don't walk on your own; there has been the occasional mugging round here. Once at New Bridge, you'll have to climb that big hill mentioned in Stage 1 all the way via Jhinu Danda to **Chhomrong** (2170m).

Note that the jeep track from Syauli is expected to reach Ghandruk soon, but for the time being the climb up from **Kimche** (1640m) to **Ghandruk** (1940m) is quite a hot, sticky affair. From Ghandruk it's a tough day to **Chhomrong**, with some surprisingly steep ascents and descents, making this option the preferred route *back from* rather than *into* the Sanctuary (see Stage 4).

Woman and child in Chhomrong

STAGE 2
Chhomrong to Annapurna Base Camp (ABC)

Start	Chhomrong (2170m/7117ft)
Finish	Annapurna Base Camp (4130m/13,545ft)
Distance	21km (13 miles)
Time	3 days
Altitude range	2170m/7117ft (Chhomrong) to 4130m/13,545ft
	(Annapurna Base Camp)
Transport	None

Leaving behind the richly terraced and picturesque villages, the route to the Sanctuary passes through wild, untamed forests and high, empty pastures. In fog this upland region is quite reminiscent of North Wales. Only lodge settlements that cater for trekkers are encountered, since herders rarely venture up here these days. Hemmed in by the rugged sheer walls of the incredible Modi Khola gorge, there is little sunlight, giving rise to an often-eerie atmosphere. The mountains are hidden from view for much of the way – that is until you emerge into the open bowl of the Sanctuary, where a tremendous cirque of glittering peaks and spires leaves you giddy with awe.

Chhomrong to Doban (5–6hrs)
The cosy lodges of Chhomrong are left far behind today and the walk will be generally humid due to the dense undergrowth and cloud rainforest. Some sections are quite a scramble; it's a surprisingly tiring walk. It can be bitterly cold and damp in this deep canyon when the afternoon mist rolls in. Be sure to keep some warm clothing handy.

From **Chhomrong** the trail dives rather disconcertingly downhill to a side stream. Almost as soon as you've adjusted to this downward rhythm, the trail suddenly climbs steps, steeply upwards to a couple of corner teahouses. **Sinuwa** is along here. After a muddy, wet, rocky cliff section, Kuldighar is reached.

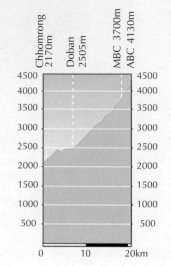

ANNAPURNA SANCTUARY – Stage 2

This **now-abandoned settlement** was once thriving, with a good lodge and weather station, before the ACAP conservation people decided to limit the places in which trekkers could stay overnight.

The isolated lodges of Bamboo and Doban can be picked out way ahead up the ever-narrowing and densely vegetated valley. On a clear day, Gangapurna can be seen at the valley's head.

For the rest of the day, the trail enters the misty underworld of the Modi Khola's thick forests. Sunlight becomes a thing of the past and the path underfoot needs care: roots, muddy areas, streambeds, overhanging bamboo branches, rotting tree trunks and slippery gullies all impede progress. The pace can be slow, so don't expect to reach **Bamboo** (2335m) early. From Bamboo to **Doban** (Dovan) is less than 1hr march. Set in small clearings,

Rhododendron forest

the lodges of Bamboo or Doban (2505m) are a welcome sight, offering warming and filling meals.

Doban to Machhapuchhre Base Camp (MBC) (5–7hrs)

This day is more varied, as the trail climbs up from the murky gorge on to the high upland meadows. On the east side of the canyon, in particular, the cliffs and lower buttresses of Machhapuchhre are sheer and imposing. At dawn the cold air of the deep canyon is bracing, especially for those camping and taking breakfast outside; that's why most trekkers choose the lodge option on this trek. Once underway, the trail soon penetrates the dense bamboo forest (one quite expects a giant panda to leap out of the undergrowth!). Watch out for the effects of altitude; the trail climbs to over 3700m by the day's end.

From **Doban** the next place for tea is **Himalaya** (2875m), with 'lodgings and foodings'.

Close by is the **shrine of Panchenin Baraha**. According to folklore, neither a lower caste menial should proceed past here, nor any chicken, cow or pig meat! Apparently the Jimmy Roberts Expedition to Machhapuchhre (see below) was required to offer 50 eggs to the deity before passing on by; the egg porter was probably ecstatic!

Not far ahead is the overhanging feature aptly named Hinku Cave (3150m). In the good old days, this sheltered spot once housed a basic lodge. Now no camps or lodges are allowed within the normal avalanche zone of Hiunchuli. That said, there is still the risk of avalanche on this stage of the trail after heavy rain or snow, so take advice from the lodge owners. After the monsoon in early October, in late December/January, and after storms throughout spring, this risk should not be underestimated.

From Hinku Cave the trail dives across a small ravine and straddles the avalanche debris to climb briefly to **Deurali** (3230m). Once above the tree line, views open up of the monumental flanks of Machhapuchhre; it's probably the most sensational buttress zone of any mountain in Nepal that trekkers can pass beneath. At **Bagar** (3300m) are the remains of what was a great spot to camp – the cliffs across the river were mesmerising to behold. Occasionally when the risk of avalanche is high, the trail is closed and trekkers have to divert across the Modi Khola and continue on the east bank before crossing back to the main track. Otherwise the stiff climb from here remains the last hurdle before reaching Machhapuchhre Base Camp. Beware of rushing on, for in this zone some may fall victim to the effects of altitude sickness.

For most trekkers, arriving at **Machhapuchhre Base Camp** (3700m) will be a relief, tinged with a feeling of slight trepidation; altitude affects every individual in a different way, and the degree of discomfort felt will be unpredictable. Going high now is ill advised; be sure to rest, drink plenty and have an early night (remembering not to indulge in a celebratory beer). There is a German-sponsored meteorological station in the vicinity. Don't be surprised if the whole base camp zone is enveloped by

thick, cold cloud – it's a rare afternoon that is clear in this haunt of the gods. Often as dusk approaches the curtains of clouds draw back and Nature reveals her artistry. Sunset on Machhapuchhre's West Face is almost beyond description.

Trekkers' views in the Annapurna Sanctuary

Machhapuchhre Base Camp (MBC) to Annapurna Base Camp (ABC) (2hrs)

Many trekkers concerned about the additional altitude of Annapurna Base Camp plan to retreat to Machhapuchhre Base Camp for another night rather than stay higher – it all depends on your time frame and how you feel. Staying at Annapurna Base Camp gives a different perspective to this great amphitheatre of mountains. It truly is a land of magical make-believe.

Although there's no great distance to travel today, it's a good idea to start as soon as the sun warms the icy platform where the lodges have been placed to capture the morning rays. Clouds are likely to swallow up the views before lunchtime. The path is clear and climbs steadily. It takes 2hrs or so to reach Annapurna Base Camp (4130m),

THE ASSAULT ON MACHHAPUCHHRE

The fishtail peak of Machhapuchhre is one of the most iconic mountains of Nepal. Standing at 6993m (22,943ft), it is a sacred peak whose summit is not to be violated. That said, an attempt was made in 1957 by a small expedition led by Jimmy Roberts.

On 24 April, Base Camp was set just inside the Sanctuary, and from there they chose a route that would take them on to the North Ridge by way of the ice flutings that from a distance looked like pleated curtain. Before gaining the ridge, however, one of the team members, Roger Chorley, was struck down with polio and was carried out to Pokhara in the care of Roberts, leaving just Noyce, Cox and Wylie to continue the attempt with support from their Sherpas. Three camps above base, the trio came on to a ridge and then settled Camp IV under the rock buttress which carries the ridge south to the upper pyramid. From there they could make out the summit obelisk, but the intervening ground was obscured by a short knife-edged ridge which fell steeply to the Seti Khola. But a glacial projection offered a possible way on to a snowy shelf, from which, it was conjectured, the upward route could be carried. Reaching the shelf was an epic in itself, and once there it was found to be 'a mountain freak', as Noyce described it. 'It is supported by nothing and one day will go crashing down into the Seti.' Fortunately it held, and Camp V was pitched above a large crevasse at about 6400m (21,000ft) on 1 June.

At 4.20am next morning, Wilfred Noyce and David Cox made their bid for the summit, which rose nearly 600m above them, 'a fluted, furrowed

Machhapuchhre before sundown

series of ribs sweeping straight up to a jagged crest'. Soft knee-deep snow led to easy step-cutting, then they continued round and above a bulbous 'onion' of ice, the size of a cottage, which took an age to pass. Out of a clear sky, long rolls of cloud gathered and engulfed the neighbouring peaks. Snow began to fall at 9am, and in worsening conditions they spent the next two hours climbing two ice chimneys, then rounded a rib to discover four or five columns of beautifully polished ice, each of which ended in a skyline pinnacle. Snow fell more thickly now, and after labouring to cut steps up one of the columns, Noyce and Cox called it a day and turned back. They were less than 50m (160ft) from the top. 'The Goddess had drawn her firm line here,' wrote Noyce, 'and with that we must be content.'

Kev Reynolds

The story of this, the sole authorised attempt to climb Machhapuchhre, is described in 'Climbing the Fish's Tail' by Wilfred Noyce (Heinemann, 1958 and reprinted by Book Faith/Pilgrims Publishing, 1998).

from where the true scale of the great glaciers below Annapurna I can be appreciated.

It was above these stupendous glacial tongues that a rock fall killed Ian Clough during the now famous **conquest of Annapurna I** by Chris Bonington's team in 1970, right after the summit successes – an irony only too familiar among these Himalayan giants. Not far from ABC is a memorial chorten to the Russian guide Anatoli Boukreev, who was also killed in 1997 by an avalanche. He was a guide with one of the parties on the controversial Everest expeditions in 1995 when so many climbers were killed.

From Annapurna Base Camp, those sufficiently acclimatised and energetic can climb up the ridge to the southwest, on the moraine, alongside the glacier that drops from Annapurna South. Gaining extra height provides yet more spectacular views. All the time the

Annapurna I seen from Base Camp

adjacent glacier is melting and crashing away. Across the Sanctuary are the peaks of Tharpu Chuli (Tent Peak) and Singu Chuli (Fluted Peak), both trekking peaks to be bagged by experienced mountaineers. To the west, the encircling cirque of Annapurna South and Baraha Shikha (Fang) forms a formidable barrier. Annapurna I finally looks like the highest of the entourage. To the east is the serrated, razor-like ridge that links Gangapurna, Gandhara Chuli, Annapurna III and Machhapuchhre, illustrating the variety of the Himalayan range at its best.

STAGE 3
Annapurna Base Camp to Chhomrong

Start	Annapurna Base Camp (4130m/13,545ft)
Finish	Chhomrong (2170m/7117ft)
Distance	21km (13 miles)
Time	3 days
Altitude range	4130m/13,545ft (Annapurna Base Camp) to 2170m/7117ft (Chhomrong)
Transport	None

The long march down to Chhomrong follows the same route, but the vistas heading south are totally different from those encountered on the approach. The rush of warmer and denser air regenerates the soul as more comfortable altitudes are reached.

The descent from **Annapurna Base Camp** to **Machhapuchhre Base Camp** can be accomplished in around 1hr. Descending from high altitude is always relaxing and refreshing, unwinding from the various stresses on body and mind. The retreat down the Modi Khola Valley is, surprisingly, little faster than the ascent, due to the twisted and tangled nature of the forest. Be sure to stop for the night well before dusk. **Chhomrong** heralds a return to modernity and time for those long-anticipated beers. From Chhomrong there is a choice of routes to Naya Pul.

Return routes to Naya Pul from Chhomrong
The shortest route, apart from the Modi Khola riverbank route already mentioned (see Alternative Stage 1), is from

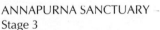

ANNAPURNA SANCTUARY
Stage 3

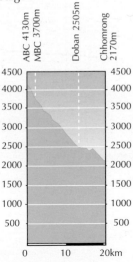

Porters on the trail

Chhomrong to Naya Pul (Birethanti) via Ghandruk (Stage 4 below). For a more in-depth appreciation of the region, head from Chhomrong to Tadapani via Kimrong Khola and then up to Ghorepani (for Poon Hill). A long day after that takes you down to Naya Pul (Alternative Stage 4).

STAGE 4
Chhomrong to Naya Pul via Ghandruk

Start	Chhomrong (2170m/7117ft)
Finish	Naya Pul (1070m/3510ft)
Distance	20km (12 miles)
Time	2 days
Altitude range	1070m/3510ft (Naya Pul) to 2250m/7382ft (Komrong Danda)
Transport	Jeep and then bus to Pokhara

Despite looking close by on the map, getting to Ghandruk from Chhromrong is quite tough, as the trail descends and climbs steeply.

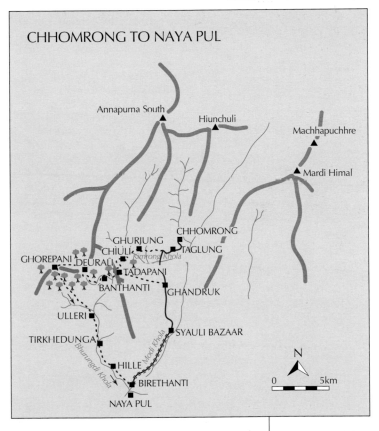

CHHOMRONG TO NAYA PUL

Annapurna South

Hiunchuli

Machhapuchhre

Mardi Himal

CHHOMRONG

GHURJUNG

CHIULI   TAGLUNG

GHOREPANI   *Kimrong Khola*

DEURALI

TADAPANI

BANTHANTI

GHANDRUK

ULLERI

TIRKHEDUNGA   SYAULI BAZAAR

Modi Khola

N

HILLE

Bhurungdi Khola   0   5km

BIRETHANTI

NAYA PUL

Chhomrong to Ghandruk (5–6hrs)

From upper **Chhomrong**, the trail heads west into the side valley of the Kimrong Khola. Make the most of a tea break at the riverside, since the climb (500m) to **Ghandruk** is 'beastly' in the humid heat of the afternoon. Fortunately there is some shade en route and the Coke sellers are out in force at the summit, **Komrong Danda** (2250m) – it's a well-earned refreshing stop. From here, head downhill on a partially rough trail to **Ghandruk** (1940m), one of the

ANNAPURNA SANCTUARY –
Stage 4

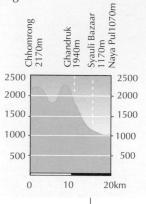

Chhomrong 2170m
Ghandruk 1940m
Syauli Bazaar 1170m
Naya Pul 1070m

most famous traditional Gurung villages of the Annapurna region (see Trek 1 Annapurna Circuit, Alternative Stage 4).

A **very pleasant trail** heads west from Ghandruk uphill into the exotic forests en route to Tadapani (another option to link with Ghorepani). The forest is spooky in places, with massive ferns, moss-laden trees, wispy lichens and big black spiders' webs (see Trek 3 Ghorepani Circuit).

Ghandruk to Naya Pul (4–5hrs)

From **Ghandruk**, head south out of the village and be sure not to inadvertently take the descending trail to Landruk. Going ahead, the way gradually loses height as it contours around a series of landslips and then relatively benign side valleys. All along the way is fertile

Annapurna South towers above Ghandruk

farming countryside, with plenty of opportunity to photograph the people and their activities: carrying water, sowing, ploughing, wood-gathering, harvesting and, often, celebrating a festival. Somewhere below Ghandruk you will encounter the advancing jeep track, making the rest of the day easier to **Birethanti** (1035m) and the scruffy trailhead at **Naya Pul** (1070m) where you can pick up a bus for Pokhara.

ALTERNATIVE STAGE 4
Chhomrong to Naya Pul via Ghorepani

Start	Chhomrong (2170m/7117ft)
Finish	Naya Pul (1070m/3510ft)
Distance	35km (22 miles)
Time	3–4 days
Altitude range	1070m/3510ft (Naya Pul) to 2990m/9810ft (Deurali)
Transport	Bus or taxi to Pokhara

It takes a couple of days to reach Ghorepani, but the route passes photogenic hill farms and heads into exotic forests. Far fewer trekkers take this route, the direct trail to Tadapani, but that in itself makes for a change around here. Don't trek alone on this route, especially in the forest sections.

Shortly after leaving **Chhomrong**, the trail descends steeply through the terraces and meadows into the Kimrong Khola Valley. Here the river is bridged near the scattered houses of **Ghurjung** (1900m), west of the Ghandruk trail crossing. Thence begins a long, long climb. The trail is quite steep and literally climbs in places over the terraces. (The porters don't like this section and neither do the farmers, who have to repair the trails, so be careful here.) Gaining height, almost brutally at times, the cool of the forest beckons as you leave the last fields near **Chiuli**. The forest is cool and inviting – at

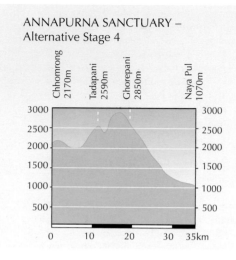

least during daylight hours – but don't get caught here after sunset. The forest clearing of **Tadapani** (2590m) is gained in about 3hrs from Kimrong Khola. Tadapani has some good lodges and it makes a change to stay in the forest for a night.

For details of the Tadapani to Ghorepani stage and down to Birethanti/Naya Pul, refer to Trek 3 Ghorepani Circuit below and Trek 1 Annapurna Circuit, Stage 4 above.

TREK 3
Ghorepani Circuit (Poon Hill Expedition)

Start	Dhampus Phedi (1130m/3706ft) or Dhampus (1650m/5413ft)
Finish	Naya Pul (1070m/3510ft)
Distance	52km (33 miles)
Time	6–8 days
Maximum altitude	Poon Hill (3193m/10,473ft)
Transport	Bus, jeep and taxi from/to Pokhara
Trekking style	Lodges

Despite the obvious attractions of other treks, this old favourite remains true to the essence of Himalayan trekking in Nepal. The views are wonderful, the village life typical and, being a short trek, it appeals to a wider audience. Such was its popularity in the 1980s that it was easily the most popular group trek and hence acquired the not-too-disingenuous title of the 'Poon Hill Expedition' among trek leaders.

Himalayan panorama near Pothana

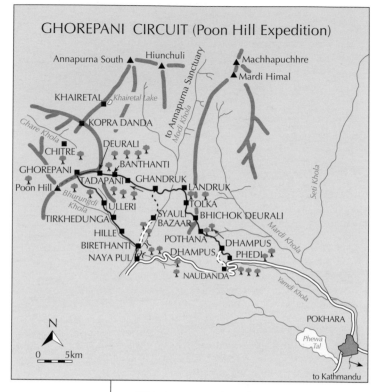

GHOREPANI CIRCUIT (Poon Hill Expedition)

Annapurna South ▲ Hiunchuli ▲ Machhapuchhre ▲

Mardi Himal ▲

KHAIRETAL ■ *Khairetal Lake*

to Annapurna Sanctuary

Modi Khola

Chare Khola

KOPRA DANDA ■

DEURALI ■

CHITRE ■ BANTHANTI

GHOREPANI ■ TADAPANI ■ GHANDRUK ■ LANDRUK ■

Poon Hill ▲ *Bhurungdi Khola*

ULLERI ■ TOLKA ■

TIRKHEDUNGA ■ SYAULI BICHOK DEURALI ■

HILLE ■ BAZAAR

POTHANA ■ DHAMPUS ■

BIRETHANTI ■ DHAMPUS PHEDI ■

NAYA PUL ■ *Seti Khola*

Mardi Khola

NAUDANDA ▲

Yamdi Khola

POKHARA

Phewa Tal

N

0   5km

to Kathmandu

With the construction of new jeep roads, the trek distance is slightly less than it used to be, but the route still enjoys the timeless attractions of the picturesque Modi Khola Valley. Annapurna South, Machhapuchhre and Dhaulagiri are the main ingredients of this feast of mountain vistas. For a shorter trek, duck out at Ghandruk direct to Birethanti and benefit from some deluxe lodges on the way. Ker and Downey have a series of inns, one located 20mins' north of Birethanti, others in Ghandruk, Dhampus and Thanchok. Some of the stages of this trek are described in more detail in Treks 1 and 2 (Annapurna Circuit/Sanctuary).

GHOREPANI CIRCUIT

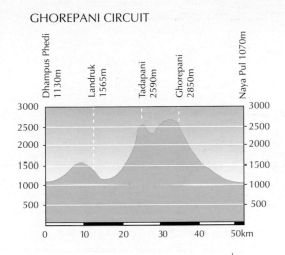

Dhampus Phedi to Landruk (6½–7½hrs)

From **Dhampus Phedi** (1130m) the route ascends to **Dhampus** (1650m), then climbs along the ridge up to **Pothana** (1890m) and **Deurali** (2100m). The path for Landruk descends through forest to Bheri Kharka. Contouring around the hillside, the trail reaches **Tolka** (1700m) and continues to **Landruk** (1565m). At sunset you are likely to get a superb view of Annapurna South and Hiunchuli.

Landruk to Tadapani (6–7hrs)

It may not be far 'as the crow flies' between Landruk and Ghandruk, but the Modi Khola Valley is a formidable obstacle on this stage. Almost before you've put your boots on, the path plunges steeply down in a series of turns. It takes about 1hr to reach the Modi Khola bridge (watch out for the 'honey hunters' in the river canyon). There's a bigger altitude gain up to Ghandruk and for much of the season it's a hot, sweaty climb. Drink stops are frequent. The typical Gurung village of **Ghandruk**

(1940m) provides all the reasons to stop for a lingering lunch – the old quarter is a 'must see' attraction.

Once clear of the fields, the climb to Tadapani begins in earnest. The forest is eerie and beguiling, with rhododendron, magnolia, larch and moss-covered decaying vegetation. Wispy lichens hang from gnarled trunks, and every conceivable design of fern is to be observed. Elusive cicadas are heard but not seen; however, monkeys will make themselves known. The forest enclave of **Tadapani** (2590m) is a welcoming spot. At night this dank haunt seems to come alive.

Tadapani to Ghorepani (4–5hrs)

From Tadapani the way almost immediately descends steeply, with mostly ascents through the little-disturbed forest later in this stage. In spring this section is ablaze with flowering rhododendrons. After the small forest clearing and settlement of **Banthanti** (2520m), the next stage can get icy, especially after snowfall and beside a waterfall, so be very careful under such conditions. Once clear of the woodlands, the path contours along a high moorland ridge to **Deurali** (2990m) and on to **Ghorepani**, with its plentiful but chilly lodges.

Ghorepani to Naya Pul via Tirkhedunga (7–9hrs)

Joining the classic Annapurna Circuit, this stage offers a return to warmer climes as the trail drops almost 1200m to Tirkhedunga (or almost 1600m from the summit of Poon Hill!). An abbreviated description of the descent follows (for more details see Trek 1 Annapurna Circuit).

> The **Poon Hill Expedition** – the daily ritual of sunrise – should not be missed. Enjoy the panoramic plethora of peaks – Churen Himal, Dhaulagiri, the Nilgiris, Fang (Baraha Shikar), Annapurna South and the Kali Gandaki gorge.

From **Ghorepani** the trail snakes down in forest and around to another place called Banthanti (2300m), with views of Machhapuchhre's fishy tail. The trail descends

The incredible view from Poon Hill

to **Ulleri**, a good lunch break. A knee-exercising drop on the staircase of a few thousand steps leads to **Tirkhedunga** (1540m). With warmer weather, enjoy the last unwinding stage. Soon it's almost too warm through **Hille** (1475m), where there is a jeep track being pushed up from **Birethanti**. A bus or taxi to Pokhara can be picked up above **Naya Pul** bazaar.

TREK 4

Annapurna–Dhaulagiri Trek

Start	Dhampus Phedi (1130m/3706ft) or Dhampus (1650m/5413ft)
Finish	Naya Pul (1070m/3510ft)
Distance	70km (54 miles)
Time	10–12 days
Maximum altitude	Khairetal Lake (4200m/13,780ft)
Transport	Bus, jeep and taxi from/to Pokhara
Trekking style	Camping, basic lodges and homestay

With only limited lodge development north beyond Tadapani at present, the trek is generally experienced as a fully supported camping expedition. This 'old style' of trekking is an attraction in itself and the feast of panoramic views from the Kopra Ridge makes it an outstanding option. Trekkers heading for the pilgrimage lake of Khairetal currently need to camp. The basic route can be done in 10 days, but it's worth adding a day on the Kopra

Curious villagers at a campsite en route

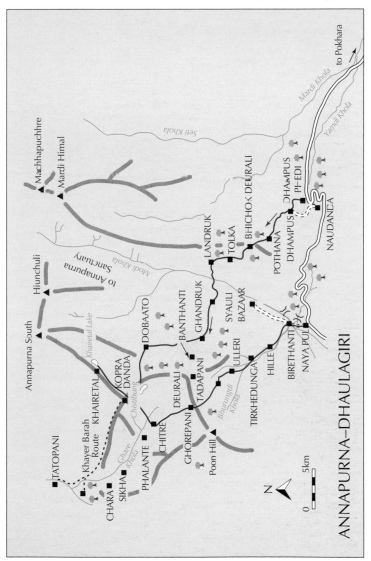

ANNAPURNA–DHAULAGIRI

ANNAPURNA–DHAULAGIRI

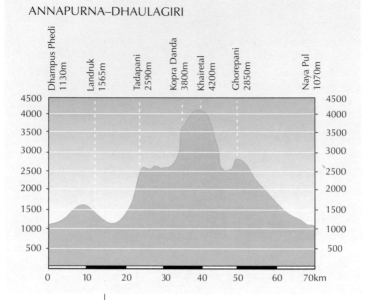

Ridge in case of heavy snowfalls, which seem to plague the route for part of the season.

In snow the whole ridge above the Kopra viewpoint is a more daunting and very occasionally dangerous task, with a slight risk of slipping off the trail in one section. However, failing to reach the quiet tarn known as Khairetal is not a disaster if the skies are clear, because the views are amazing. Most groups allow extra time for an intermediate camp on the way to the lake.

Currently homestays are possible in Baiyali, on the Kopra Danda Ridge and in the village of Swanta. Rumour has it there are homestay developments in Dobaato and in Chistibung now. A new trail is being developed from Kopra to Tatopani, the Khayer Barah Trek (see below).

The following stages on this trek correspond roughly to the daily marches. For more detailed notes on some, refer to Trek 2 Annapurna Sanctuary and Trek 3 Ghorepani Circuit.

Dhampus Phedi to Landruk (6½–7½hrs)
From **Dhampus Phedi** the route goes through Dhampus (1650m), **Pothana** (1890m), **Deurali** (2100m), down to Bheri Kharka, around to **Tolka** (1700m) and on to **Landruk** (1565m) (see Trek 3 Ghorepani Circuit).

Landruk to Tadapani (6–7hrs)
In Nepal there is hardly a level section of trail. An easy downhill section is always followed by a steep uphill grind – and so it is with Landruk to Tadapani.

> Referring to two villages on the Arun to Everest Trail, **HW Tilman** (in his book *Nepal Himalaya*) exclaimed, 'For dreadfulness, naught can excel, the prospect of Bung from Guidel.' The same can be said of 'Ghandruk from Landruk'!

The route plunges steeply down to the bridge over the Modi Khola then makes a challenging, sweaty climb to **Ghandruk** (1940m). From here it ascends through a woodland wonderland to the forest enclave of **Tadapani** (2590m). At night this eerie haunt is more alive than are the sleepy trekkers.

Tadapani to Dobaato (5–6hrs)
Breaking away from the main trail here, the route is northwards through thick forest and highland scrub reminiscent of the Scottish moors. This trail has no obvious destination for anyone except trekkers.

From **Tadapani** the morning's hike is through the cool, damp forests on a rough and little-used herders' path. There is little sunlight but a plethora of exotic plants and trees – rhododendron, magnolia and a myriad of orchids – and more bird life here than on busy tracks. Be careful navigating among the gnarled trees and twisted roots. Clearings below some rocky crags offer the best places for lunch, where the warmth of the sun is much appreciated. The afternoon walk is once again in thinning forest with a few significant ups and downs. Camp is usually set up beyond the tree line at the isolated *kharka* (herders' shelter) of **Dobaato** (3420m). Mist may hide the snowy summits of Annapurna South, Machhapuchhre and distant Himalchuli in the afternoon, but come the dawn they sparkle brightly. Apparently a new homestay/community lodge is developing at Dobaato, but check this in Tadapani.

Dobaato to Chistibung (3–4hrs)

It makes a wonderful change to be trekking so close to nature. With so few people on this trail, the wildlife is less wary, giving quiet trekkers a chance to see the shy creatures of the forest.

The route continues through remote wilderness in the shadow of the lower ramparts of Annapurna South (7219m). Here and there are isolated *bhattis* (primitive dwellings), where wild-eyed, roughly dressed men cut wood, herd their goats and forage in the forest. **Chistibung** (3000m), just below Dharamdanda, is the usual night's stop, being little more than a few terraces, a couple of houses and maybe a new homestay with an eye on the future.

Chistibung to Kopra Danda (3–4hrs)

The chill of a misty dawn soon burns off and the distant peaks gain in clarity. The trail climbs and descends almost disconcertingly; the path is often overgrown and muddy underfoot. The final climb to Kopra Ridge is demanding, seemingly never-ending and wild.

From **Chistibung** the route contours around the vast hillside high above the Kholang Khola then drops into the densely forested upper reaches of the Dhasta Khore Khola, a beguilingly complex network of tributaries and gullies. Far below, the deep ravines and damp canyons are disturbed only by the echoing sounds of screeching birds. After a daunting descent, the trail makes a determined effort to gain height via a long and taxing climb: the top is always just a bit further on. And so it goes, with

some anticipation of the views to come and the camp ahead already manned by the trekking cook crew; the prospect of hot tea and biscuits can work wonders. One cannot fail to be moved by the staggering vista at today's destination: the **Kopra Danda** (about 3800m). Lammergeyers, Himalayan Griffons, vultures, eagles and other large raptors often circle camp here.

Fang and Annapurna South from Kopra

Trek to Khairetal/Baraha Lake (8–10hrs, 2 days)
From the camp or homestay lodge near the ridge top, the route basically climbs steadily all the way, with the tantalising peak of Annapurna South periodically screened by the rocky outcrops. The intermediate campsites vary according to the availability of water and the season. Because of deep snow, the authors have twice failed to make it to the lake in the past (giving a 65 per cent chance of success).

At dawn, as mist obscures the valleys, a sweeping panorama of floating Himalayan giants appears: Churen

Himal, Dhaulagiri, Tukuche Peak, Dhampus Peak, Upper Mustang peaks, the Nilgiris, Annapurna I, Fang, and Annapurna South. The Kali Gandaki Valley is far below. Countless hazy blue ridges stretch as far as the eye can discern, towards the Indian border. Tearing yourself away from the vistas, begin the long and arduous climb up the formidable crest of the ridge.

Given a clear path, getting to the isolated pilgrimage lake of Khairetal and the Baraha shrine (4200m) is rarely insurmountable, so long as you are well acclimatised.

> **Khairetal Lake** is holy to Hindus, who come here for the Janai Purnima festival in August (a difficult expedition at that time of year, with monsoonal

Khairetal/Baraha Lake

leeches and muddy trails). Dramatic cliffs surround the beautiful, tranquil waters – it is a remarkable place of great serenity, where only the squawking of predatory eagles and vultures pierces the silence. It is not hard to understand how this spot became a significant religious pilgrimage site.

Take great care retracing your steps, descending the occasionally exposed ridge. The panoramic vistas along this hairy belvedere are spectacular in all directions.

Be sure to stay at Kopra for sunset; long before the last rays of sunlight desert Dhaulagiri, the sensational colours of dusk are displayed in all their glory: hazy blue tints, jet-black couloirs, silvery cornices, the crisp white snow dappled with fading sunlight and the darkening shadows of the deepest gorge on earth between Annapurna I and Dhaulagiri. Annapurna South and Fang loom large, like giant ogres, to the east, while on the northern horizon millions of stars twinkle above Nilgiri, Tukuche Peak and their companions on the Tibetan border. It's a magical and memorable sight.

Kopra Danda to Ghorepani (6–7hrs)
Although a tinge of sadness is felt on leaving this lofty viewpoint, there is a certain attraction in reaching the warm climes of Chitre, far, far below.

The path drops quickly off the ridge towards the distant bright yellow mustard-filled terraces. The trail is knee-crunchingly relentless. Stop for a moment to admire the view of Ghorepani, Poon Hill and the old mule route snaking down towards the Kali Gandaki Valley. Eventually, after scrambling down the tumbling trail to Swanta (Someta), to those once seemingly tiny fields, the route joins the main trail at **Chitre** (2390m). Soon it's time to celebrate in the mountain metropolis of **Ghorepani** (2850m).

Ghorepani to Naya Pul via Tirkhedunga (7–9hrs)
Having bagged such a great view from Kopra, you may not be inclined to take on Poon Hill, but if you have any

DHAULAGIRI

Dhaulagiri at sunset from the Kopra Danda

Dhaulagiri is the world's seventh-highest mountain (8167m/26,795ft). In Sanskrit its name means 'white mountain'. Admired by thousands of trekkers from the Kali Gandaki and Poon Hill, Dhaulagiri resisted the attempts of mountaineers for longer than comparable peaks. In 1950 Herzog's French expedition had initially hoped to summit it, but after lengthy reconnaissance decided it was too dangerous, turning their attention to Annapurna I instead. Six attempts on Dhaulagiri via the west ridge followed, but it was not until 1960 that a Swiss expedition finally won through – albeit in controversial style. They used a light aircraft to ferry food, equipment and even climbers to the northeast col at around 5700m (18,700ft). The Pilatus Porter, piloted by daredevils including Emil Wick, eventually crashed on the mountain without loss of life. Austrian mountaineer Kurt Diemberger, a 'foreigner' within the Swiss expedition, reached the summit on 13 May, in company with Peter Diener, Ernst Forrer, Albin Schelbert and the Sherpas Nyima Dorji and Nawang Dorji. Two other members (Michel Vaucher and Hugo Weber) also reached the top 10 days later. Attempts since then have tried different routes, but many have perished on the killer white mountain, particularly in avalanches from the notorious Dhaulagiri Icefall.

Abridged from material by Kev Reynolds

reserves of energy, don't miss it. From **Ghorepani** the trail descends through **Banthanti**, **Ulleri**, **Tirkhedunga**, **Hille** and **Birethanti** to **Naya Pul**, for the bus to Pokhara – and the cosy lakeside nightspots of the 'big' city! See Trek 1 Annapurna Circuit for a detailed description of the route to Naya Pul.

Khayer Barah route – Kopra Danda to Tatopani

For adventurous, fit trekkers, this route offers an alternative exit off the Kopra Danda ridge. Unless you can do the 1600m of descent in one day, you'll need a camping

PILGRIMS' TRAIL – TATOPANI TO JOMSOM/MUKTINATH

Long before the 'motorable' road was constructed from Pokhara to Jomsom, the route up the Kali Gandaki Valley was the sole domain of traders taking goods to Lo Manthang and Tibet and returning with salt from the high plateau. Mule and donkey trains were still a familiar sight on the trail long after the border with Tibet closed in the 1950s. Pilgrims and sadhus also followed this deep canyon to find solace and spiritual uplift at the sacred shrine at Muktinath. Mystics sought sanctuary in the caves around Muktinath. Today the new road has eclipsed the pilgrims' trekking trail; even pilgrims and some sadhus prefer a bumpy one or two-day ride. Since the inception of the road, few walk the route from Pokhara, Naya Pul or Tatopani to Muktinath (88km/54 miles), so only a brief outline is provided in this book. Accommodation is in lodges, and transport by bus, jeep, plane or even helicopter is available. For a detailed trek description, see Trek 1 Annapurna Circuit, Stage 3 in reverse.

Expect a long, dusty, rough ride all the way to Tatopani from Pokhara via Beni. Trekking from Tatopani (1190m) to Muktinath taking the alternative trails could be quite attractive, while following the currently quiet road is also a feasible option; allow 7–9 days for the trek. Ghasa is a pleasant place to overnight. After Kalopani the trek along the road from Kokhethanti to Larjung (for Naurikot), Tukuche and Marpha is much easier and more interesting. Across the river before Marpha is Chhairo's historic monastery. Between Jomsom (2710m) and Kagbeni, take a side trek up to Lubra and its Bon community. No one should miss the trek up to Muktinath (3710m), but be careful of the altitude. Save the Jhong route for the return trip down, as it's much longer. Return to Pokhara via Jomsom.

A stimulating prayer wheel!

crew, and certainly a guide who knows the way. It's an exceedingly lonely, wild region, so do not head this way alone under any circumstances; it's not yet sufficiently developed.

From Kopra, the route drops northwest down the isolated forest ridges to the settlement of upper Narchyang. One trail descends to Narchyang Besi, joining the new Annapurna Circuit alternative trail close to the Miristi Khola confluence (see Trek 1 Annapurna Circuit, Stage 3). Another trail is marked on the Himalayan MapHouse map, cutting from the Kopra Ridge directly to Gharkholagaon near Tatopani, but the authors have no information on this option. Anyone looking across the valley from the Ghare–Sikha–Ghorepani trail will have noticed how staggeringly steep and seemingly insurmountable that exciting-looking trail appears. It is essential to take a local guide for either option. The authors have been told that, 'facilities are needed and supposedly being built, but I didn't see much progress other than a pile of wooden planks.' Beware!

2 RESTRICTED AREAS
Mustang, Damodar and Nar-Phu

Narsing valley and Damodar peaks

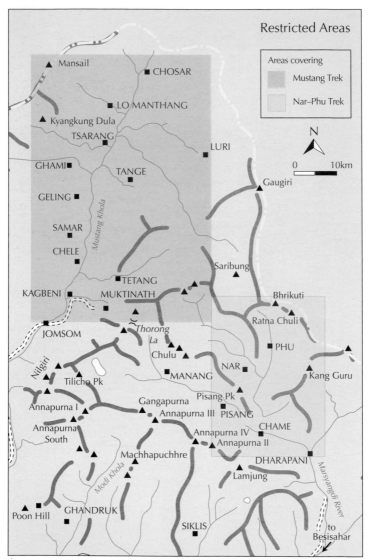

Restricted Areas

Areas covering

Mustang Trek

Nar–Phu Trek

N

0   10km

Mansail

CHOSAR

LO MANTHANG

Kyangkung Dula

TSARANG

LURI

GHAMI

TANGE

Gaugiri

GELING

SAMAR

Mustang Khola

CHELE

Saribung

TETANG

KAGBENI

MUKTINATH

Bhrikuti

Ratna Chuli

JOMSOM

Thorong La

PHU

Nilgiri

Chulu

NAR

Tilicho Pk

MANANG

Kang Guru

Pisang Pk

Gangapurna

Annapurna III

PISANG

Annapurna I

Annapurna IV

CHAME

Annapurna
South

Annapurna II

Modi Khola

Machhapuchhre

DHARAPANI

Marsyangdi River

Lamjung

Poon Hill

GHANDRUK

SIKLIS

to
Besisahar

North of the main Annapurna range are the isolated regions of Mustang, Damodar and Nar-Phu, areas that were once so remote that almost nothing was known about them. Today, trekkers can enjoy these rugged Tibetan-like landscapes with a degree of basic comfort unknown to earlier explorers.

Mystical Mustang lies north of the Annapurnas

TREK 5
Mustang Trek

Start	Jomsom (2710m/8890ft)
Finish	Jomsom (2710m/8890ft)
Distance	176km approx (110 miles)
Time	13–14 days (allow extra for flight delays)
Maximum altitude	Near Paha, and Chogo La (both 4230m/13,879ft)
Transport	Plane or bus to Jomsom and jeep from Muktinath
Trekking style	Camping or basic lodges

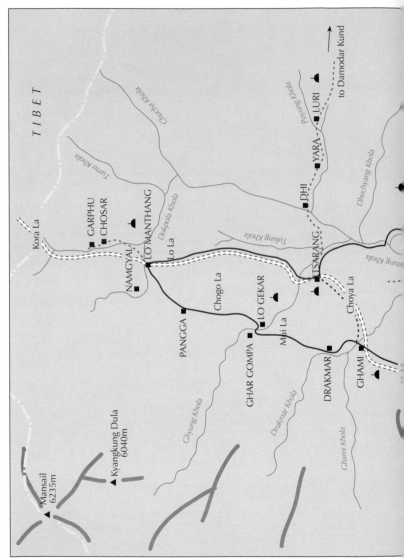

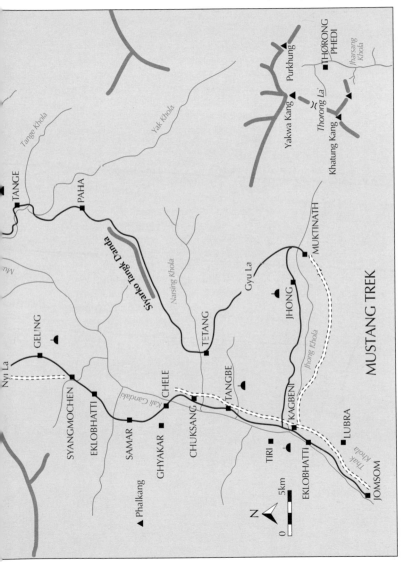

MUSTANG TREK

Mustang is magical and mysterious. The wild, rugged kingdom north of the Annapurnas hides quaint, picturesque villages, exotically located monasteries, historic treasures and a rich cultural heritage; the landscapes and mountain vistas can only be described as superlative, as befits a real Shangri-La. When Nepal first opened to foreigners, one tantalising region – Mustang – remained firmly shut. Apart from some privileged anthropologists, few other visitors were permitted until 1992.

Brief history

Mustang was first mentioned in literature discovered in AD652 in the Silk Route caves at Dunhuang, north of Tibet. It was once part of the Yarlung dynasty that stretched from Tibet into Central Asia. In the 10th century the Tibetan Bon and the Korsum dynasty of Ngari ruled. After the Menshang nomadic tribes, the Jumla kingdom and then the Gunthang kings of Tibet controlled Mustang, before the Menshang reasserted their power. Later the Buddhist master, Ngorchen Kunga Sangpo, briefly administered the region, before it fell yet again under Jumla (then ruled from Tsaparang by the Guge kings of Western Tibet). With the rise of the Sakya-pa order in Tibet, Mustang adopted the same sect.

The Mustang we see now was established under King Amapal (1388–1447). Amapal extended the rule of Lo as far as Purang in Guge. Mustang prospered through the trade between lowland Nepal and Tibet. Links with Ladakh enriched the cultural heritage until 1768, when Prithvi Narayan Shah took control of all Nepal. The Raja of Mustang joined the new state of Nepal, but ruled independently.

After 1950, when Tibet fell under new masters, Khampa freedom fighters used the isolated valleys as bases. However, when Nepalese monarch King Birendra announced the 'Zone of Peace' initiative, they left Mustang. The land reverted to its former status as a peaceful forbidden last frontier.

Festivals

- **Losar** Tibetan New Year festival (January/February).
- **Saka Lhuka** Held in the first month of the Tibetan calender; performed for an auspicious harvest.
- **Fagnyi** Week-long festival of song and dance during the seventh Tibetan month.
- **Tenchi** Three-day-long prayer for peace held in the Lo Manthang Choide Gompa.
- **Yartung** Three-day celebration including horse races held in Lo Manthang (and Manang). It takes place during the seventh–eighth month of the Tibetan year.

When to go

The optimum period to trek in Mustang is early autumn, when the skies are clear, the monsoon rains have abated and the harvest is in full swing. One possible drawback is that flights to Jomsom can still be disrupted by bad weather, entailing delays and cancellations. Winter is too cold for most; some lodges close and many residents, including the king, migrate south for the winter. Late

Trekkers and a chorten on the trail near Tsarang

spring is attractive – the higher altitudes offer pleasant trekking, clear views and cool temperatures – although winds can be a negative factor. The monsoon is often cited as the main season to visit, due to the rainshadow effect of the Himalayas, but cloud is likely, and flights and roads to Jomsom from rain and cloud-engulfed Pokhara are severely disrupted. Avoid the monsoon.

Itinerary and routes

The style of the trek and the altitude gains dictate the itinerary. Camping is more flexible, while distances between villages determine night stops for lodge trekkers. Most villages now have lodges, of varying standards. Between Chele and Ghami, altitude (3000–4000m) becomes a factor in deciding the night stops, especially for lodge trekkers. However, once acclimatised, the route is relatively moderate.

The astonishing eastern trail from Tange to Tetang is highly recommended. Few take it, citing a lack of water on the arid east side of the Mustang Khola – there is only a trickle near Paha (4210m), about halfway. Carry a huge amount of water and endeavour to do it all in one very long but thrilling day.

The stages described in the following routes correspond roughly to daily marches (based on camping), but levels of acclimatisation could modify some days. Allow a few extra days for flight delays between Pokhara and Jomsom.

There is no greater adrenalin rush than a mountain-dodging flight in the Himalayas to a stunningly located airstrip, and Jomsom is no exception. Flying between Annapurna and Dhaulagiri above the Kali Gandaki gorge is sensational. You'll need more than a few minutes to catch your breath after the dramatic landing at Jomsom before trekking on to Kagbeni.

STAGE 1
Jomsom to Lo Manthang

Start	Jomsom (2710m/8890ft)
Finish	Lo Manthang (3800m/12,464ft)
Distance	80km (50 miles)
Time	6–7 days
Altitude range	2710m/8890ft (Jomsom) to 4230m/13,874ft (Chogo La)
Transport	Jeep

Road development will surely change Upper Mustang. From Kagbeni the dirt track has already arrived in Chele and a restricted Chinese-built road crosses the Kora La (4660m) to Lo Manthang. A dirt track reaches as far south as Syangmochen. Go soon.

Jomsom to Kagbeni (3hrs)
Fortunately few suffer any ill-effects adjusting to the sudden altitude gain experienced on landing at Jomsom. The trek crew needs to check all the loads/permits, so tea is in order. The trail from Jomsom follows the Kali Gandaki Valley past the Lubra Valley through Eklobhatti to **Kagbeni** (2800m). Kagbeni, like many villages in Upper Mustang, has low tunnel alleyways that give protection from the wind.

Kagbeni to Chele (6–7hrs)
With formalities over, great excitement ensues after **Kagbeni**, the last frontier (or lost horizon) before entering the domains of Shangri-La.

Soon the east bank trail climbs steeply and traverses a number of gullies characterised by eroded turrets and dry cliffs. Looking back, Kagbeni is framed by the fluted spires of Nilgiri. Local horsemen splash happily along the riverbed. ▶

After about 2hrs the trail crosses the small Tangbe Khola into the fields of **Tangbe** (3060m). Tangbe (3½–4hrs) is a typical Mustang village with narrow alleys, whitewashed walls, chortens and prayer flags.

The new dirt road will undoubtedly alter the route described where it cuts the trail or utilises bridging points.

213

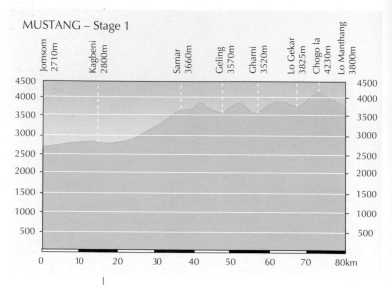

MUSTANG – Stage 1

From here the path climbs to about 3100m, with views dominated by multi-coloured cliffs before descending to the village of **Chuksang** (2980m). The major side canyon of the Narsing Khola is an example of the amazing eroded landscape of Mustang, where the soft layers of rock have been modified into chimneys, 'organ-pipe' features and fairytale gullies. The trail skirts below a ruined fort and soon reaches a striking red canyon. The route bridges the Kali Gandaki (now the Mustang Khola) as the river struggles to find a way through the narrow defile. It's a short climb to **Chele** village (3050m).

Chele to Eklobhatti (6hrs)
Keeping west of the Mustang Khola on another startling day, this stage negotiates a dramatic canyon and visits rarely seen villages. Anyone suffering from the altitude might wish to stay the night at Samar, since the trail ahead is generally above 3700m. A night in Geling is too far at this point, so stay in higher Eklobhatti if you are camping,

Local Mustang child and baby

or a Syangmochen lodge. The peaks of Damodar Himal are visible to the east.

The morning exertions involve a steep climb through a dramatic canyon west of the main valley. The village of **Ghyakar**, set among fields of buckwheat, lies across the main gorge here, as the path hugs the canyon walls. Be careful; the drops are scary as the path continues to climb. Salt oozes from the cliffs. Panoramic views to the south from a pass (3550m) reveal Nilgiri, Tilicho Peak and Yakwa Kang – the peak above the Thorong La. A short descent to the larger settlement of **Samar** (3660m) follows.

The route continues from the chorten of Samar and negotiates a couple of deep side canyons, before passing through an isolated zone of ancient juniper and the remnants of a long-denuded woody glade. It then climbs to a small col at about 3750m. About 2hrs from Samar on the descent is a teahouse. **Eklobhatti** (3820m), with a flat area for tents and shelter, is a further 1hr walk after yet another canyon.

Eklobhatti to Ghami (4hrs)

Constantly inspiring views make this another day to savour. Geling and Ghami have small monasteries. In October the buckwheat harvest is underway and is fun to watch. If you have any surplus energy, you might like to join in!

From **Eklobhatti** the trail crosses a small pass at 3870m before dropping through pleasant, lusher surroundings to **Syangmochen**, an alternative camp/lodging spot. For another 45mins there is a slight rise, then a chorten with views of Geling village. However, a further 45mins are needed to reach the settlement, because another side canyon interrupts the rhythm. Take an extended break in **Geling** (3570m), with its intriguing, dingy alleys and a monastery to explore.

After Geling the route climbs to the substantial pass of Nyika La (or Nyi La) at 4010m. The descent is equally long and even steeper down to **Ghami** (3520m). There is a monastery to visit, but beware of big growling dogs after dark.

Ghami to Lo Manthang via Drakmar and Lo Gekar (9–11hrs)

When Mustang first opened in 1992, little literature was available, apart from the writings of Michael Peissel; few people had explored southwest of Lo Manthang. Today another route links Ghami to Lo Manthang through this area, avoiding the new dirt track that runs between Tsarang and Lo Manthang. To avoid repetition, try this route northbound if you plan to return through Tsarang to Muktinath via Tange and Tetang.

THE LEGEND OF DRAKMAR

Once upon a time there was a demoness called Balmo, who put the fear of god into the people – only Guru Rinpoche could vanquish such a powerful evil spirit. During their tussle, so it is said, her blood was spilt, creating the red-coloured cliffs. Her intestines transformed into a long mani wall. A chorten holds down her heart, with smaller chortens covering the spots of her spilt blood, hiding the remnants of her powers.

From Ghami the trail runs north along the Drakmar Khola and on to **Drakmar** (3820m), an astonishingly spectacular place with incredible brilliant red and ochre cliffs.

After Drakmar, the route climbs to the **Mui La** (4170m), then descends to the upper reaches of the Tsarang Khola before continuing to **Ghar Gompa** (3950m) and **Lo Gekar** (3825m).

> **Guru Rinpoche** visited Mustang and, to commemorate this, his metal image is found in Lo Gekar. Other visitors of note were Milarepa and Rinchen Zangpo, the 11th-century translator who initiated 108 monasteries.

From Lo Gekar this stage crosses the **Chogo La** (4230m) to **Pangga** (Samdrupling). Samdrupling (4090m) was once a sacred Buddhist centre, noted for sky burials. Little more than 5km northeast from Pangga is the fabled city of **Lo Manthang** (3800m).

Ghami to Lo Manthang via Tsarang (8–9hrs)

Ghami to Tsarang (4hrs)

This used to be the main trail to Tsarang, but with the arrival of a dirt road in the vicinity, some may wish to use the new trail north via Drakmar. Tsarang has an exotic, ancient ambience displaying the cultural uniqueness of Mustang and should not be missed. (It can be visited on the return from Lo Manthang to Kagbeni.)

From **Ghami** the trail passes a trio of chortens, then crosses a gully by a bridge. About 30mins from Ghami is a very long mani wall. From the trail junction, a dramatic red-walled cliff area can be seen rearing up in the direction of Drakmar. About 2hrs from Ghami is a small pass, the **Choya La** (3770m), followed by a couple of hours of pleasant, easy ambling to **Tsarang** (3560m). The mud-walled ramparts of the tremendous fortress-citadel dominate the village. The stunningly located monastery has some amazingly intricate murals and mandalas,

Tsarang

gradually being restored. A much-revered, wooden statue of Chenresig (Avalokiteshvara) in the gompa was brought from Lhasa. East of Tsarang are the monastery of Dri, the Yara caves and the Luri Cave retreat en route to Damodar Kund, a sacred pilgrimage lake – mentioned in the box below.

Tsarang to Lo Manthang (4–5hrs)
The prospect of reaching the fabled walled city of Lo Manthang – the highlight of the whole trek – makes this a fabulous day full of anticipation.

The deep canyon beyond **Tsarang** ensures the knees wake up quickly today. Climbing out of this substantial ravine reveals a splendid Himalayan panorama to the south: Annapurna I, Nilgiri and Tilicho; and Bhrikuti Peak to the southeast. About 2hrs from Tsarang the route passes a much photographed, isolated, beautiful chorten. The gently ascending trail passes spectacular cliff caves and crosses a stream. Cliffs of yellow conglomerates and dark bands flank the route as it climbs to the next pass

– the **Lo La** (3850m). Within minutes a wonderful window opens over Lo Manthang – the fabulous city below, a spectacular sight greeted with incredulity.

Virtually untouched by modernity, the walled city is an extraordinary sight, with its white houses, red monasteries and palace. This viewpoint reveals other treasures: Tinghar Gompa, Namgyal Gompa – the red and grey-coloured edifice on a promontory – and Phuwa village. The Mustang Khola, hemmed in by a veritable sea of coloured cliffs, lies to the east. To the northwest, Mansail peak rises in a crescendo of barren ramparts to its white cap. The rapid descent is short and, once across the river, the gates of **Lo Manthang** (3800m) await.

Time in Lo Manthang

The extraordinary walled city of Lo Manthang is due to receive UNESCO World Heritage Site status soon. Roughly 180 houses exist within the 8.5m-high walls, built by the Amapalas. The big chortens of Lo Manthang house relics of the Buddha. The four-storey palace of

The Lo La is crossed on the way to Lo Manthang

Lo Manthang is the last remaining walled city in Nepal

the Mustang monarch, King Jigme Dorje Dradul (his Nepalese name is Jigme Palbar Bista), was constructed in 1440. In the early days, when Lo Manthang first opened, the King and Queen of Mustang invariably entertained trekkers and visitors at the Royal Palace; its quaint medieval atmosphere is impressive. Visitors fortunate enough to be given an audience with the gracious monarchs should delight in their generous offer of quality Tibetan butter tea. One cup should be enough to show gratitude, but anyone leaving their tea decades ago might have feared for their head!

Monasteries of Lo Manthang
As the oldest, the red-walled, three-storey Jampa (Champa) Gompa is devoted to Maitreya, the Buddha of the Future. The Sakya-pa structure was consecrated in 1448 under the auspices of Ngorchen Kunga Sangpo. The painted image of Maitreya was completed in 1663. The monastery is famed for its abundant and now restored mandala images, originally produced by Newari

artists under King Kunga Zangpo. The Sakya-pa Tugchen Lhakhang (Mahamuni) or 'Great Sage' Gompa was initiated in 1468 under King Tsangchen Trashigon. It has a magnificent image of the fifth Dhyani Buddha, Vairocana, above the entrance facing east. There are prominent images of Guru Rinpoche, Ratna Sambhava, Vajradhara and a bird-like Kirtimukha. The main icon is Mahamuni, flanked by Shadukshur Lokeshvara and Manjushri. A major restoration programme was conducted here in 1999–2004 under the auspices of the American Himalayan Foundation. The Choide Gompa (1710) was initiated by King Tsewang Phuntsok Tsugyen Norbu. It features an impressive Mahakala. Choprang Sakya-pa Gompa is the newest structure. The last two monasteries are located in a corner of the city famed for its ferocious guard dogs.

Allow a couple of days in and around Lo Manthang. So long as permits allow, visit the troglodyte villages of Chosar, Nyphu and Garphu, north of Lo Manthang. Namgyal Gompa and the Tingkhar Palace are about 1hr

Typical Lo Manthang gompa

walk up a different valley. Further north, a rarely permitted long circular day trip takes in Kimaling and Nyamdo as well.

Chosar and Garphu (5–6hrs)

Leave **Lo Manthang** from its northeast corner and cross the Dokpola Khola. Head along beside the diminishing waters of the Mustang Khola for 1hr to a long mani wall and isolated buildings. The trail is ill defined but stays on the west side of the main river for most of the way. About 2hrs' walk from Lo Manthang is the cave village of **Chosar** on the right across the river, with the red monastery of Nyphu set in a rock face beyond. From a chorten ahead there is a view of the monastery settlement of **Garphu** (3900m). The Mustang Khola can be crossed on a couple of bridges. The road from Tibet can be seen along the way; periodically trucks are permitted to bring goods from China.

CAVE DWELLERS

Across Mustang, where geological strata are soft and friable, there are many caves. Some of the more elaborate caves are at Nyphu, Yara, Chosar, Tange and Drakmar. The extensive Chosar cave system (including Sijha Dzong cave) dates to 800BC, with 40 or more chambers. In the Mahzhong cave anthropologists discovered 13th-century paintings and manuscripts executed in silver and gold. The Luri Cave Gompa has some amazing frescoes painted by Newari artists from the Kathmandu Valley in the 12th century.

Excavations have revealed that a substantial civilisation inhabited much of the Trans-Himalayan region, encompassing the Lo region, Damodar Himal and Tsaparang in Western Tibet. From 1992–97 digs around the Mehbrak caves revealed the grave of a mother and baby along with food offerings. It was dated to around 450BC. Since then over 60 more such corpses have been discovered, some with food items in ceramic vessels.

Initially the finding of mass graves or burial sites was attributed to landslides, but the theory was soon discounted. Now it is almost certain that the cave dwellers practised sacrificial rituals.

STAGE 2
Lo Manthang to Muktinath via Tange

Start	Lo Manthang (3800m/12,464ft)
Finish	Muktinath (3710m/12,170ft)
Distance	75km (47 miles)
Time	5–6 days
Altitude range	3040m/9970ft (Tetang) to 4230m/13,879ft (near Paha)
Transport	Jeep from Muktinath

The return route to Tsarang is described in Stage 1, in reverse. From Tsarang it is possible to return directly to Jomsom, continuing to follow Stage 1 in reverse. The alternative return is via Tange.

MUSTANG – Stage 2

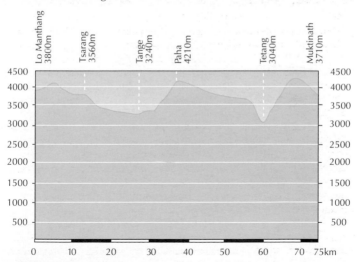

Crossing the Tange Khola

Tsarang to Tange (5–6hrs)

The day is full of unworldly, amazing sights: the rugged canyons of the Mustang Khola, and the picturesque, atmospheric village of Tange – a place far removed from reality.

The trail from **Tsarang** (3560m) to Tange departs from near the monastery, southeast through the fields. A gap in the wall heralds the start of a sensational descent into the Mustang Khola riverbed (300m). Initially in a hidden ravine, the steep, loose track descends into a colossal dry gully dominated by weirdly eroded chimneys and turrets. The very narrow, deep defile virtually spits the trail out into the Tsarang Chu canyon, leading eventually to the wide and stony Mustang Khola. A small chorten marks the spot about 1hr from Tsarang.

Following the valley floor, the trail comes to a river junction with the Dhechang Khola (3200m) and continues south. The canyon of the Mustang Khola is about 200m wide here and on both sides are towers, hermit caves, cliffs and organ-pipe features. The undisturbed riverbeds are famed for their fossils, particularly ammonites.

Continue along the Mustang Khola before turning left into the canyon of the Tange Khola. The valley floor is criss-crossed by rivers and streams, necessitating a number of wading sessions. About 1hr along the valley, the trail climbs left into **Tange** (3240m). The village is an astonishing sight, with multiple chortens of bright red and white. Framing the whole medieval mud-walled scene is an amazing, dry, fluted sandstone cliff with troglodyte caves favoured by the hermits and sages of old. It's a little-visited wonder of Mustang.

Tange to Tetang (10hrs+)
Don't expect an easy day from Tange (3240m) to Tetang (3040m), but enjoy the stupendous sights – the deepest gorge in the world between Annapurna and Dhaulagiri along with the strange geological apparitions of the ghostly upper Narsing Khola. A packed lunch and plenty of extra water should be carried today.

Tange chortens and the valley of the Tange Khola

Leaving the village just before sunrise, head down to a bridge across the Tange Khola and then climb the bluff to the south. Where black soil and oozing salt are encountered, there is a good view back over Tange as it wakes from its slumbers. Meanwhile, the dogs are no doubt retiring for the day. After crossing the Yak Khola, the way is soon steeply up for around 900m, a very long climb indeed. Fortunately tantalising views north of high, rugged and barren peaks unfold en route.

Nearly 4hrs after leaving Tange, the trail reaches a pass at about 4050m and suddenly the pain of the ascent dissipates (for a while) as the sharpened spire of Dhaulagiri rises skywards. Prayer flags adorn the pass cairn and it's possible to pick out the inbound trail between Samar and Syangmochen west across the chasm of the Mustang Khola. About 30mins on is the only feeble waterhole on the route at **Paha** (4210m). The trail ahead climbs and contours around various bluffs, reaching an estimated altitude of 4230m about 6hrs from Tange. To the west are the forbidding, serrated ridges that enclose Mustang and divide it from Tibet.

Contouring for another hour brings you to the rim of the Narsing Khola canyon. The breathtaking scenery is so fantastic that there is a risk of drifting off the narrow trail. In places drops of over 1000m on one side or the other are mind-boggling, with considerable exposure. This stage has the most sensational scenery of the whole trek; a series of gigantic organ-pipe features cascade into the contorted chasm below, topped with turret-like towers. In this vast zone of extraordinary natural sculptures mysterious holes in the soft conglomerate walls of the turrets reveal alarmingly sheer drops into the murky Narsing Khola defile below. It's a truly unbelievable sight.

The canyon rim here is sometimes less than 20m wide and the trail snakes around it for a while. Don't stray too close to the edges; the rock is soft and unstable. Eventually the trail leaves these ungodly zones and crosses a flat region, where the V-shape of the Kali Gandaki gorge slashing through the Himalayas can be seen. Well into the afternoon, the path eventually makes its descent into the cones of the organ pipes again. The trail is rough, loose and steep and, after such a long day, care is essential. At a junction, take the left fork (the right fork goes down to Chuksang). The never-ending descent continues, still on the rugged path, until with great relief you cross the river into the willow trees. Carry on up the creek to **Tetang** (3040m).

Tetang to Muktinath (6hrs)

Tetang is amazing; the walls of the outer houses are 10m high, giving the place a fortified appearance. The village has a good drainage system and a maze of mysterious dark alleys, low archways, tunnel-like lanes and eerie doorways. After Tetang you might think the trek is all but over, but there's one final surprise in store. ▶

The trail out is above the willow creek, passing a mani wall towards the southeast. A much longer mani wall keeps company with the path for a while to a rocky area. A small dam appears on the left, then it's onwards and upwards through bands of dark scree and shale. Head east into a narrow valley, where more shale and oozing salt lie underfoot, as well as a spring surrounded by greenery. The trail now leaves the main valley, turning south up a smaller tributary valley and climbing for 1hr to the **Gyu La** (4080m). A magnificent view of Tilicho Peak unfolds, one of the most beautiful, glittering snowy walls of the Annapurnas, with its delicately cascading fluting. Its sheer size is staggering – grandeur unsurpassed at such close range. It is the highlight of the day.

The hike down is pleasant and easy via Chhyonkar village before joining the main trail at **Muktinath** (3710m), with its good lodging and 'fooding', heralding a return to the busy byways of the Annapurna Circuit.

Muktinath to Jomsom (5–6hrs)

Back on familiar territory now, there remains only the ambling descent to Jomsom to complete the trek; or take a jeep if you dare! See Trek 1 Annapurna Circuit for fuller details on this stage. Most Mustang trekkers then normally fly to Pokhara.

An ancient salt mine lies about 2hrs along the Narsing Khola.

The evening bus from Jomsom

DAMODAR KUND TREK

This high and wild trek links Upper Mustang with Nar-Phu and has only very recently been opened to trekkers and mountaineers, because it is very close to the Tibetan border. The trek involves the crossing of the high Saribung La (6020m). With a glacial zone en route, it's probably only an option for those with some mountaineering background. The same permits required for travel to Upper Mustang also apply to this adventurous and very demanding region.

The route can be tackled from **Tsarang** by heading east. The trail goes via Surkhang, **Yara** and the **Luri** cave monastery, with its exquisite Buddhist art, before continuing to Ghuma Thanti. A very wild, isolated stretch heads to the focal point of the trip, **Damodar Kund**, a lake and shrine at 4890m. The next section involves an ascent across glacial zones to the Saribung pass between the peaks of Saribung (6330m), Kumlang Himal (6335m), Sonam Peak (6255m) and Kharsang Peak (6225m). The long descent via Nagoru (4600m) eventually descends to Phu (4080m) and back to earth at Koto on the Annapurna Circuit. Another unknown trail links Tange to Ghuma Thanti and then over the Tiri La (5600m) southeast via the Yak Khola and down the Labse Khola to Nar (4110m) and Koto (2600m).

TREK 6
Nar-Phu Trek

Start	Koto (2600m/8530ft)
Finish	Koto (2600m/8530ft)
Distance	70km (45 miles)
Time	7–8 days
Maximum altitude	Nar (4110m)
Transport	None
Trekking style	Camping, homestay and basic lodges

Nestling against the Tibetan border is one of the most mysterious and extraordinary destinations in the Annapurnas: the Nar-Phu region. It has a lot to offer curious and adventurous trekkers. Far, far removed from modern times, the hidden valleys have retained their ancient Tibetan-orientated culture, something that is virtually lost in mainstream Tibet. Pisang Peak and Kang Guru, a

The Phu Valley and Kang Guru Peak

229

rarely seen peak, dominate the horizons. Only opened to trekkers in 2002–03, these magical valleys are now attracting attention. With so few inhabitants, the Nar-Phu region is a naturalist's paradise.

The trek is characterised by remote, exciting and challenging trails that most will enjoy. However, be aware that many sections are narrow, loose underfoot and exposed. There are, of course, sections of path that are a pure delight; through cool pines, across dry meadows dotted with sweet-smelling juniper and beneath towering snowy ranges. The wild terrain is contorted and uncompromising. Obtaining proper insurance is vital for both trekkers and staff. This is no place to have an accident, so care and concentration on the way are vital.

When to go
It is possible to trek in the region during the usual post-monsoon season, late October to early December, but don't come too early after the rains in case heavy snow remains. Late December is very cold and, if snow comes early, many people migrate from Phu and Nar to warmer zones, meaning the few lodges could close. The authors began their trek in late March, but at this time snow lingers in some shady corners and below frozen waterfalls, making the first day from Koto to Meta testing in a few places. Wind is a particular feature of the spring, usually gently down-valley from the north in the morning and gusting wildly uphill in the afternoon. By April the trail is cleared for ponies, making this month and May attractive (although the approach march from Besisahar will be hotter). The monsoon period is recommended by some, because the villagers are busy with the growing season, meadows blossom for grazing animals and the two schools are open. However, the walk into Koto from the leech-infested and rain-soaked middle hills will be very taxing, and landslides could disrupt plans.

Planning
There are three ways to plan this trek. All require a guide or porter/guide, and taking an extra porter from Koto is

advisable. Don't expect your staff to carry much more than 12–15kg, due to the nature of some sections of the trail. Carry emergency food supplies that do not require cooking, so that you can have a picnic lunch any time, anywhere.

The most comfortable way to trek is with a fully supported camping crew. This gives much more flexibility, with altitude, accommodation and food issues eliminated, but it does cost more. Western trekking companies and a few local agencies can organise this style of trek.

It is perfectly feasible to arrange this trek as a lodge trek, and it doesn't cost much more than 'lodging treks' on the main trails, once permits are sorted. However, there are some complications. Only Meta and Nar have lodges of a quality similar to the main areas of Annapurna. Lodging in Phu is far more basic. The main problem is that there is no lodge in Singenge Dharmasala (meaning you need to get up to Meta the first day), or in Kyang.

The trail near Kyang

In Kyang a vandalised ACAP porter shelter with an open doorway is the only option. For much of the season, the old Khampa settlement here, used by seasonal herders, is abandoned. There is water in Kyang, but no kitchen, and the toilet is unusable. The authors cooked their own food outside the shelter, bringing back memories of scouting days long past. In Nar Phedi there is currently only a three-bedded room at the new monastery complex guardian's house, but it's very simple, smelly and bug-ridden. It is better to plan on staying that night at Meta, despite the extra distance (1hr), until (or if ever) the new monastery accommodation is completed. It could be a while yet, years perhaps.

Bring a cooking pot, mugs or bowls, spoon, penknife and matches/lighter. Bring three or four tins of meat or fish, instant mashed potato/noodles, muesli, peanut butter, marmite or sandwich spreads for lunches. Don't forget a small thermos flask for tea or coffee, as well as sugar, and loads of chocolate/glucose tablets for energy. There is no food anywhere between lodges. Apart from a few streams, water is located at Singenge Dharmasala and Kyang. Sometimes there is water at Gulung en route to Nar. There is no water at the seasonal herder settlements of Chyk, Junam or Chyako. Remember the sterilising tablets. Since lunches may be only chapattis, daily expenses are comparable with the Annapurna Circuit.

A compromise on the above would be to bring a lightweight tent for one or possibly two nights (including Nar Phedi). Of the five other trekkers the authors encountered, three were fully supported and two stayed in lodges, carrying a tent but no cooking equipment. Food in the lodges is simple but adequate for a week or so, particularly if supplemented with your own reserves and favourite goodies.

Whichever way you do it, be sure to ask whether your crew members have been there before. The authors' guide and Koto-employed porter had both done the trek several times and were fully conversant with the conditions and availability of water/accommodation. This was not the case with the other teams encountered.

There is currently no electricity anywhere on the trek, so bring extra camera batteries or even back-up slide film. You can extend the life of your batteries by warming them inside your clothing.

Yaks on the bridge to Nar

Itinerary and routes

The seven-night itinerary described is the one planned and followed by the authors. On the walk-in from Besisahar, we spent a night in Timang, the highest overnight spot before reaching Koto, and also allowed ourselves the luxury of a day off in Koto, visiting Chame from there for the morning. It is possible that spending three nights at around 2600–2700m before entering the Nar-Phu area helped our altitude acclimatisation. Ideally, given time, going to Pisang for acclimatisation would be the best option.

The first day from Koto to Meta is long and gains over 900m. From Meta, it is not recommended to go to Nar first, because of the altitude gain and very steep ascent. A day trip to Nar does not really allow enough

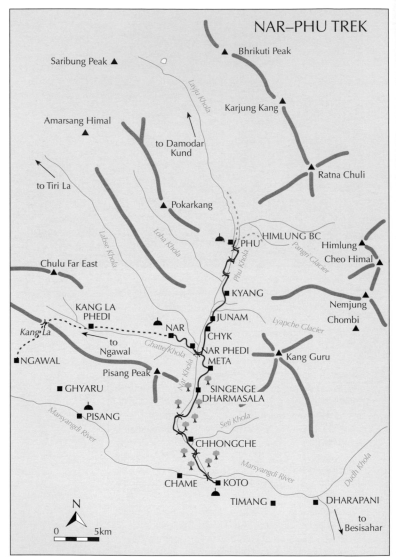

NAR–PHU – Stages 1 and 2

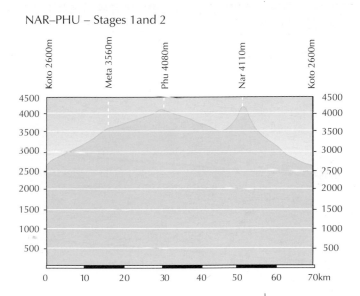

time to savour the delights of the village. The trail to Phu makes an intermediate stop in Kyang, with altitude gains of no more than 300m per day. It's perfectly possible to descend from Phu to Nar Phedi or Meta in one long, punishing day.

Beyond Nar the Kang La is often snowbound and is said to be desperately steep down into Ngawal. Our experienced climbing guide (and cook) suggested trekking teams would be advised at the very least to carry an ice axe and ideally have ropes and crampons.

Access to Koto
To access the start of the trek at Koto from Besisahar, please refer to Trek 1 Annapurna Circuit for details of the route.

STAGE 1
Koto to Phu

Start	Koto (2600m/8530ft)
Finish	Phu (4080m/13,380ft)
Distance	32km (20 miles)
Time	3 days
Altitude range	2600m/8530ft (Koto) to 4080m/13,380ft (Phu)
Transport	None

The level of anticipation is almost unbearable as you contemplate the incredibly narrow entrance to this domain of lost horizons. It's a day of mostly 'up', but there is some respite with a few short descents. Remember to take chapattis and snacks as well as a thermos today, because there's nothing en route.

Koto to Meta (8–9½hrs)

From the checkpost and kani, the trail heads steeply down to cross the Marsyangdi River. Immediately the trail is quiet and peaceful through forest of blue pine and larch. Within 30mins there is an overhanging sheer cliff where the way has been carved out of the rock face. If you find it too intimidating, consider turning back now! An easier forest section and a steady climb follows to another narrow zone about 2hrs from Koto. Look back for a glimpse of Lamjung. Soon spindly bamboo blocks out the steep drops to the side of the path.

About 2¼hrs from Koto, the trail crosses to the east bank and, shortly after some zigzags, crosses the foaming white side stream of the Seti Khola. There is a toilet and camping area here, with water. The trail climbs rigorously now for 30mins to a glade of massive trees. Shortly a sign directs the walker on to the lower path to the cave shelter of **Chhongche** (2935m), reached in 4hrs or so.

From here the trail mostly climbs as the route approaches a narrower part of the canyon with sheer walls towering to the sky far above, totally unimaginable

in scale. About 5½hrs from Koto the trail crosses to the west bank and shortly comes to an overhang called Hulaki Odar, beside a beautiful waterfall and ravine. The ACAP sign implies it's only 1¼hrs to Singenge Dharmasala, but don't believe a word of it. Through the narrow defile there is some more exposure.

About 15mins up from Hulaki, the route crosses back to the east bank. Here there is a small hot spring (although how one is supposed to access it down a precarious carved log staircase is anyone's guess). Ahead the path crosses the first of two evil and exposed snow chutes from avalanche areas thousands of metres above. Take care here! A short narrow section follows to another snow chute, but here trees below provide a reassuring buffer. About 6hrs from Koto, the trail dives behind a

Lamjung from Meta

dramatic waterfall with the path protected by a rock tunnel blasted out of the cliff. **Singenge Dharmasala** (3210m) is little more than 30mins ahead, but is a dreary, damp and uninviting place to stay. Campers concerned about the altitude might be forced to spend the night here. The ACAP shelter, sponsored by the Hong Kong Kadoorie Foundation, is sadly in ruins.

There is a brief glimpse of the elusive Kang Guru. Since leaving Dharapani (on the way to Koto from Besisahar) you have virtually encircled the peak without ever seeing its main summits. The dreaded steep climb to Meta begins now and it's tough at the end of the day. As encouragement, the welcome chorten of Meta can be seen in 30mins, but still perched very high above. There is a rough open shelter in 15mins and, after crossing a side stream, the path climbs the ravine on a path characterised by loose detritus. The last stage is across the meadows through juniper to the slopes of **Meta** (3560m).

Meta is a permanently inhabited settlement formerly used by Khampa guerrillas after the Chinese move into Tibet in 1959. Today it has two already-functioning lodges, a new modern one and a more basic place near the checkpost. This is not always manned, but from time to time catches those who try to sneak into the area without permits. There are around 20 stone houses here and a small school. The food is excellent and the two lodges comfortable, with 'deluxe thickness' mattresses and acceptable toilets!

Meta to Kyang (5–6hrs)

The day begins with a pleasant contour around the hill-side, but this is not indicative of the day overall, which is almost all uphill. The views ahead towards the Tiri La, which links Nar to Tange in Mustang, are incredible and well illustrate the typical terrain of the region. Nar village is hidden behind the high bluffs to the northwest, and far below is the strange new red monastery of Nar Phedi.

Within 1hr the trail passes above the temporary set-tlement of **Chyk**, where herders graze their goats and yaks on the meagre grasses and bushes. Ahead is a mountain that's off the map and northeast of Phu, called Ratna Chuli. Huge Himalayan Griffons glide above in search of prey. The stiff climb continues through patchy areas of ancient juniper trees and bushes to Junam (2½hrs from

Traditional nomadic weaver in Chyk

Meta). **Junam** (3670m) is a waterless, abandoned settlement of crumbling stone shelters. Shortly beyond the grassy meadows, the path plunges abruptly into a deep ravine characterised by moraines that drop from the western glacier of the hidden Kang Guru. In the dry season the path snakes down around the moraine and climbs back out of the twin ravines, but there is also a new bridge for the summer high-water period.

From Junam the trail climbs steadily to a chorten of three parts (Rigsum) and past the abandoned houses at Chyako/Chyakhu (3735m, 4hrs). The spire of Annapurna II soon appears. Beyond Chyako the path continues up to a ridgeline and a rather narrow, exposed stage. Fortunately it's down next through a glade of silver birch on a slippery, muddy path. A large steel bridge waits at the bottom (about 5hrs into the walk). The Mruju Khola here drains from the well-hidden Lyapche Glacier of the Nemjung peaks. Massive moraines dominate the zone ahead. Here is the highest point of the day at 3950m. It's quite a struggle to climb across not one but two of these obstacles before the welcoming sight of **Kyang** (3840m). After a short descent the 'deluxe' ACAP shelter here is attained.

Kyang to Phu (4–5hrs)

The sunrise view of Annapurna II from the shelter defies description, making even the most sleepless night fade into insignificance. Leaving **Kyang**, the route contours towards the main canyon, where it drops dramatically on a path carved out of the brilliantly coloured, sheer-sided cliffs. Throw a backwards glance at Annapurna II and Lamjung, fantastically framed by the dark walls of the canyon. After 1hr is the western side valley of the Loha Khola, the domain of snow leopards. The path leads on to the isolated shrine of a deceased lama of the Khampa people, marked by a beautiful painting on the rock face (1½hrs from Kyang). Alongside the stone staircase here is a narrow defile, where the Phu Khola squeezes between weirdly shaped outcrops. The trail climbs up around a small bluff and descends to a side stream. Here the trail divides, the lower one keeping to the riverbank via a

Phu 'entry gate' tower

mani wall. The upper one climbs to a beautifully decorated old chorten and crosses a bridge to rejoin the main route in a few minutes.

About 3hrs from Kyang, sheer walls begin to close in on the trail. Oozing salt surrounds a strange outcrop and around a bluff is the most bizarre blood-red natural feature where red and white 'corpuscles' bleed from a gaping gash in the rock. Around the corner is another astonishing spectacle, a gigantic monolithic rock tower.

In the **folklore of Phu**, great power has been attributed to this tremendous tower. It is said to depict the face of evil, where the spirits have been trapped. The river is also virtually trapped here, as it bubbles under this outcrop through a crack barely 1m wide.

The trail quickly runs away from this tower of evil into a small side gully, where the route climbs a seemingly impossible obstacle of sheer rock barring the way to Phu. It is steep, dramatic and rigorous up to the first kani gate. The narrow trail contours around the cliffs opposite an abandoned fort. Incredibly deep fissures in the eroded sandstone plunge down to the tortured river far below. Picturesque lines of larger chortens beside the now calm fresh clear waters of the Phu Khola herald the first astonishing view of Phu. High on the cliffs are long-abandoned hermit caves. Various brightly coloured mani walls grace the final stretch to the main suspension bridge that leads to **Phu** citadel and village (4080m).

Time in Phu

One day is definitely desirable and preferably two, as there is so much to enjoy in the area. Apart from the Trashi Gompa, there are three options for extended walking from Phu – heading east, west or north.

The first settlements at Phu date back around 800 years; exploring involves ferreting about in narrow alleys, under low doorways and through tunnels that protect against the cold. Most of the citadel area can be accessed from the lane near the village monastery. Take time to climb up to the entrance way of the old fortified zone above, but be very careful of the structures that are near to collapse; beware of any dogs. The people of Phu spend their days spinning, weaving and yak or goat herding. Many migrate to the lowlands for the winter, when Phu is cut off from the outside world for several months, but some still spend the long, cold, dark winters here. There is a small seasonal school for about 20 children.

Phu has three basic lodges in the main area, as well as a shelter and ACAP camping site on the east bank. The Himalayan Border Lodge and the Karma Lodge were both temporarily closed at the time of the authors' visit, but the brightly coloured unnamed lodge on the west side of the main citadel was open. Four beds in a converted animal shelter make a welcome place of respite above the cosy kitchen. The lockable toilet is up a very steep loose

Phu, seen across the monastery prayer flags

pathway above, so try to avoid a night visit or work out some other devious solution. There is currently no electricity in Phu or anywhere else on the entire trek in the restricted zone.

No one should miss the Trashi Gompa. The path to the monastery hillock goes around the south side of the citadel. Climb to the small Samdu Gompa in the village and head around on the main street, passing two lodges. Once around the Phu outcrop, there are two bridges leading over the stream to the monastery hill path. It's a steep ascent of over 100m and takes roughly 30mins from Phu. Beyond the kani gate are 13 small chortens in a long row – a classic picture with Phu below. Beware of the guard dog whose first instinct is to be ferocious, but he is soon placated. On the first cloudy afternoon here the authors spotted a herd of blue sheep, perhaps seeking protection from prowling but elusive snow leopards.

Visitors should explore the hill in a clockwise direction where possible, following Buddhist conventions.

Dramatic trail down from Phu

For a fabulous all-round view, it's best to head first along a dry ridge to the northern end of the hill. The valley to the north is dominated by Karjung Kang (Chako), a mountain similar to the Matterhorn in shape. Further north is Bhrikuti peak, named after the Nepalese princess who married King Strongsten Gampo, a major historic figure of Buddhist Tibet. Covering the monastery hill are numerous bright blue mani stones set in various banks and displays of devotion. Looking east, the great jumble of the Pangri Glacier dominates the panorama, while beyond lie mysterious peaks that no map has been able to name. Himlung is the highest named peak, but that is hidden behind the nearer barren hillside. To the south are three great massifs, the peaks and fluted walls of Nemjung, Chombi and the ridgeline of Kang Guru (6981m), glinting in the morning sunlight like a great icy whaleback.

TRASHI GOMPA

Dedicated to the lineage of the Ktienchen Thrangu Rinpoche, the latest incarnate died in January 2012. The main chamber is dedicated to Guru Rinpoche, but the gompa follows the Karma-pa sect of the Kagyu-pa school. Left of Guru Rinpoche is the Sakyamuni Buddha and Maitreya, the Buddha of the Future. Below is the curious idol of Guru Dragpo. To the right is a white Tara. Snellgrove referred to an image of the lion-headed dakini, Senge Dongma, but it's not in evidence now. Buddha and another version of Guru Drakpo are on the right. Various thangkas and paintings adorn the walls, including a prominent Medicine Buddha and some fearsome Mahakalas. The reincarnate lamas of the Trashi Lhakhang are known as the Amchi, meaning revered healer or medicine man.

Above this chapel are more chambers. In the left-hand room is a Buddha icon with many books. The next chamber is very interesting, being the home of a large white Tara and the medical dispensary. Tibetan and more contemporary samples are displayed here. In the next chamber is another Sakyamuni Buddha with some stupas. The right side room is the Gonkhang and houses a red image of Tsapame. Females are not permitted to enter this chamber of horrors.

Guru Rinpoche icon in Trashi Gompa, Phu

West of Phu

High above Phu is a private monastery from where rough, dangerously exposed tracks lead into the western valley. The views might open out to reveal the mysterious knot of peaks east of Phu – Himlung, Cheo Himal and Nemjung – that dominate the Larkya Himal of the Manaslu Trek.

East of Phu

The vast moraines of the Pangri Glacier completely dominate the view east from Phu. Most of the hike is rather ugly and frustrating, since the vistas only open out after much toil. There is no exact trail, but what there is begins across the main suspension bridge below Phu. Once past the ACAP camping shelter, keep generally close to the base of the hillside. Berberis and scrub struggle to survive here on the rocky moraines. With the hillside on your right, continue to climb relentlessly up and eventually around to the east.

The authors did not follow this route, but their guide, who was the cook on a few Himlung expeditions, said the route eventually comes to the ridgeline of the moraine where the contorted rubble of the glacier and Himlung appear. North of the vast moraine complex is said to be a track to the Phu Goth herders' shelter, but it looks a rather chaotic and difficult route to find.

To viewpoint north of Phu (1½hrs+)

The northern option is perhaps the more enticing. It follows the trail along the Layju Khola Valley, part of the route from Mustang via the Saribung (or Saibung) La and the Damodar Kund (Lake), briefly mentioned in the Damodar Kund Trek (end of Trek 5).

From the two bridges below the Trashi Gompa, turn right. The trail climbs a little and contours around near a mani wall. It's rather narrow and contours above a chorten before continuing around the base of the Trashi Gompa hillock. Care is needed here, since the trail crosses a couple of steep, loose sandy sections that lurch towards the edge. Just beyond the monastery hill is a water tank cover (about 30mins from Phu). Continue steadily and slowly uphill on to the moraine top and a small cairn. From here the view east is better than from Phu. Ratna Chuli is the long snowy peak, and south of it is Himlung (7126m).

The path contours up to a bluff of red and yellow rocks, (1hr). The climb ahead is tough, very steep and quite narrow. It takes at least 30mins to reach the high sandy plateau area. Looking back, Kang Guru and Lamjung are formidable. Looking west are amazingly ominous-looking contorted black rock walls that guard the peak of Pokarkang. To the north are the spire of Karjung Kang and the great faces of Bhrikuti. Crossing the impossible-looking terrain below Bhrikuti Peak is the enticing-looking trail continuing north – an addictive prospect for those unavoidably attracted to the far horizons of the Trans Himalayas and Tibet.

The trail to Damodar Kund north of Phu

It's worth just crossing the plateau briefly here to peer down into the forlorn abyss of the **Layju Khola canyon**, peppered with oozing salt, organ-pipe features, strange outcrops – and a sensationally sheer drop. Do not get too close to the edge as it's constantly falling away.

The estimated height here is 4400m, so don't hang about or the altitude might begin to kick in. The return trip is surprisingly quick (around 1hr), but be careful on the steep, loose sections. With more time and clear weather, one might continue north to Nagoru and further, but beware of staying high for too long unless you are very well acclimatised.

STAGE 2
Phu to Koto

Start	Phu (4080m/13,380ft)
Finish	Koto (2600m/8530ft)
Distance	40km (25 miles)
Time	4 days
Altitude range	4110m/13,480ft (Nar) to 2600m/8530ft (Koto)
Transport	None

It's a long and surprisingly hard day to Meta, considering the altitude to be lost. Those with a tent can stay at Nar Phedi, but lodge trekkers are currently advised to head for Meta.

Phu to Nar Phedi or Meta (7–8hrs)
Following the outward trail, be careful dropping down past the monolithic tower. Just after the junction where the alternative trails via the chorten or the mani wall join there is an alternative route on the west bank. A small bridge (almost 1½hrs from Phu) allows access. Cross

The trail near Kyang

the rocky areas of riverbank below fantastically sheer cliffs. About 15mins on is a frozen waterfall, where dripping daggers of ice dangle over an overhanging feature. In another 15mins the trail crosses another photogenic bridge to rejoin the main route at the Lama shrine.

Kyang is about 3½hrs down from Phu. Be sure to take a break here, because the next section is a killer. The moraine crossed on the way into Kyang is now a formidable and exhausting obstacle; the next hour is hard. However, from Chyako (5hrs) there is some respite until the canyon before **Junam**. An hour from Chyako is **Chyk**. From here the trail divides. The one above the meadows goes to **Meta** (see outward route above). The route for Nar Phedi goes down to the Chyk meadows. In a few minutes around the hillside the sandy path takes a dramatic turn, dropping through some weirdly shaped outcrops on a very unnerving path. At one point logs have been used to bridge a gaping lack of ground, and loose stones underfoot are the main difficulty. Luckily the descent is short to the two bridges that provide the only access to Nar Phedi, Nar and the Kang La. The attractive Chinese-looking cantilever bridge has been recently restored and makes a great picture. Just above the cataclysmic defile are the ruins of the ancient fortress of Zampo Cho Dzong (the sacred fort of the bridge).

The chasm below the bridges is phenomenally deep and barely 10m across. **Nar Phedi** and its extraordinary new red monastery are just uphill, but the path is cruel at this late stage of the day. The new monastery at Nar Phedi is funded from overseas, but the posh-looking monks' lodgings may remain without floors or windows. Apparently the guardian can provide cooked food if/when in residence.

Meta to Nar (3½–4½hrs)

Start early from **Meta** (or **Nar Phedi**) to take advantage of the morning calm, as the wind can be ferocious on this hillside. If staying in Meta, head down to the bridges on the signed path.

> Those with bags of energy should divert from the two bridges on the path south to the ancient, virtually abandoned **monastery of Yunkar** (Yung Kar Lhacho) and its very stylish large chorten. The name suggests some historic connection with the Bon people of Tibet, but today it's mostly all locked up. This detour might take 30mins; be aware that the narrow path climbs back up to the two bridges rather steeply.

The first part of the climb to Nar is steep and then becomes rocky underfoot as it zigzags up to the first small chorten (1hr from the bridges). About 15mins later is a small kani gateway and from here the less steep meadow offers some respite. The teahouse of Gulung is ahead, but water is not guaranteed. Up to the next small chorten the way is steep; however, the view north to the Tiri La Valley is fantastic.

On this trail make way for the ponies that keep Nar supplied with firewood, as there is only dried dung for fuel above Nar Phedi. After another small chorten, the muddy trail is almost level as it sweeps around the hillside with an evil drop. About 4hrs from Meta is the fourth small chorten; soon after the trail heads into a walled

View along the Labtse Valley towards Tiri La

zone. The North Face of Pisang Peak dominates the route, with its maze of odd-looking pyramid-structured rock bands. Outcrops of boulders accompany the trail to the photogenic line of chortens that are watched over by Kang Guru, which bears more than a passing resemblance to a mirror image of Mont Blanc at this point. From here it's an easy amble to **Nar** (4110m) around the hillside. A lower path heads into the heart of the village, while the other path leads directly to the lodges.

> Before the trail from Koto was cut about 16 years ago, the **Kang La** was the main way into Nar. Snellgrove used the pass during his 1956 explorations of the area. According to a teacher from Tal who spent a year in Nar recently, the hair-raising ancient trail from Koto was only passable during times of low water, when temporary log bridges were in use. These were then taken to higher, safer spots above the riverbank and stored until the next season of low water.

Nar

Although it doesn't have the setting of Phu, medieval Nar sits on a dramatic hillside with Manangi-style stone houses and log-cut ladders for access.

To explore the narrow alleys and streets of Nar, follow the lane heading from the main mani wall through the upper levels to a chorten on the west side; another path leads back along the lower levels. There is a large colourful chorten near the mani wall and big prayer wheel. The local people will be busy weaving and spinning wool for much of the day. Buckwheat, barley and potatoes are the main crops. Nar has four good lodges (Shanti, Laxmi, Nar Guest House, unnamed lodge), although only one or two might be open at any time. A fifth is called Hotel Karma, set in a large mansion house that isn't sure if it is really open for business. Sadly, the hydroelectric plant that used to work was not functioning when the authors visited. It should be fixed 'soon'.

There are also four small monasteries, once of the Nyingma-pa order, but the Karma-pa lamas are also revered here. The one in the village was not open, but a squint through the window revealed an eight-armed Buddha and Guru Rinpoche. The monastery near the lodges is also closed and there's no hope of seeing inside. The monastery below the village is also closed, but it has some penetrating

Nar village

eyes on its top turret. The monastery well below the village in the meadows is also closed, but through various dusty windows idols of the main protecting images, Yamantaka and Mahakala, along with six central icons, two stupas and an impressive Sakyamuni Buddha flanked by his two disciples can be seen. The school operates for about six months, but many children are sent to Buddhist monasteries across Nepal and even as far as India.

Nar to Meta (3–4hrs)

With only a short trek to Meta to follow, it's definitely worth getting up early to explore Nar again and the valley west before departing down that big hill. Heading towards the **Kang La Phedi** meadows are a series of chortens about 15mins from Nar. The second square set of chortens house water-driven prayer wheels. The stream is the village water source; it's a long slog to get water. Climb up past three chortens near the defunct hydro plant to a viewpoint displaying Pisang, Kang Guru, Chombi and Nemjung. Chulu Far East is visible from the other meadows. The trail to Kang La Phedi appears to be a steady, gentle but no doubt exhausting climb.

Before leaving **Nar**, it might be worthwhile to climb the small hills east of the lodges for an uninterrupted view down. The trek down is accomplished with a lot less effort, but loose sections are waiting to catch you out occasionally. Be careful! Views are dominated by the West Face of Kang Guru.

Meta to Koto (7–8hrs)

This stage is a long walk down, but surprisingly many small ups are encountered all day long. However, the return to warmer climes, masses more oxygen and the thought of the first shower in a week can aid the pace. By the beginning of April, the potentially lethal snow chutes on the path should have been cleared by ACAP staff for the benefit of long trains of goods-laden ponies.

Crossing the Marsyangdi bridge and arriving back on the main trail is like spinning out of orbit and suddenly landing back on Planet Earth. At the checkpost life continues as

Kang Guru and chortens below Nar

before, with a steady stream of afternoon trekkers registering their progress on the Annapurna Circuit. It's a definite culture shock to be back in the 'real' world at **Koto**.

CROSSING THE KANG LA TO NGAWAL

To the west of Nar and Kang La Phedi lies the 5300m Kang La, a formidable barrier, not yet attempted by the authors. Note that it is not recommended to access Nar from the Ngawal–Manang side owing to the extreme altitude gain over the Kang La, unless you are exceedingly well acclimatised.

Nar to Kang La Phedi is an ascent of around 450m (3–4hrs); the trail is not unduly steep most of the way. The jagged walls of the Yungregang Ridge that runs from Pisang Peak dominate the hike. Apparently there is a rough shelter at Phedi, but camping with a fully equipped crew will make the whole project much safer.

The trek from Kang La Phedi to Ngawal takes 6–9hrs. The climb involves an ascent of around 600m, followed by a very steep and often icy descent of 1700m to Ngawal. The pass is invariably snowbound and icy. The trail heads up towards the icy ramparts of Chulu Far East and the rocky flanks of the Kangla Himal. From the Kang La (5300m), hope for a superb view of Annapurnas II, VI and III and Gangapurna. On the very steep descent, this panoramic vista will be a constant companion, so watch your footing carefully. Ngawal (3660m) will be a welcome sight, as will the luxuries of trekkers' lodges and plentiful food. From Ngawal you can either descend to Pisang and then head to Besisahar, or go to Mungji and up to Manang (see Trek 1 Annapurna Circuit).

3 OTHER TREKS

Dhaulagiri from near Chitre

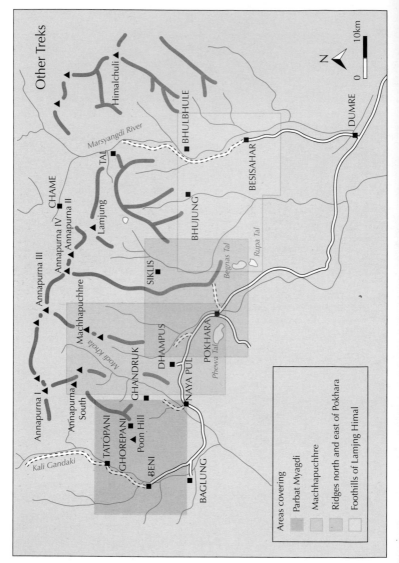

This section briefly outlines less familiar treks in the Annapurna region: two routes for trekkers to 'assault' Mardi Himal below Machhapuchhre; a new eco-homestay trek below Poon Hill; quiet ridge treks northeast of Pokhara; a route little-used today, Panchase Hill; and some new homestay options below Lamjung Himal.

MACHHAPUCHHRE REGION

View across the ridges towards Mardi Himal and Machhapuchhre

Hardly on the radar yet for most trekking visitors to Nepal, these two short but tough treks will be a revelation to frequent Annapurna region explorers. Mardi Himal (5600m) is the rocky peak that guards the southwest flank of Machhapuchhre; it is also the eastern guardian of the Annapurna Sanctuary–Modi Khola 'entry gate'. The approaches to Mardi Himal are along the airy, lofty ridges that run north of Pokhara. Panoramic views from the ridges are magnificent: vistas west to Dhaulagiri and Churen Himal and east to Annapurna II, Lamjung, Himalchuli and Baudha. The fantastic rock triangle of Machhapuchhre completely dominates other views, but look south for uninterrupted panoramas of dazzling, blue-rinsed ridges.

Because both the ridge trails climb quickly, the main risk on these sometimes-exposed belvederes is of altitude sickness. Scrambling around Mardi Himal Base Camp needs care: remember it's a trek, not a climb! Currently the trek is suitable for camping, because the daily marches can be varied to suit the conditions and acclimatisation levels. It is likely that rustic lodges will be developed soon, as more trekkers discover these pristine routes. Check with the Pokhara trekking agencies. The two routes and the terrain crossed can be observed from Sarangkot Hill near Pokhara. A guide who knows the way intimately is needed for both routes.

Currently the typical cost of a fully inclusive trek to either Mardi Himal or Machhapuchhre Korchon is US$50–60 per day. This will include guide, cook, porters, all camping equipment and full board food on trek. Permits, drinks and personal equipment will be extra.

Information compiled with many thanks to K B Nembang in Pokhara, of both Mountain Tiger Outdoor Adventure and Eastern Light Trekking.

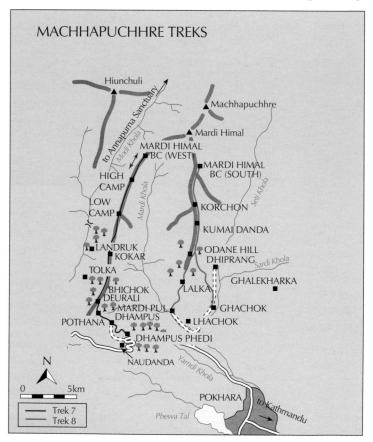

TREK 7
Mardi Himal Trek

Start	Dhampus Phedi (1130m/3706ft)
Finish	Dhampus Phedi (1130m/3706ft)
Distance	48km (30 miles)
Time	7–8 days
Maximum altitude	Mardi Himal Base Camp West (4500m/14,760ft)
Transport	Bus, jeep and taxi
Trekking style	Camping

Water supplies on this high ridge are often an issue, depending on the season, so you may not necessarily have a lot of choice of camp location. The following

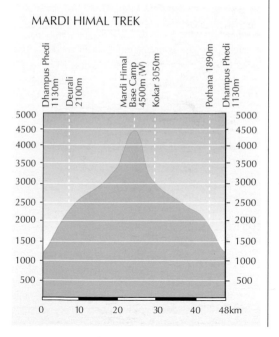

MARDI HIMAL TREK

information is given only in outline, with estimated altitudes and timings.

Dhampus Phedi to Pothana (3–4hrs)

Take transport from Pokhara to Dhampus **Phedi** (or Dhampus). It's a classic walk with variety and memorable views of the 'Fishtail' peak. After climbing up the hill or taking a jeep to Dhampus, the path climbs along the ridge to good lodges at **Pothana** (1890m). It's better to stay near Pothana if camping, as Deurali has few flat camping areas.

Pothana to Kokar Forest Camp (5–6hrs)

Beyond **Deurali** (2100m), the trail leaves the busy route to Landruk and begins the long, wild climb along the Kali Danda Ridge. Fleeting views of the mountains ratchet up the anticipation of getting closer to Machhapuchhre. This cool forest stage is magical and strangely quiet: rhododendron and magnolia, larch and moss-covered, decaying vegetation are encountered. Ancient gnarled trunks host dripping, wispy lichens. There is apparently a functioning rustic forest lodge at **Kokar** (about 3050m).

Kokar Forest Camp to Low Camp (3–4hrs)

There are few landmarks along this route, the sole domain of woodcutters, herders, monkeys and very few foreign trekkers. The trail continues to climb in varying degrees of steepness; the path, being rarely used, is not always good. The normal overnight stop is at a place called **Low Camp** (about 3050m), where the water source is sufficient for groups.

Low Camp to High Camp (4–5hrs)

Breaking free of the dense forest, the route climbs steadily upwards into the high pastures and open moorland. Assuming the clouds keep at bay, the closer you get to the Fishtail, the more amazing its towering buttresses become. The trail (such as it is) makes a considerable height gain. How long the walk takes will depend on the ability of the group and acclimatisation. Water sources

on the ridge determine which particular **High Camp** (about 3900m) is used.

On the trail

Mardi Himal Base Camp and return
Base Camp (4500m) is the high point of the trek in all senses, as the route climbs to within a whisker of the great rocky outlier of Mardi Himal (5553m). The effects of altitude need to be remembered, as going too high is always a temptation on these exciting days.

The return march to Pokhara is generally the same way to **Pothana**, then on to either **Dhampus/Dhampus Phedi** or Australian Camp/Khare. However, according to trekking agent and guide K B Nembang, who has years of experience in Pokhara and beyond, a difficult route off the ridge goes down east into the Susel/Mardi Khola Valley. Check in detail about this if you want to vary the return.

TREK 8
Machhapuchhre Korchon (Model) Trek

Start	Mardi Pul (1160m/3804ft)
Finish	Ghachok (1260m/4132ft) or Mardi Pul (1160m/3804ft)
Distance	40km (25 miles)
Time	7–8 days
Maximum altitude	Mardi Himal Base Camp South (4120m/13,513ft)
Transport	Bus, jeep or taxi from Pokhara
Trekking style	Camping

A variation on the Mardi Himal trek, this route is along a ridge further east, offering equally awe-inspiring panoramic views. With the Mardi Himal ridge blocking the mountains to the west, you can enjoy the 'eastern light' and the peaks of Annapurna IV and II and Lamjung.

MACHHAPUCHHRE KORCHON
(MODEL) TREK

Himalchuli and distant Ganesh might show their shining faces. Only an outline itinerary is shown below, since the authors have not done this route.

Mardi Pul to Lalka (2–3hrs)

From Mardi Pul (or Ribban), the first day involves a climb up the steep ridge, possibly as far as **Lalka**, but the availability of water, an important factor on the whole route, will determine the exact camping place.

Lalka to Odane Hill (3hrs)

The trekking must be tough, as the trail continues to ascend the ridge to Odane. Occasionally shade is on offer, with some forest cover. Rhododendrons bloom in spring and woodcutters shelter in isolated kharkas. **Odane Hill** (2515m) is the usual camp, making it a half-day march.

Odane Hill to Kumai Danda (5–7hrs)

The next day, the trail continues mostly uphill; it's that sort of trek when you are heading for Machhapuchhre.

Machhapuchhre at sunset

At least there are great views when you leave the cover of the forest. Owing to the altitude gain, you need to stop in **Kumai Danda** (3245m).

Kumai Danda to Korchon (2–3hrs)

Although in distance it's not far, you will soon be reminded of the height gain to be made to **Korchon** (3680m). Even if you are fit, remember to go slowly for the sake of your acclimatisation. With more open pasture to cross, the views distract you from looking at your feet all day. From Korchon you can either return the same way or attempt the trail west down to the Mardi Khola via Naudhoke, but make sure your guide knows this trail. Most will continue on to Base Camp.

Korchon to Mardi Himal South Base Camp (4–5hrs)

Given a clear dawn, it will be hard to get moving on this day. You can't get much better panoramic viewpoints in Nepal for sunrise on the peaks, floating above endless valleys, often shrouded in mist. With the **South Base Camp** located at 4120m, you need to take it very steadily along the ridgeline. With trails rarely used, don't expect the ground underfoot to be as forgiving as on a regular route. At the South Base Camp you are no more than 5–6km from the sheer unconquered South Face of Machhapuchhre. The summit gods gaze down at you from a vertical drop of over 2800m (9180ft).

Return to Ghachok/Mardi Pul

There is a route marked on the maps between South Base Camp and the West Base Camp, but taking this means a colossal descent and ascent that is quite impossible – so don't expect any trekking agency to plan this one. From Mardi Himal South Base Camp you have to retreat down to **Korchon**. It is apparently possible to leave the ridgeline and descend to the Seti Khola Valley and end the walking in **Ghachok** (1260m) for an array of second-class transport options to Pokhara. The descent is much quicker, but watch those knees. Otherwise retrace your route from Korchon to Mardi Pul.

PARBAT MYAGDI

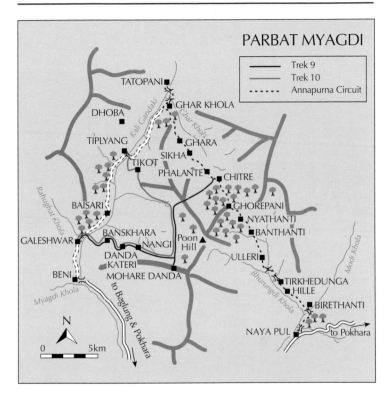

Southwest of Poon Hill and Ghorepani is an area of great potential for those trekkers seeking to leave the crowded trails behind. The hillsides of the developing Parbat Myagdi region, also known as the Mohare Danda Trekking Area, face towards the west and northwest, with outstanding views of Dhaulagiri.

With quiet, rural pastoral scenes and virgin forests, this new trekking area now has a series of village-based homestays and community lodges.

One option is to access the area from Phalante (near Chitre) on the main trail between Tatopani and Ghorepani and walk down to meet the Tatopani–Beni–Pokhara road (see

Typical houses

Trek 9 below). Although not currently marked on the maps, a trail also links these homestay villages with Poon Hill.

You can also do a circular trek without going into the Annapurna Conservation Area (at the moment, at least) by the following (7–8 day) itinerary: Pokhara–Beni–Galeshwar–Ghumaone–Banskhara–Danda Khetri–Nangi–Mohare Danda–Tikot–Tiplyang and then back to Beni along the motorable road of the Kali Gandaki Valley (see Trek 10 below).

Times and descriptions are estimated for guidance only, as the authors have not done these routes.

TREK 9

Parbat Myagdi Link

Start	Phalante (2300m/7544ft)
Finish	Galeshwar (1020m/3345ft)
Distance	24km
Time	4–5 days, various options
Maximum altitude	Mohare Danda (3225m/10,580ft)
Transport	Bus, jeep, taxi from Galeshwar/Beni
Trekking style	Homestay

Phalante to Mohare Danda (6–7hrs)

Starting near **Phalante** (2300m), the trail climbs up generally southwest for 1hr or so to cross a ridge at Nakako Bisaune (about 2990m). It then contours to a community lodge at Danda Kharka before making the climb to the **Mohare Danda** Ridge (3225m), an exciting new viewpoint, with a stunning vision of Machhapuchhre. Much of the way is through forest of pine, rhododendron and chilaune trees. Keep a lookout for birds such as the White Owl, Himali Kokale, Nyauli and Dundul. Fleet-of-foot wildlife includes deer, fox and the elusive leopard.

Mohare Danda to Nangi (3–4hrs)

From **Mohare Danda** the way heads down to **Nangi** (2300m), a Magar village which has homestays as well as a typical oval-shaped community structure for schoolteachers and visiting volunteers; see www.himanchal.org. Nangi is noted as the 'Internet village' because of its enterprising locals and international donors.

Oranges grow on the warm, sunny hillsides surrounding the village, which also has a small temple. There are good views of Dhaulagiri and Churen Himal.

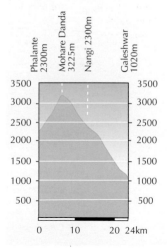

PARBAT MYAGDI LINK

Meeting the local children

Nangi to Danda Kateri (2–3hrs)

For a shorter trek down the next day, you may overnight in the settlement of Danda Kateri (2009m), with a community dining hall and homestay options. The Pyari Barah temple is near here.

Danda Kateri to Banskhara (2hrs)

Some 800m below Mohare Danda is another Magar village called **Banskhara** (1526m), with more new homestays.

Banskhara to Galeshwar (1–2hrs)

The descent to Ghumaone Tal is relatively short but quite steep. **Galeshwar** (1020m) is 15mins downstream along the road to Beni and expanding rapidly. It's worth a break to see the temple – a large complex built upon a mound of rock. There are a couple of reasonable lodges in Galeshwar near the suspension bridge on the north side.

TREK 10
Parbat Myagdi Circular

Start	Galeshwar (1020m/3345ft)
Finish	Tiplyang (1040m/3410ft)
Distance	33km (21 miles)
Time	6–8 days, various options
Maximum altitude	Mohare Danda (3225m/10,580ft)
Transport	Bus, jeep, taxi
Trekking style	Homestay

Galeshwar to Banskhara (2hrs)
To avoid all the main trails and do this as a circular trek, start near **Galeshwar**. Cross the Kali Gandaki at the Ghumaone bridge and trek up to **Banskhara** (1526m).

Banskhara to Danda Kateri (2–3hrs)
Continue uphill to **Danda Kateri** (2009m). Homestay is possible here.

Typical farmhouse of the middle hills

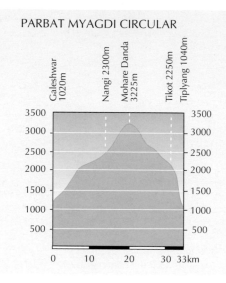

PARBAT MYAGDI CIRCULAR

Danda Kateri to Nangi (2–3hrs)

It's pretty much all uphill through farms and isolated woods to **Nangi** (2300m), the famed Internet village.

Nangi to Mohare Danda (4–5hrs)

The trail climbs ever higher and into the beautiful forests that characterise the upper slopes of Poon Hill. Continue to **Mohare Danda** (3225m), an exciting newly discovered panoramic viewpoint.

Mohare Danda to Tikot (6–7hrs)

Since the authors are unfamiliar with the trail, it has to be assumed that, mostly, it contours around the hills and then drops down to **Tikot** (about 2200m).

Tikot to Tiplyang (2–3hrs)

With a bigger descent today to the Kali Gandaki Valley floor, the trail zigzags down around the cliffs to **Tiplyang** (1040m) and then it's back to Beni and Pokhara along the road.

Apparently, homestays are also being opened in the villages of Khiwang and Swat, both on the hillside west of Sikha. Khiwang is quite a large settlement, with around 800 inhabitants, while Swat has roughly 50 houses. The people here are known locally as the Pun Magar.

Having an experienced local guide is definitely necessary. Route-finding through settlements, across the hillsides and in forests is impossible with so many junctions and trails; the forests are certainly not places in which to be alone. Thanks are due to Alonzo Lucius Lyons for help with the information on this trek.

A woman's work is never done

271

RIDGES NORTH AND EAST OF POKHARA

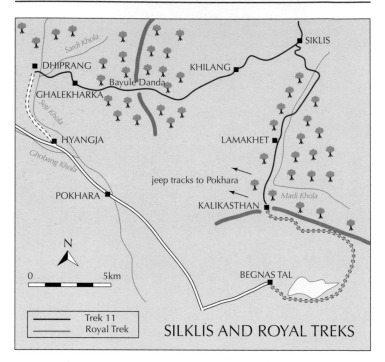

SILKLIS AND ROYAL TREKS

For many years, before the coming of the motor vehicle to the hills north of Pokhara, a variety of short trekking routes were popular on these ridges. All offered great views of the Annapurnas and kept to relatively low altitudes, making for easier, stress-free hiking. A route along the ridges from Pokhara to Begnas Tal became known as the Royal Trek. Being only 3–4 days in duration, it proved very popular with trekkers who wanted a taste of

Nepal's mountain attractions without needing to be excessively fit.

Another trek – the Siklis Trek – was a little longer, climbed higher, but did not deviate too far from civilisation. Siklis is a major Gurung village, nestling on a high meadow, dominated by the slumbering giant of Lamjung peak. These days few trekkers venture to Siklis; those who do, however, have reported that it is still a tranquil place to visit.

Porters on the trail, with Annapurna IV beyond

Both routes start or finish in the resort lake area of Begnas Tal, about 15km east of Pokhara, on a road that leaves the main Kathmandu highway at km10. These days better hotels have been developed to cater for the increasing numbers of foreign, Nepalese and Indian tourists.

ROYAL TREK

HRH Prince Charles famously undertook this trek in the early 1980s along with all his bodyguards, guides, cooks, porters, porters' bodyguards... and bodyguards' porters! Then the trek encompassed all the traditional features typical of a moderate hike in the farming countryside: picturesque rounded ochre and red-coloured houses, undisturbed forests singing with cicadas, grubby children rushing to greet the strangers and women in brightly coloured saris washing clothes, while the men pondered on the future of the country...

Today a jeep track climbs up on to the Kalikasthan Ridge, so reducing the Royal Trek to a gentle amble east to the lakes of Rupa and **Begnas Tal**. That said, the views have not changed; on a clear day the Himalayan giants on display include Machhapuchhre, Annapurna IV, Annapurna II and Lamjung. Allow three days for a gentle stroll along this ridgetop, and check whether you still need to take a tent or if homestays have developed.

TREK 11
Siklis Trek

Start	Dhiprang (1440m/4750ft)
Finish	Near Lamakhet (1020m/3347ft) or Kalikasthan (1400m/4593ft)
Distance	35–45km approx
Time	5–6 days
Maximum altitude	Bayule Danda (2900m/9570ft)
Transport	Bus to Hyangja, then jeep or tractor – really!
Trekking style	Camping, some lodges

Sunset over Pokhara

For a region so close to Pokhara, this trek rarely attracted many takers, and as a consequence remained little changed by the march of modernity. It illustrated well the typical, rural farming life of the hills. Untouched rhododendron forests and mountain views

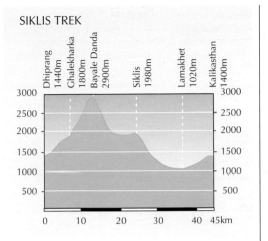

of Machhapuchhre, Annapurna IV, Annapurna II and Lamjung, added to the mix. For a while groups enjoyed its serenity. Camping was the only option, but now Dhiprang and Siklis have lodges. Check with trekking agencies in Pokhara in case homestays are opening elsewhere. Note that you will need the usual TIMS and ACAP permits for this area.

A jeep track reaches Dhiprang and beyond, but basically from there it's all boot-wearing trail. The end of the trip has changed, as a jeep track reaches close to Siklis, north of Lamakhet, along the Madi Khola, The Kalikasthan Ridge is crisscrossed by tracks of poor quality, so there is little point in concluding the walk after this. Find a jeep and hop off to Pokhara – good luck! Only an outline itinerary is provided.

From Pokhara the jeep track meanders around rice fields and farmhouses overshadowed by the sheer buttresses of Machhapuchhre. Take transport as far as the road will allow – normally that is Dhiprang. Trekkers used to enjoy an evening of cultural entertainment here, with singing and dancing. It's a leisurely introduction to the village life of the Annapurna foothills.

Dhiprang to Ghalekharka Ridge (3–4hrs)

From **Dhiprang** (1440m) in the Seti Khola Valley, the route crosses the Sardi Khola tributary heading east, then climbs vigorously. Luckily it's a short day, due to the lack of water higher up the ridge. The high point of the day is the camp on the **Ghalekharka Ridge** (1800m), with a surprising panorama – hazy blue-tinged ridges roll away far to the south.

Ghalekharka Ridge to Forest Camp/Nauli Kharka (6–7hrs)

Leaving behind the misty dawn views, the trail climbs into dense, undisturbed rhododendron forest. Invariably it's muddy underfoot and only woodcutters are encountered. There are tantalising glimpses of Machhapuchhre through the dense forest.

Lamjung seen from Siklis

Forest Camp to Siklis (6–7hrs)

The path slips and slides up to the **Bayule Danda** (2900m), the high point of the trek. The descent is much the same. Some trekkers make an intermediate camp after the forest near Chipli or **Khilang**, allowing for a half-day hike through Parche to **Siklis** (1980m). Siklis is surrounded by rich farmland and the view of Lamjung Himal is pretty impressive.

Siklis to Lamakhet

Before leaving, most trekkers explore the meadows and view Lamjung from a closer hillock north of the village. Once having left **Siklis**, the trail descends rather quickly and steeply down to the valley of the Madi Khola. Kingfishers and other birds delight in the abundant food of the lush, forested riverbank. Somewhere before **Lamakhet** (1020m), the jeep track should be encountered, thus the time taken for this walk will vary as the jeep track develops.

The return to Pokhara involves crossing the surprisingly high ridge of Kalikasthan (adding 10km if walking). Following the old Royal Trek route via Shaklung to **Begnas Tal**, which eventually drops off the ridge past an old fort, is a longer possibility.

PANCHASE TREK

Once quite popular, this trek sees hardly any visitors now, owing to road and jeep track construction. It's only really done by those wanting an easy 2–3 days from Pokhara. The route heads along the ridge from the Peace Stupa and west to a viewpoint before dropping to the Khare/Lumle area.

FOOTHILLS OF LAMJUNG HIMAL

The Annapurnas rising above the Lamjung district

Bound by the Marsyangdi River and stretching west towards Pokhara is the Lamjung district, a major new area for trekking within the Annapurna region. New routes (and dirt roads) are being rapidly developed in this area, destined for a different type of visitor. Through homestay programmes, modest trekking is being combined with cultural interaction, eco-tourism and village development. Hikers looking for a more authentic, intimate experience of traditional rural Nepal will want to check out these new routes. Homestays with local families are being encouraged in order to spread the visitor's dollars into areas where,

until now, only subsistence agriculture has sustained the way of life.

These 'new' trails do not require quite such a high level of fitness, and enable visitors to enjoy perhaps a more genuine Nepal, away from the more comfortable trekkers' ghettos of the main trails. Bizarrely this latest, almost fashionable, initiative is a kind of reinvention of the 'good old days' of early trekking 40 years ago. Note also that when you 'travel back in time' you can't expect the level of luxury and standard of toilets that modern lodges provide on the main trails. These trails offer fine scenery, tranquillity and equally spectacular views

Your homestay host

but are not yet ideal for independent trekking; the trails are not marked, so taking a guide with specialist knowledge, and porter, is vital.

Be warned that if you come in late spring the lower foothills can be hot and humid. Late autumn and into December probably offers the best season. The main areas of interest in the region are the Chowk Chisopani–Tandrangkot–Puranokot cultural treks

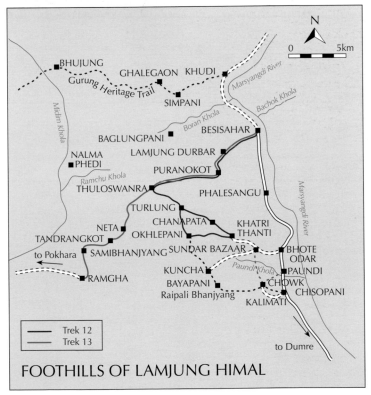

FOOTHILLS OF LAMJUNG HIMAL

and the longer Gurung Heritage Trail (Trek 14).

These new eco-cultural treks are eminently suited to visitors interested in meeting the local people, interacting with their culture and, in so doing, helping to alleviate rural poverty. Those who enjoy the challenge of a long, sustained trek would probably find these treks too relaxing. The routes are graded as easy, with moderate stretches, since the hikes are short (2–4hrs). Views of Lamjung and Annapurna II are spectacular, while across the Marsyangdi Valley, Baudha, Himalchuli, Ngadi Chuli and Manaslu pierce the sky. Almost nothing remains of the 15th-century settlements, which had historic links to the ruling Shah dynasty.

Choice Humanitarian Nepal is developing and supporting the area. They provided information on the trek, ably assisted by Kate Hargadon; see www.choicehumanitarian.org.

There are various trekking options on offer. The first is to begin from Dumre and head to Khatri Thanti on local transport, then trek to Besisahar across the ridges via Puranokot. To extend the trek, why not start in the fledgling homestay area of Chowk Chisopani? A second option starts from Pokhara, bumping along dirt roads east towards Nalma, then a trek from Ramgha to Puranokot and on to Besisahar. Some altitudes are estimated and walking times are approximate.

In the Lamjung foothills – Marsyangdi river below Himalchuli (Trek 12)

TREK 12
Khatri Thanti–Besisahar Trek

Start	Khatri Thanti (760m/2500ft)
Finish	Besisahar (760m/2500ft)
Distance	26km (17 miles) approx
Time	4–5 days
Maximum altitude	Puranokot Hill (1750m/5775ft)
Transport	Bus, jeep and taxi
Trekking style	Homestay

This trek runs from Khatri Thanti to Turlung, Thuloswanra, Puranokot and on to Besisahar. Access to Khatri Thanti from Kathmandu is via Dumre to Sundar Bazaar, off the road to Besisahar (7hrs' drive). There are microbuses (Rs350) direct to Sundar Bazaar from Kathmandu, but avoid the back seats! From Sundar Bazaar a local bus sometimes goes to Khatri Thanti.

Khatri Thanti to Okhlepani or Chanapata (2hrs)
From **Khatri Thanti** (760m) one track/trail heads off via Printibeshi (bus Rs100) and then on foot to the beautiful

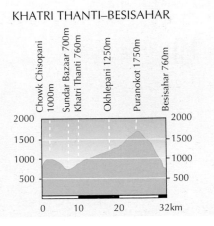

KHATRI THANTI–BESISAHAR

village of **Okhlepani** (1250m), southwest of Chanapata. It has a community centre and a rice mill. The village is surprisingly clean, with impeccable sanitation. Another trail also heads from Khatri Thanti to **Chanapata** in about 2hrs.

Okhlepani to Thuloswanra (3hrs)

It's about a 1hr walk from **Okhlepani** to Turlung (Turlungkot) and is a good work-out. You can generally avoid the jeep track by keeping to the path and then head up stone steps. **Turlung** village is a pleasant village with a new school. The children are always excited to see a foreigner. The homestay hospitality and enthusiasm is very welcoming, especially if you come prepared with some useful Nepali phrases. From Turlung it's an easy walk to **Thuloswanra** and more hospitable homestays. Fresh honey from the local bee farm is a speciality. Annapurna II and Lamjung can be seen from the village. Thuloswanra was under the former Ghale fiefdom, with its strong traditions of song and dances. A new jeep track from Thuloswanra allows you to take the local bus in the morning to **Khatri Thanti** and **Sundar Bazaar**. It's also possible to head straight to Puranokot from Turlung.

Quiet trails typical of the region

Thuloswanra to Puranokot (3–4hrs)

The trail heads across the Manange Danda area to **Puranokot** (1750m), a larger village. Puranokot has roughly 110 houses and is striving very hard to make its new guests feel at home.

> The star attraction, apart from the superb ambience, is the **new climbing wall**. Two local young men have been trained in professional rock climbing by Tyler Cline, a rock climber from Salt Lake City, who spent six months living in Puranokot village, teaching safety and techniques. The 100m-high wall utilises the dramatic cliff face near the village.

People in Puranokot call themselves the Duras, a mongoloid group from the Dura Danda Ridge, but there are also Gurungs.

Puranokot to Besisahar (4hrs)

Leaving **Puranokot**, the route descends along the wooded ridges and terraced ricefields to **Lamjung Durbar** for **Besisahar** (760m). Lamjung Durbar is an intact Newari-style substantial former fiefdom palace.

Chowk Chisopani variant (1½–2hrs)

Off the road north from Dumre to Besisahar is the traditional hill village of Chowk Chisopani, accessed by jeep from Kalimati (about 22km from Dumre) or 2hrs' walk uphill. It is one of those unusual places where Newari people have migrated to the hills from their ancestral home in the Kathmandu Valley. The village is also home to Gurung, Chhetri and Magar people. The locality offers panoramic views. Visitors could also overnight in Bandipur, a beautiful hill town near Dumre, en route to Chowk Chisopani.

The following description should enable trekkers to take a day walk here, but for most visitors having a guide and porter is essential across this entire region, both for safety and to avoid getting utterly lost.

From the west side of central **Kalimati** there is a dirt road to Chowk Chisopani, or take the steep path from the north end. Following the dirt road is easier. The 'road' loops up to a banyan and pipal tree grove. Beyond the trees there is a junction (30mins). Go left uphill into a woody glade where monkeys abound. Continue to some houses, taking the old path to cut the road corners. About 1hr from Kalimati is a stupa with two white chortens. From here take the path up left, passing traditional rural houses before crossing the dirt road. Ahead soon is a white building, the post office, reached in about 1½hrs from Kalimati. **Chowk Chisopani** (1000m) is a spread-out village. To reach the upper area of the village take the small path up a narrow gully from the right side of the post office. A shop, a large school and two temples (devoted to Laxshmi, Narayan and Shiva), are located 20–30mins uphill.

Apart from the utterly untouched rural environment of the village, the main attraction on a clear day is the stunning panorama that spans almost 360° from the school and nearby. The arc, from east to west, includes Baudha, Himalchuli, Ngadi Chuli and Manaslu, as well as Lamjung to Annapurna South. Below are the lush green hillsides of the Middle Hills. Homestay is still being developed, so you need to check the status before planning an overnight stay.

The family of Sohan Shrestra own a sizeable **traditional Newari house** near the temples, with typical mud-plastered walls and pleasing wood-carved windows and doorways. It is planned to become a homestay in future. For more details see updates on www. expeditionworld.com or contact Sohan Shrestha at sohan_kgh@hotmail.com. A Gurung family may also be able to provide accommodation soon.

From Chowk Chisapani there are three alternative trails to Paundi, Sundar Bazaar or Chanapata/Okhlepani.

Chowk Chisapani to Paundi or Sundar Bazaar
From the northeast end of the school look for a pipal tree to find the trail down to Paundi and Sundar. The

path descends steeply and crosses a small 'tractor' track (5–10mins). Continue on the path down to a path intersection. Going left here leads to **Sundar Bazaar** (about 3hrs). A guide is vital for this route. From Sundar Bazaar erratic transport should be available to Khatri Thanti and beyond towards Chanapata or Okhlepani. However, you might end up walking, so be prepared, taking water and snacks.

The trail to **Paundi** basically always heads straight down from this intersection on the stone Gurung staircase. It's a lonely, almost-disused route but eventually comes down to various farms after 1hr. Cross a dirt road and go down to the Paundi Khola. Head right along the riverbed to find the main Besisahar road and go left for the bus stop or village over the steel bridge (1½hrs).

Chowk Chisapani to Chanapata/Okhlepani

A much better and more direct link to the Puranokot area is to take a trail from the temple area of **Chowk Chisapani** to the Raipali Bhanjyang pass (1hr) and west to **Bayapani** (2hrs). Descend from here through Ruksepani and down to a dirt road near **Kuncha** (4hrs from Chowk Chisapani). After crossing the Paundi Khola, the routes climb to **Chanapata** or **Okhlepani**, (at least 6–7hrs in total according to local people).

Chowk Chisopani village

TREK 13
Ramgha–Besisahar Trek

Start	Ramgha (530m/1740ft)
Finish	Besisahar (760m/2500ft)
Distance	28km (17 miles)
Time	5 days
Maximum altitude	Puranokot Hill (1750m/5775ft)
Transport	Bus, jeep and taxi
Trekking style	Homestay

It is recommended to begin this trekking route at Ramgha and work your way across the middle hills of the Lamjung district to Besisahar. From Pokhara and Begnas Tal, a series of new rough roads run over the Sarka Bhanjyang Pass to the Midim Khola and east through Karputar. Allow 6–7hrs for the drive to Ramgha (530m).

Ramgha to Samibhanjyang (1hr)
From the humid lowlands of the Midim Valley, the trail heads up through terraced hillsides to **Samibhanjyang**, a small saddle.

RAMGHA–BESISAHAR

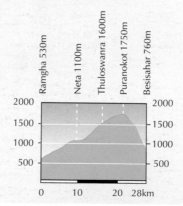

Samibhanjyang to Neta (3hrs)
Climbing more, the route reaches the hilltop location of **Tandrangkot** and then continues to **Neta** (1100m).

Neta to Thuloswanra (2hrs)
The complex series of ridges and valleys that typify the area are accessed fairly easily from Neta village as the trail leads on to **Thuloswanra** (1600m). Although a historical site, little remains of its past glories, but the views of the mountains are magnificent.

Thuloswanra to Puranokot (3–4hrs)
On a clear day, the walking is dominated by the Himalayas to the north – Annapurna II and the great whaleback of Lamjung are always prominent. See Trek 12 for outline details of the route.

Puranokot to Besisahar (4hrs)
Before leaving **Puranokot** (1750m), there is plenty of time to try your hand on the climbing wall. See Trek 12 for details of the route.

Local homestay children

TREK 14
Gurung Heritage Trail

Start	Gumle Bazaar (606m/1988ft)
Finish	Khudi (790m/2592ft)
Distance	45km (28 miles)
Time	5–6 days
Maximum altitude	Ghalegaon (2090m/6860ft)
Transport	Bus and jeep
Trekking style	Homestay, lodges, teahouses

Traditional village

Last but not least, this easy-to-moderate trek shows off the Gurung culture and some of the least-visited regions below Annapurna II and Lamjung. Villages like Bhujung have rarely been heard of – until now. This trek offers a glimpse into traditional hill country life, where little-known ethnic peoples other than Gurungs are found. The trek utilises homestay accommodation.

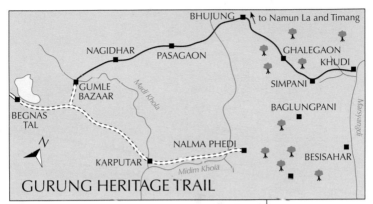

Because the ACAP area is entered you need to obtain the TIMS and ACAP Conservation Area permits in advance. Since these new areas are not used to trekkers, taking a guide from the Pokhara or Lamjung region is essential. The authors have not done this route, so timings are estimated.

The trek starts east of Pokhara at Thumsikot/Gumle Bazaar. Buses and jeeps take roughly 2hrs, departing

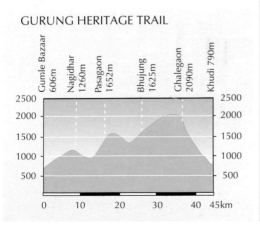

Different ethnic groups along the trail

normally four times daily from Ranipauwa in Pokhara between 7am and 3pm.

Gumle Bazaar to Nagidhar (3–4hrs)
After crossing the Madi Khola from **Gumle Bazaar**, the route climbs to Gahate and on to **Nagidhar** (1260m) for the first night, with tantalising views.

Nagidhar to Pasagaon (4–5hrs)
On the second day it's necessary to descend to the Rudi Khola Valley and climb up along the ridge to the village of **Pasagaon** (1652m), with its Buddhist kani and monastery.

Pasagaon to Bhujung (4–5hrs)
The third morning involves a climb through delightful forest to 2100m. Between here and Bhujung is the valley of the Midim Khola, which needs to be crossed. **Bhujung** (1625m) is located above the valley and is reached by a typical Gurung stone staircase trail. This aesthetically

Shady trails

pleasing traditional village is currently notable as being the largest Gurung village in Nepal. Electricity has arrived here and homestays are available.

> Reached by a long, remote and rugged trail from Bhujung is the **holy lake of Dudh Pokhari** (4600m, meaning 'milky lake'), where Shiva and Parvati reputedly bathed. This route continues over the Namun La (4850m) to Timang.

Bhujung to Ghalegaon (3–4hrs)
From **Bhujung** the trail heads to Ghalegaon, once the dominant fiefdom of the region. Before Nayan there are no facilities; the trek is through isolated country. Later there is a side trail to Ghan Pokhara, a hilltop village with panoramic views. **Ghalegaon** (2092m), a beautiful Gurung settlement, is the overnight stop, making this a relatively short day. Ghalegaon can also be reached by a dirt track from Besisahar in 3–4hrs.

Ghalegaon to Khudi (3–4hrs)

This trail also leads to a junction giving access to Baglungpani and the trekking area described below. ◄ From here the designated route descends to Khudi. ◄ The path to Khudi heads to Balamchaur, initially through uninhabited forest, and on to **Simpani**, the village of temples, used by devotees of a local deity, Thani Mai, as well as by followers of Ganesh, Krishna and his consort Radha, and Mahadev. From **Khudi** (790m) trekkers can join the main Annapurna Circuit trail (Trek 1) or head south for Dumre, Pokhara, Chitwan or Kathmandu.

For more information on this route see *The Gurung Heritage Trail* by Alonzo Lucius Lyons.

POKHARA TO KHUDI VIA BAGLUNGPANI

Those with masses of time, hoping to complete the full Annapurna Circuit from Pokhara, can follow tracks or trails linking Pokhara with Khudi, via the high ridge of Baglungpani (ideally, take a guide). From Begnas Tal, the route crosses the low saddle of Sarka Bhanjyang to Karputar and goes along the Midim Khola Valley to Nalma Phedi. An unrelenting climb follows up to Baglungpani (1595m), where there is a lodge. Descent is via the Bhalam (Boran) Khola to Khudi. Previously, trekking groups thwarted by heavy snow on the Thorong La returned down the Marsyangdi to Khudi and followed this route to Pokhara.

Farewell to the mountains

APPENDIX A

Trek summaries and suggested schedules

Grades are relative. There's hardly a flat area in Nepal – not even mountain airstrips or the odd odd lodge bed! Easy still involves some steep ups and downs. Moderate is that bit harder, including altitude, and Strenuous involves steep climbs and exposed paths with some at altitude. All treks listed require trekkers to be in good physical shape.

Trek 1 Annapurna Circuit (Moderate/Strenuous)

Day	Trekking route	Time	Alternative	Time
Note If taking the jeep from Besisahar to Chamje, start at Day 3 below.				
Day 1	Bhulbhule – Bahundanda	3–4hrs	Bhulbhule – Jagat	4–5hrs
Day 2	Bahundanda – Chamje	5–6hrs	Jagat – Tal	4–5hrs
Day 3	Chamje – Dharapani	5–6hrs	Tal – Danakyu	4–5hrs
Day 4	Dharapani – Chame	6–7hrs	Danakyu – Chame	4½–5½hrs
Day 5	Chame – Pisang	5–6hrs		
Day 6	Pisang – Braka	4–5hrs	Pisang to Mungji/Braka	5–7hrs
Day 7	Braka – Manang	½–1hr		
Day 8/9	*In Manang*			
Day 10	Manang – Churi Lattar	4–5½hrs		
Day 11	Churi Lattar – Thorong Phedi	2–4hrs (slowly)		
Day 12	Thorong Phedi – Muktinath	6–12hrs		

Trek 1 Annapurna Circuit (Moderate/Strenuous)

Day	Trekking route	Time	Alternative	Time
Day 13	Muktinath–Jharkot–Kagbeni	3–3½hrs	Muktinath – Jhong – Kagbeni	6hrs
Day 14	Kagbeni – Jomsom	3hrs		
Day 15	Jomsom – Dumba Lake side trip	4–5hrs	Jomsom – Marpha (high route)	5–6hrs
Day 16	Jomsom –Tukuche via Chhairo	5–6hrs	Marpha –Tukuche via Chhairo	4–5hrs
Day 17	Tukuche – Kalopani	3–4hrs		
Day 18	Kalopani – Dana	6–7hrs		
Day 19	Dana –Tatopani	3–4hrs		
Day 20	Tatopani – Ghorepani	6–8hrs	Tatopani – Beni	7hrs
Day 21	Ghorepani – Tirkhedunga	5–6hrs		
Day 22	Tirkhedunga – Naya Pul	2–3hrs		

Alternative Stage 4

Day	Trekking route	Time
Day 21	Ghorepani – Tadapani	4–5hrs
Day 22	Tadapani – Landruk	5–6hrs
Day 23	Landruk – Dhampus Phedi	6–7hrs

Trek 2 Annapurna Sanctuary (Moderate/Strenuous)

Day	Trekking route	Time	Alternative	Time
Day 1	Dhampus Phedi – Landruk	6½–7½hrs	Syauli Bazaar – Jhinu Danda	4-5hrs
Day 2	Landruk – Chhomrong	5-6hrs	Jhinu Danda – Chhomrong	2-3hrs
Day 3	Chhomrong – Doban	5-6hrs		
Day 4	Doban – Machhapuchhre Base Camp	5-7hrs		
Day 5	MBC – Annapurna Base Camp	2hrs		
Day 6	Annapurna BC – Doban	7-8hrs		
Day 7	Doban – Chhomrong	5-6hrs		
Day 8	Chhomrong – Ghandruk	5-6hrs		
Day 9	Ghandruk – Naya Pul	4-5hrs		
Alternative Stage 4				
Day 8	Chhomrong – Tadapani	4-5hrs		
Day 9	Tadapani – Ghorepani	4-5hrs		
Day 10	Ghorepani – Tirkhedunga	5-6hrs		
Day 11	Tirkhedunga – Naya Pul	2-3hrs		

Trek 3 Ghorepani Circuit (Poon Hill Expedition) (Moderate)

Day	Trekking route	Time
Day 1	Dhampus Phedi – Landruk	6½–7½hrs
Day 2	Landruk – Ghandruk	3–4hrs
Day 3	Ghandruk – Tadapani	3–4hrs
Day 4	Tadapani – Ghorepani	4–5hrs
Day 5	Ghorepani – Tirkhedunga	5–6hrs
Day 6	Tirkhedunga – Naya Pul	2–3hrs

Trek 4 Annapurna–Dhaulagiri Trek (Moderate/Strenuous)

Day	Trekking route	Time
Day 1	Dhampus Phedi – Landruk	6½–7½hrs
Day 2	Landruk – Tadapani	6–7hrs
Day 3	Tadapani – Dobaato	5–6hrs
Day 4	Dobaato – Chistibung	3–4hrs
Day 5	Chistibung – Kopra Danda	3–4hrs
Day 6	Kopra Danda – Camp	3–5hrs
Day 7	Camp – Khairetal – Kopra Danda	6–8hrs
Day 8	Kopra Danda – Chitre	4–5hrs
Day 9	Chitre – Ghorepani	2hrs
Day 10	Ghorepani – Tirkhedunga	5–6hrs
Day 11	Tirkhedunga – Naya Pul	2–3hrs

Trek 5 Mustang Trek (Moderate)

Day	Trekking route	Time	Alternative	Time
Note Alternatives going up to Lo Manthang (Days 3 to 6) relate to altitude issues, not stages or alternative options described.				
Day 1	Jomsom – Kagbeni	3hrs		
Day 2	Kagbeni – Chele	6–7hrs		
Day 3	Chele – Eklobhatti/Syangmochen	6hrs	Chele – Samar	3hrs
Day 4	Eklobhatti – Ghami	4hrs	Samar – Geling	4–5hrs
Day 5	Ghami – Lo Gekar	5–6hrs	Geling – Drakmar	5–6hrs
Day 6	Lo Gekar – Lo Manthang	4–5hrs	Drakmar – Lo Manthang	6–7hrs
Day 7/8	*In Lo Manthang*			
Day 9	Lo Manthang – Tsarang	4–5hrs		
Day 10	Tsarang – Tange	5–6hrs	Tsarang – Geling	5–6hrs
Day 11	Tange – Tetang	10hrs	Geling – Chele	6hrs
Day 12	Tetang – Muktinath	6hrs	Chele – Kagbeni	6hrs
Day 13	Muktinath – Jomsom	5–6hrs	Kagbeni – Jomsom	3hrs

Trek 6 Nar-Phu Trek (Moderate/Strenuous)

Day	Trekking route	Time	Alternative	Time
Day 1	Koto – Meta	8–9½hrs		
Day 2	Meta – Khyang	5–6hrs		
Day 3	Khyang – Phu	4–5hrs		
Day 4	In Phu			
Day 5	Phu – Meta or Nar Phedi	7–8hrs		
Day 6	Meta – Nar	3½–4½hrs	Nar Phedi – Nar	2½–3½hrs
Day 7	Nar – Meta	3–4hrs		
Day 8	Meta – Koto	7–8hrs		

Trek 7 Mardi Himal Trek (Moderate/Strenuous)

Day	Trekking route	Time (estimated)	Alternative	Time
Day 1	Dhampus Phedi – Pothana	3–4hrs	Dhampus – Pothana	1–2hrs
Day 2	Pothana – Kokar	5–6hrs		
Day 3	Kokar – Low Camp	3–4hrs		

Day		Time
Day 4	Low Camp – High Camp	4–5hrs
Day 5	High Camp – Mardi Himal West Base Camp – High Camp	Day trip
Day 6	High Camp – Kokar	7–9hrs
Day 7	Kokar – Dhampus Phedi	7–8hrs

Trek 8 Machhapuchhre Korchon (Model) Trek (Moderate/Strenuous)

Day	Trekking route	Time (estimated)	Alternative	Time
Day 1	Mardi Pul – Lalka	2–3hrs		
Day 2	Lalka – Odane	3hrs		
Day 3	Odane – Kumai Danda	5–7hrs		
Day 4	Kumai Danda – Korchon	2–3hrs		
Day 5	Korchon – Mardi Himal South Base Camp	4–5hrs		
Day 6	Mardi Himal South BC – Korchon	4–5hrs		
Day 7	Korchon – Odane	7–8hrs		
Day 8	Odane – Mardi Pul	5–6hrs	Odane – Ghachok	6–7hrs

Trek 9 Parbat Myagdi Link (Moderate)

Day	Trekking route	Time (estimated)
Day 1	Phalante – Mohare Danda	6–7hrs
Day 2	Mohare Danda – Nangi	3–4hrs
Day 3	Nangi – Danda Kateri	2–3hrs
Day 4	Danda Kateri – Banskhara	2hrs
Day 5	Banskhara – Galeshwar	1–2hrs

Trek 10 Parbat Myagdi Circular (Moderate)

Day	Trekking route	Time (estimated)
Day 1	Galeshwar – Banskhara	2hrs
Day 2	Banskhara – Danda Kateri	2–3hrs
Day 3	Danda Kateri – Nangi	2–3hrs
Day 4	Nangi – Mohare Danda	4–5hrs
Day 5	Mohare Danda – Tikot	6–7hrs
Day 6	Tikot – Tiplyang	2–3hrs

Trek 11 Siklis Trek (Moderate)

Day	Trekking route	Time
Day 1	Dhiprang – Ghalekharka Ridge	3–4hrs
Day 2	Ghalekharka Ridge – Forest Camp	6–7hrs
Day 3	Forest Camp – Siklis	6–7hrs
Day 4	*In Siklis*	
Day 5	Siklis – Lamakhet	4–5hrs
Extension to Kalikasthan		
Day 6	Lamakhet – Kalikasthan	3–4hrs

Trek 12 Khatri Thanti–Besisahar Trek (Easy/Moderate)		
Day	**Trekking route**	**Time (estimated)**
Day 1	Khatri Thanti – Okhlepani	2hrs
Day 2	Okhlepani – Thuloswanra	3hrs
Day 3	Thuloswanra – Puranokot	3–4hrs
Day 4	Puranokot – Besisahar	4hrs

Chowk Chisopani variant (Easy/Moderate)

Day 1	Bandipur – Kalimati – Chowk Chisapani	2hrs drive + 2hrs
Day 2	Chowk Chisapani – Okhlepani	4–6hrs
or		
Day 1	Kalimati – Chowk Chisopani	2hrs
Day 2	Chowk Chisapani – Okhlepani	4–6hrs

Continue to Besisahar as above.

Trek 13 Ramgha – Besisahar Trek (Easy/Moderate)

Day	Trekking route	Time (estimated)
Day 1	Ramgha – Samibhanjyang	1hr
Day 2	Samibhanjyang – Neta	3hrs
Day 3	Neta – Thuloswanra	2hrs
Day 4	Thuloswanra – Puranokot	3–4hrs
Day 5	Puranokot – Besisahar	4hrs

Trek 14 Gurung Heritage Trail (Moderate)

Day	Trekking route	Time (estimated)
Day 1	Gumle Bazaar – Nagidhara	3–4hrs
Day 2	Nagidhara – Pasagaon	4–5hrs
Day 3	Pasagaon – Bhujung	4–5hrs
Day 4	Bhujung – Ghalegaon	3–4hrs
Day 5	Ghalegaon – Khudi	3–4hrs

APPENDIX B
Religious and other terminology

Significant Buddhist deities

The Dhyani Buddhas face the four cardinal directions; they are often found on stupas and chaityas (small stone chortens). The Dhyani Buddhas were created from the wisdom of the Adi (first) Buddha, the primordial Buddha. Vairocana is the first Dhyani Buddha and resides in the stupa sanctum; Vairocana is the illuminator, to light the way. Akshobhya faces east; Amitabha faces west; Amoghasiddhi faces north, with a seven-headed serpent behind him; Ratna Sambhava faces south (these are the Sanskrit names).

The following are some other important deities. Sanskrit names are shown first and Tibetan names follow in brackets.

Sakyamuni (Sakya Tukpa)

The mortal Buddha, Gautama Siddhartha, born in Nepal.

Avalokiteshvara (Chenresig)

A bodhisattva having renounced Nirvana, the end of the cycle of rebirth. He embodies compassion (*karuna*) and remains on earth to counter suffering. The Dalai Lama is considered to be his earthly representative.

Amitayus (Tsepame)

The Buddha of Boundless Life, an aspect of Amitabha; he is associated with longevity.

Vajrapani (Channa Dorje)

A spiritual son of Akshobhya. He carries a *dorje* (*vajra*) and is a powerful, wrathful protector. He has monstrous Tantric powers and wears a snake around his neck.

Hayagriva (Tamdrin)

A wrathful emanation of Chenresig, guards many shrines. Blood red with a small horse sticking out of his head, he wears a garland of skulls.

Manjushri (Jampelyang)

The god of wisdom, who carries a sword to cut through ignorance. Worshipping Manjushri gives intellect and intelligence.

Yamantaka (Dorje Jigje)

The 'slayer of death', a wrathful emanation of Manjushri; a Gelug-pa deity with a buffalo head.

Tara (Drolma)

Sacred to both Buddhists and Hindus, representing the maternal aspect, symbolising fertility, purity and compassion. With 21 versions, Tara appears in different colours: red, green, white and gold, and as Kali, dark blue, representing different aspects of her nature.

Maitreya Buddha (Jampa)

The future Buddha.

Medicine Buddha

Engaged for healing the sick, often a blue colour with four hands.

Mahakala

Linked to Shiva with his trident. He tramples on corpses and is a wrathful Avalokiteshvara.

The Four Harmonious Brothers

Found in many monasteries, depicting four animals, one on top of the other: the Elephant, Monkey, Rabbit and the Bird. These represent harmony for peace and the removal of conflict.

The Four Guardians

Seen at monastery entrances. Dhitarashtra is the white guardian of the east, holding a flute. Virupaksha guards the west; he is red with a stupa in one hand and a serpent in the other. Virudhakla is guardian of the south, holding a blue sword. Vaisravana guards the north, holding a yellow banner and a mongoose, usually seen vomiting jewels.

Padma Sambhava (Guru Rinpoche)

The most famous icon of Buddhism, an Indian Tantric master who went to Tibet in the eighth century. He established the Nyingma-pa Red Hat sect. His consort Yeshe Tsogyal recorded his teachings to be revealed to future generations.

Milarepa

Tibet's poet, magician, saint, a historical figure, associated with many legends. He meditated as a hermit before achieving realisation.

Significant Bon deities

Bon has four main peaceful deities, the 'Four Transcendent Lords': Shenlha Wokar, Satrig Ersang, Sangpo Bumtri and Tonpa Shenrap Miwoche.

Others include: Kuntu Zangpo (similar to the primordial Adi Buddha of Buddhism); Kunzang Gyalwa Gyatso (very similar, and perhaps a precursor to the 1000-armed Avalokiteshvara); Welse Ngampa (a nine-headed protector representing 'piercing ferocity' and crushing the enemies of Bon); Sipai Gyalmo (a protectress called the 'Queen of the World').

Other definitions

arhat	Being who has managed to become free from the cycle of existence (samsara). Arhats are not often seen as icons, but when they are, their faces have moustaches and beards. The 16 arhats are the original disciples of Buddha.
bharal	Species of blue sheep.
bhatti	Small rural dwelling.
bodhisattva	Saint or disciple of Buddha who has delayed the attainment of Nirvana and has remained to teach.
Bon	Pre-Buddhist religion of Tibet.
chang	Home-brewed barley wine/beer, sometimes made with other grain.
chorten	Similar to a small stupa (see below) but does not normally contain relics.
dakini	Female deity who can fly.
dorje/vajra	The thunderbolt: it destroys ignorance. A complex figure-of-eight-shaped metal object found at many temples and shrines.
dzong	Fortress, castle.
gompa	Tibetan name for a monastery.
gonkhang	Small, dark and somewhat forbidding chamber housing the protecting deities: Yamantaka, Mahakala and Palden Lhamo, among others.
kani	Entrance archway to settlements.
kharka	Herders' shelter.
lama	Religious teacher and guide, male or female.
lhakhang	Temple chapel within a monastery
Losar	Tibetan New Year festival.
mandala	In art, a circular pattern made of many colours, often a square or squares within a circle. Represents 'the divine abode of an enlightened being.
mani stone	Rock covered with engraved Buddhist mantras, sometimes painted.
mani wall	Long wall made of flat stones engraved with Buddhist mantras; may also contain prayer wheels. You should always keep these on your right.
prayer flag	In five colours, on which prayers are printed; these flutter in the wind, sending prayers direct to heaven. The colours represent the five elements: earth, fire, air, water and ether.
prayer wheel	Metal wheel engraved with Tibetan script and containing prayers. Generally fixed into a wall, or hand held and spun while walking; the spinning action activates the prayers.
puja	Ceremony offering prayers.
rakshi	Nepalese alcoholic drink, not always healthily prepared.

Rigsum Gonpo	The three chortens seen above kanis and elsewhere, representing the three deities who offer protection to villages. The red chorten represents Manjushri, giving wisdom; the white chorten represents Avalokiteshvara, offering compassion; and the blue, black or grey chorten represents Vajrapani, to fight off evil. Together, they ward off many spirits found in the three worlds: sky, earth and underworld.
sadhu	Self-proclaimed holy man/ascetic.
Sago Namgo	Seen in Mustang, these strange objects give protection against bad omens. They relate to the 'Mother Earth spirits' and translate as Earth Door and Sky Door. Made from ram skulls, wood or fabric.
sky burial	Form of burial where the body is cut up and fed to the vultures and large birds.
stupa	Large monument, usually with a square base, a dome and a pointed spire on top. The spire represents the levels towards enlightenment. A stupa may often host the remains of a revered lama or teacher.
tantra	Oral teachings and Buddhist scriptures, describing the use of mantras, mandalas and deities in meditation and yoga. Commonly associated with physical methods of striving for enlightenment but equally applicable to meditation methods using the energies of the mind.
thangka/tangka	Religious painting, usually on silk fabric. Seen in all monasteries, hanging on walls or pillars.
tsampa	Roasted barley; the Tibetan staple food. Mixed with butter tea, it is made into a sort of porridge and eaten with the fingers.
Vajrayana Buddhism	The 'diamond' branch of the religion, found in Tibet and associated with Tantric ideas.
yab-yum	Depiction of two deities, male and female, in union. The male represents compassion and the female wisdom. Deities depict the spiritual union that reaches to the pinnacle of awareness.

APPENDIX C
Useful words and phrases

Hello/Goodbye	*Namaste*
Goodnight	*Suva ratri*
How are you?	*Tapaailai kasto chha?*
Very well	*Ramro chha*
Thank you	*Dhanyabad*
Yes (it is)	*Ho*
No (it isn't)	*Hoina*
Yes (have)	*Chha*
No (don't have)	*Chhaina*
OK	*Tik chha*
What is your name?	*Tapaaiko naam ke ho?*
My name is Bob	*Mero naam Bob ho*
Where is a lodge?	*Lodge kahaa chha?*
What is the name of this village?	*Yo gaaunko naam ke ho?*
Where are you going?	*Tapaailai kahaa jaane?*
Which trail goes to Bhujung?	*Bhujung jaane baato kun ho?*
I don't understand	*Maile buhjina*
I don't know	*Ta chhaina*
How much is it?	*Kati paisa*
Please give me a cup of tea	*Chiyaa dinos*
Where is the toilet?	*Chaarpi kahaa chha?*

Where is there water?	*Pani kahaa chha?*
Please go slowly	*Bistaari jaane*
I want to rent a pony	*Malaai ghoda bhadama chaainchha*
I need a porter	*Ma kulli chaainchha*
I am sick/my friend is sick	*Ma biraami chhu/ mero saathi biraami bhayo*
I have altitude sickness	*Lekh laagyo*

Other useful words

what	ke
where	kun
when	kaile
how much	kati
good	ramro
bad	naramro
cold	jaaro
hot	garam
trail	baato
steeply up	ukaalo
steeply down	oraalo
river (small)	khola

Food

food	khaana
bread	roti
rice	bhat
noodle soup	thukpa
eggs	phul
meat	maasu
yoghurt	dahi
sugar	chini
salt	nun
water	pani
b water	umaalekho pani
black tea	kalo chiyaa
hot water	tatopani
cold water	chiso pani

Numbers

1	ek
2	dui
3	tin
4	char
5	paanch
6	chha
7	saat
8	aath
9	nau
10	das
11	eghaara
12	baara
15	pandhra
20	bis
30	tis
40	chaalis
50	pachaas
100	ek say
500	paanch say
1000	ek hajaar

APPENDIX D
Books, films and music

Books

Anderson, Mary *The Festivals of Nepal* (George Allen & Unwin, 1971)

Bista, Dor Bahadur *People of Nepal* (Ratna Pustak Bhandar, 1987)

Blum, Arlene *Annapurna: A woman's place* (First female on Annapurna in 1978, repub. 1998)

Bonington, Chris *Annapurna South Face* (Cassell, 1971/Pilgrims, 1997)

Bowman, W E (Bill) *The Ascent of Rum Doodle*, 1956 (www.rumdoodle.org.uk – a great skit on the big mountaineering expeditions of the past, written long before they became in vogue)

Chandra, Lokesh *Buddhist Iconography* (International Academy for Indian Culture, Delhi, 1991)

Chorlton, Windsor and Wheeler, Nik *Cloud-Dwellers of the Himalayas* (Time–Life Books, 1982)

Dalai Lama *An Introduction to Buddhism and Tantric Meditation* (Paljor Publications, 1996)

Fleming *Birds of Nepal* (reprints by Indian publishers only)

Gibbons, Bob and Pritchard-Jones, Siân *Kathmandu: Valley of the Green-Eyed Yellow Idol* (Pilgrims, 2004)

Gibbons, Bob and Pritchard-Jones, Siân *Mustang – A Trekking Guide* (Pilgrims, 1993)

Gilchrist, Tom *The Trekkers' Handbook* (Cicerone Press, 1996)

Gordon, Antoinette *The Iconography of Tibetan Lamaism* (Munshi Ram M Delhi, 1978)

Govinda, Lama Anagarika *The Way of the White Clouds* (Rider and Company, London, 1966)

Hagen, Toni *Nepal: The Kingdom of the Himalayas* (Kümmerley and Frey, 1980)

Handa, OC *Buddhist Western Himalaya* (Indus Publishing, New Delhi, 2001)

Herzog, Maurice *Annapurna* (Jonathan Cape, 1952)

Kalsang, Ladrang *The Guardian Deities of Tibet* (Winsome Books India, 2003)

Kawaguchi, Ekai *Three Years in Tibet* (1909, reprints only)

Kumar, Rai Ratan *Along the Kali Gandaki* (Book Faith India)

Lachenal, Louis *Carnets du Vertige* (Editions Guérin, 1996)

Landon, Perceval *Nepal: Vols I and II* (Pilgrims, 2007)

Lhalungpa, Lobsang P *The Life of Milarepa* (Book Faith India, 1997)

Lonely Planet *Nepali Phrasebook* (frequently published)

Lyons, Alonzo Lucius *The Gurung Heritage Trail* (Himalayan Map House, 2011)

Messner, Reinhold *Annapurna* (The Mountaineers, 2000)

Mierow, Dorothy and Shrestha, Tirtha Bahadur *Himalayan Flowers and Trees* (Sahayoga Prakashan/Pilgrims)

Powell, Robert *Earth Door, Sky Door* (paintings of Mustang) (Serindia Publications, London, 1999)

Pritchard-Jones, Siân and Gibbons, Bob *Kailash and Guge: Land of the Tantric Mountain* (Pilgrims, 2006)

Pritchard-Jones, Siân and Gibbons, Bob *Ladakh: Land of Magical Monasteries* (Pilgrims, 2006)

Pye-Smith, Charlie *Travels in Nepal* (Aurum Press, 1988)

O'Connor, Bill *Adventure Treks: Nepal* (Crowood Press, 1990)

Roerich, Nicholas *Altai Himalaya* (1929, reprinted by Book Faith India, 1996)

Snellgrove, David *Buddhist Himalaya* (Himalayan Booksellers, 1995)

Stainton, Adam and Polunin, Oleg *Concise Flowers of the Himalayas* (Oxford University Press, 1987)

Stevenson, Andrew *Annapurna Circuit* (Constable, 1997)

Tilman, HW *Nepal Himalaya* (Cambridge University Press, 1952/Diadem Books–The Mountaineers, 1983)

Tucci, Giuseppe *Shrines of a Thousand Buddhas* (Pilgrims, Varanasi, 2008)

Tucci, Giuseppe *Transhimalaya* (Nagel Publishers, Geneva, 1973)

Films

A wonderfully evocative film about the people of Dolpo in Nepal, *Himalaya* portrays the life of traditional village yak herders in the remote regions. Not about Nepal but good background is *Seven Years in Tibet*, about Heinrich Harrer's life as a fugitive from World War II and his life in Lhasa close to the Dalai Lama. *Kundun* is a more esoteric look at the life of the Dalai Lama in Lhasa before 1959.

Music

There are a lot of new CDs on Himalayan themes. A few are folk songs, others are amalgams of Tibetan chants, songs and 'Western Oriental'. These tunes resonate with calming and meditative music. Some of the authors' favourites are *Tibetiya*, *Sacred Buddha*, *Karmapa: Secrets of the Crystal Mountain*, *Journey to Tibet*, *Sacred Chants of Buddha*, sound track of the film *Himalaya*, *Nepali Folksongs*. All these can be found in Kathmandu for Rs100–400.

APPENDIX E
Useful contacts

Tour operators in the UK

Classic Journeys www.classicjourneys.co.uk

Exodus www.exodus.co.uk

Expedition World www.expeditionworld.com (travel site run by the authors)

Explore www.explore.co.uk

Intrepid Travel www.intrepidtravel.com

KE Adventure Travel www.keadventure.com

Mountain Kingdoms www.mountainkingdoms.com

Peregrine www.peregrineadventures.co.uk

Sherpa Expeditions www.sherpa-walking-holidays.co.uk

The Adventure Company www.adventurecompany.co.uk

Walks Worldwide www.walksworldwide.com

World Expeditions www.worldexpeditions.co.uk

Tour operators in Nepal

Ama Dablam Adventures
www.amadablamadventures.com, www.adventure-himalaya.com Email: himalaya.sales@amadablam.wlink.com.np

Asian Trekking
www.asian-trekking.com (Ang Tshering, Bob's first sirdar in 1975)

Eastern Light Trek
www.easternlight-trek.com Email: easternlight@wlink.com.np (Pokhara area)

Himalayan Encounters
Email: himenco@wlink.com.np (in Kathmandu Guest House courtyard)

Nepal Nature dot com Travels
www.nepalnaturetravels.com (Rajendra Suwal)

Nepal Trans Himalayan Explorer
www.himalexplorer.com

Pokhara Mountain Tiger Outdoor Adventure
Email: knembang@hotmail.com

Sherpa Adventure Travel
www.sherpaadventure.com Email: sat@wlink.com.np (Pasang Dawa)

3 Sisters Adventure Trekking
www.3sistersadventure.com (specialist with female guides)

The authors have either worked with these providers or know them from experience; many more can be found online.

Online information

www.fco.gov.uk/travel – travel advice and tips
www.immi.gov.np – immigration department for visa and permits
www.taan.org.np – Trekking Agencies' Association of Nepal
www.welcomenepal.com – tourist information
www.info-nepal.com – general background
www.visitnepal.com – travel information
www.mnteverest.net/trek.html – list of trekking companies
www.kmtnc.org.np – conservation themes
www.ekantipur.com – news
www.nepalnews.net – news
www.nepalnow.com – news
www.stanfords.co.uk – maps and books
www.themapshop.co.uk – maps
www.nepalmountaineering.org

NOTES

NOTES

LISTING OF CICERONE GUIDES

For full information on all our
guides, and to order books and
eBooks, visit our website:
www.cicerone.co.uk.

Walking – Trekking – Mountaineering – Climbing – Cycling

Over 40 years, Cicerone have built up an outstanding collection of 300 guides, inspiring all sorts of amazing adventures.

Every guide comes from extensive exploration and research by our expert authors, all with a passion for their subjects. They are frequently praised, endorsed and used by clubs, instructors and outdoor organisations.

All our titles can now be bought as **e-books** and many as iPad and Kindle files and we will continue to make all our guides available for these and many other devices.

Our website shows any **new information** we've received since a book was published. Please do let us know if you find anything has changed, so that we can pass on the latest details. On our **website** you'll also find some great ideas and lots of information, including sample chapters, contents lists, reviews, articles and a photo gallery.

It's easy to keep in touch with what's going on at Cicerone, by getting our monthly **free e-newsletter**, which is full of offers, competitions, up-to-date information and topical articles. You can subscribe on our home page and also follow us on **Facebook** and **Twitter**, as well as our **blog**.

Cicerone – the very best guides for exploring the world.

CICERONE

2 Police Square Milnthorpe Cumbria LA7 7PY
Tel: 015395 62069 info@cicerone.co.uk
www.cicerone.co.uk